LOW MAN RIDES AGAIN

Books by H. Allen Smith

ROBERT GAIR: A STUDY

MR. KLEIN'S KAMPF

LOW MAN ON A TOTEM POLE

LIFE IN A PUTTY KNIFE FACTORY

LOST IN THE HORSE LATITUDES

DESERT ISLAND DECAMERON

RHUBARB

LO, THE FORMER EGYPTIAN

LARKS IN THE POPCORN

WE WENT THATAWAY

LOW AND INSIDE (*with Ira L. Smith*)

PEOPLE NAMED SMITH

THREE MEN ON THIRD (*with Ira L. Smith*)

MISTER ZIP

SMITH'S LONDON JOURNAL

THE COMPLEAT PRACTICAL JOKER

THE WORLD, THE FLESH, AND H. ALLEN SMITH

THE REBEL YELL

THE AGE OF THE TAIL

WRITE ME A POEM, BABY

THE PIG IN THE BARBER SHOP

DON'T GET PERCONEL WITH A CHICKEN

WAIKIKI BEACHNIK

LET THE CRABGRASS GROW

HOW TO WRITE WITHOUT KNOWING NOTHING

TO HELL IN A HANDBASKET

TWO-THIRDS OF A COCONUT TREE

A SHORT HISTORY OF FINGERS

POOR H. ALLEN SMITH'S ALMANAC

SON OF RHUBARB

BUSKIN' WITH H. ALLEN SMITH

THE GREAT CHILI CONFRONTATION

RUDE JOKES

THE VIEW FROM CHIVO

THE BEST OF H. ALLEN SMITH

LOW MAN RIDES AGAIN

H. Allen Smith

Low Man
Rides Again

Doubleday & Company, Inc., Garden City, New York, 1973

ISBN: 0-385-03390-7
Library of Congress Catalog Card Number 73-76220
Copyright © 1973 by H. Allen Smith
Printed in the United States of America
First Edition

For
RUFUS BLAIR
and
FRED BECK

CONTENTS

8 CONTENTS

THE LOVE LIFE OF A GALLOPING GOOSE

(A Preface)

Most of the articles and stories contained in this volume were published in a gallimaufry of magazines and newspapers. Several of the pieces have never been published before, meaning that editors looked at them and decided against them, saying they were no damn good.

Publications represented herein (and I hope the list is complete) include:

True, Playboy, Family Weekly, Variety (the Bible of Showbiz), *Reader's Digest, Travel, McCall's,* the Chicago *Tribune, Contact* (a Ford Motors publication), *The Saturday Evening Post,* the Washington *Post, think small* (a book of Volkswagen comedy), *Holiday, The National Observer, Cosmopolitan, Westways,* the El Paso *Times, Odyssey* (published by the Gulf Travel Club), the *Authors Guild Bulletin, Venture,* the Los Angeles *Times,* NOVA (a publication of the University of Texas at El Paso), the Denver *Post, Golf, This Week, Rx Sports and Travel,* and Martin Levin's "Phoenix Nest" in the *Saturday Review.*

There have been minor alterations here and there, usually to correct anachronisms. Because it is my nature to do so, occasionally I have dropped in a little strong language which would not likely have been permitted in some of the magazines. This sort of thing irritates a woman reader who lives in St. Louis and she writes me intemperate letters about it. I answer her by writing her that she can go micturate up a flagpole.

Now, I need to explain the title at the head of this prefatory note. It is a title I have been trying to put on one of my books for twenty years. Year after year I have sent in book manuscripts with the first page reading: *The Love Life of a Galloping Goose*. And year after year the publishers have rejected it, out of ignorance or because they lack poetic feeling, or both. I do not want to pass to Higher Realms without somehow using that title; if it is thrown off of this Preface, I will figure out some way of using it on a Christmas card.

It derives from an ancient vituperative taunt known to vulgarians of the Midwest and South. This common execration or curse instructs the tauntee exactly what he can do with respect to a goose that gallops. It is a physical act which I suspect would be impossible of achievement. By a concupiscent gander, perhaps; by a male humanoid functioning in midair, no. For the male humanoid it would be more difficult of execution than the assignment given the St. Louis lady with respect to a flagpole.

I once worked for a brilliant city editor on a New York newspaper and this gentleman sometimes took on more grog than was warranted by the sorry condition of the world, at which times he would speak loudly to anyone within hearing, telling them to do thus and so to a galloping goose. He somehow managed to give the command great vigor and pungency; he always put the word "flying" in its correct position; once in a sober moment he told me he had first encountered the barnyard proverb in Indiana—that's where I learned it and I felt vaguely (and proudly) that it made the two of us kin.

In a modified drawing-room form, the malediction might be phrased with formal and cultivated *politesse* as: "A galloping goose awaits your aeronautical service, sir." I'm sorry not to have given the reader the full classic phrasing, but then Tennessee Williams didn't give us a complete figure in the title of his play *Cat on a Hot Tin Roof*. He neglected to tell us what that cat was trying to accomplish on that hot tin roof. So I am moving in good company. Or am I?

Richard Bissell, the Iowa-born author, gave me some assistance when I was investigating the range of the galloping goose through Midwestern folklore. Mr. Bissell first declared that he certainly had heard the correct phrasing many times in Iowa and all along the Mississippi and Ohio Rivers.

He said to his wife, Marian, on my behalf: "Does the expression 'galloping goose' mean anything to you?"

She replied: "Certainly. It's the name of a narrow-gauge railway in Colorado."

He said to his son Sam: "You ever hear of a galloping goose?"

"Sure," said Sam. "He's a football player in the Big Ten."

I inquired in many places and tried my question on the Leibsons of El Paso, and son Mark spoke feelingly of a racing hound then running at the Juárez dog track.

I entertained the notion that neither Marian Bissell nor Sam nor Mark Leibson had been given a proper upbringing. And I'm happy that my galloping goose has finally made it, if only at the head of a Preface.

H. Allen Smith

LOW MAN RIDES AGAIN

CHAPTER 1

A TRAIPSIN' TOTEM POLE

Not long ago a letter came from Ken McCormick saying:

"On the jacket of your latest book is a photo of you standing beside a handsome totem pole. Could this possibly be the same totem pole that was carved for you in Alaska all those years ago? If so, it appears to be in a remarkable state of preservation. And so do you."

For answer, let me say that my totem pole has been a traipsin' totem pole and is indeed the same one mentioned by Mr. McCormick, who is a boss editor at Doubleday & Company. It stands today above a stone wall a few steps from the main entrance to my house in the mountains of West Texas. It is a little over seven feet tall, set in concrete, painted in gleaming colors, and it faces westward toward the Pacific Ocean.

The story goes back to 1940. In that year I composed a book which was published the following year by Doubleday under the title *Low Man on a Totem Pole*. The book became a fat best seller and set me on the road to some easy living, and it tied my name to the totem pole forever and a day. Up to the publication of that book I doubt if I had ever seen a totem pole in the flesh, or in the grain. To this day when I am introduced to strangers the chances are strong that they will say, "Oh, the totem pole man." I am identified with the totem pole as immutably as Albert Payson Terhune was identified with dogs, Jimmy

Durante with a nose, Herman Melville with a whale, and Howard Johnson with ice cream.

After *Low Man* had become a hit in the marketplace my agent, Harold Matson, hit upon the notion of having a totem pole carved surreptitiously and presented to me for the decoration of my newly acquired premises near Mount Kisco, New York. Mr. Matson consulted with executives at Doubleday and a treaty of procedure was drawn up and ratified. The conspirators wanted to have real people depicted on the pole and for the sake of authenticity, they agreed that it should be carved by a professional in Alaska. Summit conferences were held to determine whose likenesses should be carved on the pole and in the end these men were chosen (beginning at the top): Fred Allen, James Street, Don Elder, Cedric Crowell, Harold Matson, and the bottom man, me. Fred Allen was accorded the peak position because he had written the introduction to my book, and a line from that introduction had provided the totem pole title. Jim Street, the Confederate novelist, was one of my closest friends; Don Elder, biographer of Ring Lardner, was my editor at Doubleday; Cedric Crowell was boss of sales for the publisher; Matson, as stated, was my literary agent and still is, and I . . . well, I wrote the book.

Photographs of these six were collected and handed to an artisan in New York and he constructed a model totem pole about a foot high. It was sent to a grizzled old guy, non-Indian and un-Eskimo, in Alaska. I once had a photograph of this Yukon Praxiteles with a toad-stabber in his hand. In former times the most celebrated carvers of totem poles were Indians with such names as Oyai, Hasemhliyam, and Hlamee. Mine was Eli Tate.

In early research I established that the totem pole was invented in Russia, along with the telephone conference call, the electric backscratcher, the litter barrel, crewelwork, and *enchiladas con queso*. The anthropologists say that when the Russians were running Alaska they brought in their own tools and techniques and revolutionized the native craftsmanship. They showed the people around Sitka how to put grizzly bears and witchetty grubs and killer whales and dominecker hens at the top of cedar poles, and they told them to carve eagles and more eagles and still more until they were able to reproduce the Russian Imperial Eagle. That's why you see so many eagles on totem poles. All these birds and animals and witchetty grubs came to represent the ancestors of the owner, and the owner was never to eat his totem-creature. It would be much the same as eating his grandmaw.

Old Man Tate, up there in Alaska, carved well and the likenesses of the people on the pole were very good, but he missed the main point completely. He carved me at the bottom and then further down the pole, underneath my portrait, he put an Indian chief, high feathered war bonnet and all.

His second mistake, I thought, was my nose.

The nose figured prominently in the travels of my totem pole which were almost as extensive as the journeyings of Lowell Thomas. When it was finished and painted, the pole proper was shipped by freighter from Alaska to New York by way of the Panama Canal. My nose, a five-inch beak painted a boozy red (that old man didn't even *know* me!) was shipped separately, later to be doweled and glued to the middle of my face.

Within a couple of months the pole and the nose had reached Garden City, Long Island, where Doubleday had offices and a big bindery. I was still ignorant of the whole plot and remained so until the day Harold Matson drove me to Garden City and led me up to my tribal monument, which stood in a wooden base beside the main entrance to the book factory. Someone took a picture of Mr. Matson and me in squatty positions beside the pole, while other people stood around making big brags about how it had been carved clean the hell and gone up yonder in Alaska and how it had actually been through the Panama Canal.

A short time later a Doubleday executive, Milton Runyon, had the pole wrapped in a tarp and roped on top of his car, which he drove from Long Island to my house in Westchester. And after that I set it in concrete above the pool, taking care that only the Indian chief's feathers were showing. For his sinful usurpation of my place as low man on the totem pole, the handsome Indian's face was buried underground. I took care also to instruct my dog in basic totem pole etiquette after I caught him sniffing around the nose of the low man.

There the pole stood, unshakable, for twenty-three years. Fred Allen was photographed several times standing beside it. So was Jim Street, up from Chapel Hill for his annual visits. Also Harold Matson and all his considerable kin, over from nearby

Greenwich. Visitors from near and far always wanted their pictures taken by the pole, usually making with the comical faces. One I remember whose photo showed him looking solemn and perplexed was Peters, my agent in London. He understood about the sarsen trilithons at Stonehenge but he was a trifle bewildered concerning my bloodline affiliations with this tall stump. So was I. Yet he posed beside it as sedately and as reverently as was possible under the circumstances. As it stands today, that totem pole has been photographed ten times more than its owner, often by cameramen from the newspapers and magazines.

The dowel at the rear of my nose had been smeared with glue before it was set into the pole, but within a few years it had worked loose. It was always working loose. From time to time the pole had to be repainted and this involved the feathery application of five colors, delicate work usually executed by my daughter or by me. Picasso could not have done better.

The ancient wood carver who flubbed the nose (I've resisted saying he blew the nose) could never have anticipated my great raging hordes of grandchildren. The red nose fascinated these kids and, since it was loose in its socket most of the time, they were inclined to remove it and use it for a plaything. My god, they had playthings more intricate than a lunar module, yet whenever they arrived on the premises they headed straight for my nose. If it was not loose at the moment, they simply wrenched it off my face.

We lived on the edge of a deep forest where the children loved to explore and usually they carried my nose off into the timber. And lost it. By good fortune I had respected the integrity of the original artist and I kept the nose painted a bright red. The color made it easier to locate out there amongst the briers and the ferns and the poison ivy.

The years marched, and the time came for us to move to a more salubrious climate and we ended up choosing West Texas. The totem pole would, of course, go with us. Sir Galahad would never have left his armorial bearings behind if he departed Camelot to go a-grailing in Brewster County, Texas.

I took a sledge hammer and shattered the concrete base and lifted out the pole. On the instant the population of my hilltop home increased by ninety-six thousand. That was my personal estimate of the number of termites buzzing inside the base of my pole.

I slaughtered most of them with insecticide. I got a ten-gallon bucket and soaked the mildewed Indian up to his eyebrows in triple-strength bug-killer and after that I let him marinate for a week in creosote. At last it was time to amputate the infested wood and I approached this task with apprehension. Happily, the termites had not penetrated past the Indian's forehead and my own noble sculpture was undamaged. I wrapped the pole in a tarpaulin again and it traveled West by moving van. The nose I managed to fit into my travel kit.

The cedarwood obelisk has been repainted twice in Texas, but time and the sun and the wind have taken their toll. Deep cracks have developed and grow deeper with each passing season. The end is not too far away. Here today and gone tomorrow. I confess without qualm that I have an abiding affection for my totem pole, and I have undertaken the customary arrangements. I have talked to the people who conduct such matters in our town.

"How big is he?" asked the man, not understanding the question. I explained that the patient, or client, was not a person, but a totem pole.

"He," I said, "is a trifle over seven feet."

"How broad?"

"Nine and a half inches at the bottom. Narrower at the top."

"The casket would have to be custom-made. We haven't yet run into anybody quite that narrow. Some pretty close to it though. Look, Mr. Smith, since he is a totem pole maybe we could keep the cost down. A plain pine box might do. We could get a local carpenter to run it up for you."

"No, by god. Nothing's too good for him. Could I get a cedar casket?"

"If you insist on a casket, how about bronze?"

"No. Cedar. His body is cedar and cedar would be appropriate."

"Okay. No sweat. It'll run eight feet in length and a little over a foot wide. Want me to order it?"

"Oh, he isn't . . . he hasn't . . . he's not ready yet."

We then went into the matter of a cemetery lot and I thought this would be troublesome, but it wasn't, except that the man said he didn't think they would sell me a parcel eight feet long and one foot wide. A grave of those dimensions would impair cemetery symmetry.

I got up to leave, well satisfied with the way things had worked out. As I reached the door the man called out to me.

"You want the lining to be satin?"

"Velvet," I answered. "I told you nothing's too good."

While I was on this funereal kick I thought of composing my totem pole's obituary for the New York *Times*. My first newspaper job, fifty years ago, was the writing of obituaries and funeral notices and I make bold to suggest that I do a bang-up job in that area of journalism. I went to the library for some more research, and I stumbled upon a startling theory advanced by a writer named Ruth Brindze. She asserted: "It is possible that a decorated pole actually was carried by winds and ocean currents to the American coast from one of the Pacific islands, where the people were also expert wood carvers."

Shortly after I read those lines an inspiration struck me. I got to thinking of all those rafting expeditions that have been cluttering the oceans since the voyage of the *Kon-Tiki*. I realized that here, in the realm of pure science, lay a far better fate for my totem pole than a grave in Elm Grove Cemetery.

I would dig the pole out of the concrete again and transport it to Hawaii or Tahiti or Bora Bora and set it adrift in the Pacific. Keep in mind the voyage of the *Kon-Tiki*, which was intended to prove something about sweet potatoes, and the journey of the *Lehi* VI to prove that the Book of Mormon is true. And somewhere I've read of a rafting expedition in the Pacific, organized to show that California peanut butter originated in the mountains of Peru.

My totem pole might well serve as the instrumentality for proving the Ruth Brindze hypothesis and putting the Russians to shame. It could wash ashore in Alaska or Vancouver or Oregon and American anthropologists would be so delighted they would leap about like exultant goats.

Think of the fun in it for me, going again to Hawaii or Tahiti or Bora Bora. And on top of that, perhaps an award of the Na-

CHAPTER 2

BLACK DEATH ON THE LIVING ROOM FLOOR

Back yonder in the Jurassic Age when I was courting her in the hammock-lands of South Florida, she told me the story of The One, You Know, Who Ate the Doily.

This remarkable incident, which demonstrates one of the special vagaries of the human race, dated back to her high school days in a small town in middle Missouri. There was an afternoon party for girls of the sophomore class. One girl—let us call her Myrt Bagnell—achieved irrevocable immortality at that party, solely through accident. There were small plates, and in each plate a tiny lacy-edged paper doily, and on the doily a mound of strawberry ice cream. Miss Myrt Bagnell came of good stock—quality, you might say—but she was a high-strung nervous girl, self-conscious in public yet eager to make a good impression. So she ate the ice cream, and then she ate the doily.

From that unhappy day forward she was often pointed out, especially to visitors in the town, and everyone knew the story, and she was frequently referred to as The One, You Know, Who Ate the Doily. She was, in a sense, the town celebrity. That's the way it goes in life—one little no-account doily, and a girl is marked for life.

I did not visit my wife's home town until many years later. When we did finally make it, I expected to find a community of retired rubes and snuff-dipping chawbacons. Not so. It was a neat,

tional Medal of Science, given by the President of the Uni
States to me and my totem pole jointly.

Hell, why wait! I think I'll go out and dig it up and get ou
the tarp and start for Bora Bora next Tuesday.

trim, well-ordered town of neat, trim, and well-ordered people. They gave a party for us at the home of a prominent businessman and after things had started rolling, a handsome woman came up the granitoid walk and entered the house. Immediately people began congregating around me and whispering, "Here she comes. The one, you know, who ate the doily." They knew I had expressed an interest in this lady, and so I made her acquaintance and found her to be witty and intelligent and charming. I confess that I felt some compassion for her because I knew that the misadventure of the doily would follow her unrelentingly to the grave.

Still, down through the years I continued to josh my wife about the caliber of the people who lived in her home town, with special reference always to The One, You Know, Who Ate the Doily. Then I began, in a figurative sense, to eat a whole series of paper doilies.

One of the first unhappy incidents was The Awful Night of the Ball-Peen Hammer. We were living in a small house in a commuter town snuggled up against the Hudson River. One night I was awakened by a noise below stairs, a rattling sound as if someone were trying to force open a door. I got out of bed and went to a window and established that no wind was blowing. I thought of wakening my wife, so she could witness my heroics, but I didn't do it. I crept down the stairs in my bare feet, made a left turn into the kitchen, gentled open a closet door, groped inside, and came out with a ball-peen hammer in my grip. I hefted it a couple of times, noting its nice balance. What a weapon! Armed with that hammer alone, I felt that I could have won for Custer at the Little Big Horn.

Now I heard the rattle again and I moved slowly into the living room and glanced toward the front door. There was a quarter moon and I could move about without banging into furniture, and I could detect shadowy objects outdoors. The front door was a full-length sheet of plate glass and as I fixed my eyes on it, I detected something moving on the porch. I lowered myself into a crouch to diminish the target in case of gunfire. I moved slowly across the room, ball-peen hammer poised above my right shoulder, ready for a skull-shattering blow.

As I inched closer to the door I was able to get a better idea of The Presence outside. It was a man all right. I could only see him as a blob of ectoplasm, but he was there. He was not aware of the trap that was being set for him because he was now creeping up close to the door. I continued moving forward. Never before or since have I displayed such magnificent courage. I shudder and chill today just thinking about it.

I now arrived within a couple of feet of the plate glass, and he was in striking distance on the other side of the door. I thought I saw his hand move toward the doorknob. I began talking in a low voice, something on this order: "All right, you sneaky son-of-a-bitch! You asked for it, here it comes!"

I poised myself on the bare balls of my feet, moved the hammer backward a couple of inches to increase the murderous arc, took a deep breath, tensed my muscles, and . . .

Somebody grabbed my arm from behind, and then came a shrill cry: "No! Hold it! *Don't . . . do . . . it!*"

I almost fainted. I let out a yowl of pure fright and turned and in the dimness saw it was my wife. I shrieked at her and whirled around to tackle the intruder on the porch. My wife now yelled at me: "There's nobody out there! You were about to hit your own reflection in the glass!"

I couldn't believe it for a moment, couldn't believe that I had been so stupid, but then I saw that it was true. I had broken out in a cold sweat and I was trembling. I turned on the light and went to the kitchen and fixed a beverage. Not a soft beverage.

After that, whenever in company I maligned my wife's native town with the tale of The One, You Know, Who Ate the Doily, she would retaliate a detailed account of The Awful Night of the Ball-Peen Hammer.

It was a sort of game, and I didn't particularly enjoy playing it. I knew I had a job ahead of me. I had to catch *her* in one, a real good one, a classic piece of egregious blundering. But years went by, and while her mistakes and misjudgments were beyond numbering, they were all quite minor league. Meanwhile I, the perfect man, embarked on a series of bumbling botcheries that could only be explained by eccentric sun spots, voodoo, or a heady infusion of strontium 90. I remember especially the case of The Red Rain From Outer Space.

We bought a home in the country and one day I was sitting on

a stone wall beside the driveway when I noticed that the top of
the wall was sprinkled over with a strange, brownish, granular
substance. I picked up a few of the grains and examined them and
crumbled them, and I now saw that they were spread evenly all
along the top of the wall. It was obvious that they had fallen
from somewhere, rained down on my premises. I thought back
to Charles Fort and his theories about "teleportation"—rains of
strange objects from outer space. The more I speculated on the
phenomenon, the more I found myself thinking in Fortean, supernatural terms. I walked around to the kitchen door and spoke
to my college-bred wife.

"Look at these," I said, extending my hand. She looked at
them.

"Most astonishing thing," I said with Sherlockian poise. "This
stuff must have rained out of the sky. I've eliminated every other
possibility—and I'm the guy who poked fun at old Charles Fort."

"Where did you find it?" my wife wanted to know.

"It's scattered all over the top of the stone wall, all over everything."

She started laughing. "You are a dope," she said, "and you are
also a kook. What you've got there is Grape Nuts. Nothing but
old, stale Grape Nuts. I sprinkled them out there for the birds."

I thought I'd never be able to live that one down—me, the
raucous crusader against superstition in any and all forms. I
still hadn't trapped her in a single misadventure that could compare, in dramatic quality, to the mounting list of my own. And
then just recently I added another. We were watching a play
on television. The telephone rang and I hopped up and caught
my foot on a hassock and sprawled at full length on the floor;
struggled to my feet and made it to the phone and picked it up
and said, "Hello." Nothing. Nobody. A dial tone. God damn.
She howled with laughter. It had been, of course, a phone ring-
ing on the television show.

Later that same evening it happened. We had quit television
(at my earnest urging) and were reading. I recall that I went to
the kitchen and got a thick slice of watermelon and brought it
back to the living room. As I savored the melon's rich and juicy
sweetness, I considered how things had been shaping up. I could
never win. The score was too lopsided. I was trying in my mind

to formulate the terms of an armistice. I would never again kid her in public about the intelligence quotient of those people in Missouri, about The One, You Know, Who Ate the Doily.

Our house was surrounded by meadow and deep forest. We were continually subject to invasion by small varmints—field mice, little black spiders, small crickets of an ebony color, occasional beetles. Whenever we'd spot one of these creatures parading insolently across the floor, we'd move fast and pounce. We'd swat them or slam down a sheet of tissue on them, or if they were moving we might even stomp them.

So, suddenly my wife put her book aside and stood up. She had spotted a dark invader off to her left. She moved swiftly and stomped. "Got him!" she announced, and stomped hard a second time, and then a third just to make certain. Now she grabbed a piece of tissue and picked up the corpse and moved back to the light and examined it.

It was a black watermelon seed that had somehow squirted away from me.

I had her. Oh, how I had her!

The armistice is now in effect. I am no longer to mention The One, You Know, Who Ate the Doily. She in turn is not to tell people of The Awful Night of the Ball-Peen Hammer or about The Red Rain From Outer Space.

And finally I have agreed that I won't even tell our closest friends about The One, You Know, Who Stomped the Watermelon Seed to Death.

CHAPTER 3

DOG AT THE KITCHEN DOOR

Subsequent to the awful slaughter of the watermelon seed, an account of that incident appeared in *The Saturday Evening Post*. A lady in Teaneck, New Jersey, read the article and informed the *Post* that Mrs. Smith had her sympathy, because she had recently banged a parsley leaf to death with her husband's shoe.

And there was a fresh incident that put me in the driver's seat for all time to come. Since the death of Rufus we had never kept a dog, but certain neighborhood Fidoes made a practice now and then of calling at our back door. We had a box of dog biscuits handy and always tossed one out when our canine visitors scratched on the door.

One evening I got a can of beer from the refrigerator and when I had finished it, I put the empty can outside near the kitchen door. Now, I suppose that other people who drink beer from cans know that after cold metal warms up a bit, it often goes *clank* in a loud and unseemly manner.

Three minutes after I had discarded that can, it did just that. *Clank!* My wife got out of her chair and went to the kitchen and I heard her open a cabinet. Then she opened the kitchen door and called out, "Here you are, boy!"

She is The One, You Know, Who Threw a Bone to a Beer Can.

CHAPTER 4

A SAMPLING OF WORRIES

Those philosophers who are qualified to get into our books of quotations are almost unanimously opposed to worry. Nobody says anything nice about it. They tell us that a good strong fret, if it is not curbed, can put us under the sod quicker than a bullet between the eyes.

I have so many worries pestering my mind from the time I get up until I go to bed that I don't see how I keep alive five minutes.

Recently I put in an entire day, neglecting my work, worrying about who gets to call President Nixon "Dick." From all that appears in the public prints and on television, the moment the ballots are counted a man ceases to be "Dick" to his long-time buddies and becomes "Mister President," the same as with Ike and Jack and Lyndon. The same, no doubt, with Zach and Millard and Abe and Rutherford and Chester.

In the privacy of his office, with the door closed, does Mr. Nixon say to Senator Scott, "Look, Hugh, ixnay on that Mister President talk; call me Dick the way you always have." Question mark. Or does the Secretary of State call him "Mister President" at a Cabinet meeting and then, that evening at cocktails over to Fulbright's house, address him as "Dick"?

A major worry to me is the book trade, since that is my principal business. Is McLuhan right? Is the printed word vanishing? Is technology putting me out of business? It comes at me from all sides. An essay contest was held in New York not long ago with the young people under instruction to write down what they thought about books. One boy wrote: "A book is a hunk of bull." I tell you, I could have taken that kid and . . . well, I'll bet he had sideburns halfway to his ankles and was drooling.

At that time an old friend of mine named Fred Beck wrote me a discouraging letter, discouraging because Mr. Beck himself is the author of several books.

He said that he had run across a book in the Palm Springs library called *The Hen,* containing a schematic illustration showing how a hen goes about laying an egg. Said Mr. Beck: "I have read that hen book five times, and try and strain as I will, I haven't been able to lay a single egg. Furthermore, I have read a book by Tommy Armour about how to play golf as good as Tommy Armour plays it. I am still unable to play golf anywhere near as good as Tommy Armour, and I can't lay an egg fit to fry. Books ain't any good."

Pretty convincing, hey? And in my own adopted homeland, West Texas, where almost everybody kills deer and antelope and doves with happy abandon, they have a saying that borders on the biblical: "Readin' books ruins yer shootin' eye." I know from personal knowledge that no shootin' eyes are being ruint.

I worry about when-to-kiss. In our modern era a man is supposed to kiss a woman on the cheek whenever they meet, especially in public and on television programs. But how well must I know a woman before I administer the kiss of greeting, even when it consists merely of banging dimples? This whole procedure, unknown when I was a rake and a libertine, gets to be a habit, and just a few days ago, when I was introduced to a handsome girl from San Diego, I gave her a quick kiss on the cheek. She looked startled, alarmed. Perhaps the rules of etiquette are more rigid around San Diego than elsewhere; perhaps civilized ways have not penetrated that far. I once consulted a young woman who worked for a Madison Avenue conspiracy, asking for guidance. "Who do you kiss, and when?" I wanted to know. "Anybody and everybody," she said. "Never kiss on the first meeting but on the second, it is legit, and expected. Try not to make actual contact. Fouls the makeup."

Here is a seemingly trivial matter that gives me the whimwhams. Or gave them to me in former times. A man who is still enslaved takes out a cigarette and puts it in his mouth. Then he fumbles out a book of matches and tears off one match and at that precise moment his companion strikes a match of his own, or whips out a lighter, and applies the flame to the cigarette. This leaves the poor guy standing there with phosphorus all over his chin. It used to happen to me all the time. I suspect that this recurring, clumsy embarrassment, and not fear of cancer, was the real reason for my giving up smoking. It is almost possible to read a man's character from the way he reacts to the excess match situation. If he's inclined to be wishy-washy, he'll try to snake his own unstruck match back into the book from which it was torn, and he'll try to do it surreptitiously, as if in shame. On the other hand, if he's a dynamic and forceful creature, as I would like to be, he'll say to the companion who proffered the light: "You off your rocker? Didn't you see me pull out my match? Take yours and go somewhere and light yourself a candle."

All manner of incidents and impending disasters pester me. I worry that the dog down the street will eventually bite me. I worry that I'll lock myself out of my car, somewhere far from home. I worry that Jacqueline Susann will quit writing and leave me in a state of utter desolation.

I sometimes sit and think that next to war the biggest problem before this country is highway traffic, and I worry about it and try to work out systems for making it safe. The simple way to solve the problem would be to make it impossible for the Stupids to drive. Only the Brights. But it can't be done. The Stupids hold the balance of power at the voting booths; there is some evidence that they constitute a majority.

Still another worry that plagues me steadily has to do with the curdling of my memory buds. I'm getting so I'm not sure if a thing really happened or if I merely saw it on TV last night. I spent half an hour the other day trying to remember which of my friends had quit drinking and got a job as a manager of a hardware store. The answer finally came. No friends of mine had quit drinking. It was a character named Gregory in a TV drama.

Then I fret over a thing my father once told me. Out of the deep well of his wisdom he said: "The stren'th goes outa things." I apply his precept to everything. The stren'th goes outa the pills in my medicine chest—sometimes I have a feeling that the stren'th begins to ebb before I can get them home from the drugstore. The stren'th goes out of insecticides and buttermilk, out of corned beef that has been in the refrigerator more than a month or two, out of strong drink if I leave it standing around too long. This thing bothers me so deeply that sometimes I think the stren'th is going outa *me*.

As I've suggested, I could go on interminably about my little worries which loom so big at the time I was worrying them. If I run out of problems I can go clear back to the 1930s, when I read that Franklin D. Roosevelt shaved himself for eight days with his safety razor before changing the blade. How did he remember which day to put in a fresh blade? I have a mantel clock which has to be wound each week. I wind it every Sunday night, just before I go to bed. It has become second nature to me that on Sunday night I wind that clock. Yet, if I were obliged to wind it every eight days, I would be in trouble. Sometimes I wish that Franklin Roosevelt had never lived; or at least that he could have been sensible about his razor blades and changed them once a week—once every Sunday night.

I keep thinking about a story that was going around a few years back. A woman, disturbed by her husband's continual worrying, said to him: "You should have worries! How would you like to be the President of the United States and be saddled with all *his* worries?"

"Listen, dear," said the husband. "Don't you realize that I have to worry about what the President of the United States worries about, and in addition to that I have to worry about all my own worries too?"

I'm content to stay with my own. They are ample.

CHAPTER 5

MY POOR CHRISTMAS LEG

Here it is December again, and the Yuletide is approaching, and
already I seem to be taking on that pleasant glow that comes with
the best of holiday seasons. It is the best of times, it is the friend-
liest of times, and I like everything about it. Wup! Not everything. There's the matter of those confusing and unsettling mystery cards.

In common with almost everyone else, I get piles of Christmas
greetings in my mailbox day after day, and before the flood has
ended I could count them in the hundreds. I enjoy them. I must
confess that I don't read all the words of the engraved inscrip-
tions, though I knew a Tahitian woman a few years back who
considered these factory-made sentiments to be the most glorious
and lyrical prose ever produced in any language. Each Christmas
she gets half a dozen cards from movie people she met when they
were on her island filming *Mutiny on the Bounty*. She carries
those cards around with her clear up to Eastertime and whips
them out and recites the graven sentences to anyone who will listen, always exclaiming over the beauty of the language and the
splendor of the sentiment. If, in addition, there happens to be a
white bird pictured on one of her cards, she gets the dizzies and
has to lie down for a while. White birds send her. I am not that
deeply addicted.

I enjoy the cards mainly for the lines that have been scribbled on by the senders—usually just enough to tell me what they've been doing since last we communicated. What exasperates me are the mystifiers. Each year we get at least a dozen of these and they almost ruin the entire holiday season. They are from people we don't know, never knew, never heard of . . . *but they know us.* Almost intimately!

I pick up a handsome card, a fifty-center at least, and find a formal engraved greeting and then underneath it, written in ink, will be:

CRAIG, MILLIE, RODGE, AND JACKIE

And under that, also in ink, the line:

HEY, HOW'S THAT LEG?

I stare at this writing for a long time and then I call out to my wife: "Who's Craig, Millie, Rodge, and Jackie?"

She looks up from her lapful of cards and responds: "Craig, Millie, Rodge, and Jackie WHO?"

With considerable heat I now declare: "If I knew who Craig, Millie, Rodge, and Jackie were—if I knew their last name—would I have asked *you?*"

In her mothering tone she now says, "Why don't you look on the outside—the return address?"

There is no return address on the outside.

"Well," she says, "try the postmark. That might give you a clue."

It must be noted that Christmastime is a rough season for post-office cancelling machines; they get bone-tired and take on that dried-out feeling and tend to smudge up their work. So that's usually no help.

Now I tell my wife about the leg part. Where they say, "HEY, HOW'S THAT LEG?"

I got no leg. That is, I got no leg worth mentioning—worth talking about in a Christmas card. This surely must be a reference to some leg other than my own two; this card definitely was meant for some person who's got a bothersome leg. It's not me. Still, it's addressed correctly to me, right down to the ZIP code. Maybe they got the cards mixed up and put them in the wrong envelopes. No . . . there is just nobody in our circle of acquaintances named . . .

My wife's voice suddenly sounds in the room. "You know somebody named Fenway Gorsley? The postmark looks like Pensacola, Florida."

"I don't know a single human being named Fenway Gorsley," I say, and the meanness is now beginning to jangle around in my bloodstream. "I don't even *want* to know anybody named Fenway Gorsley. I don't know anybody in Pensacola, Florida, and nobody in Pensacola, Florida, knows me, and I'm getting just a little . . . let me have a look at it. Fenway Gorsley. *Fennn*-way Gorsley."

Staring at it doesn't help a bit, so I put it aside and almost immediately another Gordian knot appears before me, a card from . . .

THE STANLEYS

Nicely engraved, in gold on black, and then written in white ink beneath it:

HEATHER SAYS MERRY CHRISTMAS, TOO!

There is an address on the outside of the envelope. The Stanleys live on Round Hill Road in Greenwich, Connecticut. I used to know some people named Swayze on Round Hill Road, but no Stanleys. I'm sure of it. And their mystery card creates a special apprehensiveness growing out of past experience. I sometimes try to get these problems unsnarled by writing notes to the people, hoping to get a clue or even a full explanation in return. Once there was a card similar to the Stanley greeting, with the handwritten line: "Henrietta says hello." I wrote a polite note of acknowledgment, with the intention of getting these people identified, and I ended with the line: "I seem to be losing track all the time—what grade is Henrietta in now?" It turned out that Henrietta was a cocker spaniel. So always beware of this kind of bluffing. That Heather creature at the Stanley house could be a cat, or even a sheep.

I think of another mystifier I got a few years back. A nice card from someone named Vesta Kastner, with the message:

"Hi! No, I can't believe it! Not YOU!"

Any way I looked at it, I couldn't figure it. I hadn't taken on a mistress. I hadn't contracted any social diseases. Or any unsocial ones for that matter. In all my life I had never heard of anyone named Vesta Kastner. So I just kept her card around to spring on people when I hear them say that we live in a well-ordered universe with divine purpose behind it.

Given about three of these brain-clouding problems in a row, I usually find myself growing restless and fretful, unable to sit still. So my wife says, "Will you please quit torturing yourself over those people we don't even know or can't remember? It's the same thing every year. Forget about them. Put them out of your mind. You know them or you don't know them. Forget them!"

Easy said.

We have a sizable forest at our back door and I take my mystery cards and put on my boots and head into the lonely woods. The birds and the beasts out there are accustomed to my presence in normal times, but not at this season of the year. I wander amongst them, now and then bumping into large trees, uttering strange words over and over, maybe cussing just a little, saying, "Craig, Millie, Rodge, and Jackie. God eternally damn! Craig, Millie, Rodge, and Jackie. I'll be blowed! Spose it coulda been those people in Tulsa that time? No. Maybe that nice family out near Brackenridge Park in San Antonio. They had two kids. No. *Cuidado*. That Jackie might be a simpering schnauzer, or a saddle horse. Fenway Gorsley. Fennn . . . way Gorsley. Nope. Couldn't be. If I ever met a Fenway Gorsley, even fleetingly, I'm sure I'd remember him for the remainder of my days. Even as matters stand, I'll never forget Fenway Gorsley, and I don't even know him."

And at this juncture I am likely to begin feeling sciatica pains or knee-throb in that leg of mine—the leg that was clinically sound until CRAIG, MILLIE, RODGE, AND JACKIE had to come along and fling it in my face.

I return to the house, limping slightly, and find my wife sitting in the spot where I left her. She is staring at the floor.

"DeVoe," she says. "Mildred DeVoe." She looks up at me with a pitiable expression and asks, "Who is Mildred DeVoe? She's a cousin of Thelma Trotter."

"Wait a minute," I answer. "Who is Thelma Trotter?"

"How should I know? Here, look."

The card bears the engraved name of the sender: Mildred DeVoe. And underneath in ball-point script the pellucid, clarifying, identifying, explanatory line: "Cousin of Thelma Trotter." Great Christ! What a perplexity! I don't know Mildred DeVoe. Never heard of her. But I know her twice as well as I know her cousin Thelma Trotter!

They tell me that during the holiday season it is sometimes a good idea to stir up a fat wassail bowl. I have moments when I suspect this to be a laudable idea. For I simply cannot come up with a solution to this mystery card problem. Right at the moment, now in December, I am toying with the idea of moving to Pensacola, Florida, and leaving no forwarding address.

CHAPTER 6

THE FATHER OF OCTOPUS WRESTLING

The American people are blessed with a near surfeit of athletic pursuits, both indoors and out, and it is today a difficult matter to bring a new form of sporting activity to public acceptance. I need only call attention to how boomeranging didn't make it, and how quickly the Hula Hoop petered out. And yet today a new and thrilling sport is developing and showing staying power along the golden California littoral. I refer to octopus wrestling.

There would appear to be enough novelty as well as sufficient real hazard in this sport to allow it to achieve great popularity. At the present writing, however, I am not inclined to think it will ever become as big as football, baseball, deer killing, golf, bowling, or fish fishing. It cannot outdistance these firmly established sports for one basic reason: there are not enough octopuses. I mean within ready reach.

Nevertheless, I hope and pray that this new sport will prosper and become an important element of the American cultural pattern. I hold such hopes for the reason that I have in my possession an outline history of the man who would surely become celebrated as The Father of Octopus Wrestling. I would be the one to tell his heroic and inspiring story. His name was O'Rourke. I don't know his given name. But he is to octopus wrestling what Abner Doubleday was (or wasn't) to baseball, what Dr. James Naismith was to basketball, and what Lord Halliwell Jefferies was to crokinole, sometimes known as squails.

I first heard about the great O'Rourke from my friend Idwal Jones, the California critic, historian, and gourmet. Mr. Jones knew O'Rourke and furnished me with most of the details of his story, and I picked up additional information about him in Los Angeles and San Francisco. All this historical data has been reposing in my files for nigh twenty years. I had, indeed, forgotten about O'Rourke until just recently when I heard about the renascence of octopus wrestling on the Pacific Coast.

Idwal Jones met O'Rourke through a man named Vanderhoeven, a soldier of fortune who looked and acted the part; he was a crack shot, a sybarite, a boulevardier, an explorer, a gunrunner, somewhat interested in girls, and he wore a pointy beard. Back in the 1920s this Vanderhoeven came upon lean times while living in Southern California and it became necessary for him to find employment. The idea of steady work was revolting to him, but so was the idea of going hungry.

During sober consideration of his need for funds, Vanderhoeven recalled the fact that the meat of the octopus is a delicacy among the Chinese who live in large numbers along the Pacific Coast, and he knew that there was always a shortage of this commodity. He schemed out a plan, and kismet moved into the picture, and he made the acquaintance of our hero O'Rourke, a former diver in the Coast Guard, who also was on his uppers. Idwal Jones, always a fine hand with words, described O'Rourke as being "a kobold with one eye and vast brawn, five-foot-five, built like a redwood stump."

The dashing Vanderhoeven and the hebetudinous O'Rourke put their heads together and organized what was later known as the Octopus Monopoly. They built themselves a large and sturdy raft and acquired some old diving equipment and a rusty windlass. They informed themselves about those areas of the Pacific which were the known haunts of the eight-armed monsters, and they set out to get them in quantity.

Vanderhoeven was the brain, the mastermind, of the project and O'Rourke had what would appear on the surface to be a somewhat lesser role. He was live bait.

The operation was simplicity itself. The two men took their raft into the octopus grounds. Once over a likely field, O'Rourke stripped himself naked and fitted a diving helmet over his squarish head. Then Vanderhoeven, puffing on a stubby brier pipe, manned the windlass and lowered his partner to the ocean's floor.

O'Rourke was never sensitive about his part in the business; he did not think of himself as the equivalent, in a sense, of a fishing worm. He'd grope his way along the bottom while overhead Vanderhoeven puffed brier and worked the ancient air pump. O'Rourke was good at his job. He probed into submarine crevices and canyons, a shining white mark for all manner of hideous sea beasts—the voracious dog salmon, the man-eating abalone, the night-growling grunion, and the spike-toothed pilchard. All of these O'Rourke brushed aside, for he sought more profitable quarry. Sooner or later, there in the watery quiet, an octopus would come at him, and O'Rourke, a man of magnificent guts, would stand quiescent while the beast began wrapping him in fond embrace. There are no bigger octopuses in the world than those that flap around in the waters off California, and O'Rourke's meaty body sometimes brought forth specimens with an unpleasant reach of twelve or fourteen feet.

An octopus has great confidence in himself and generally goes about his work with care and deliberation, the same as a boa constrictor. It is never advisable for unskilled personnel to fool around with an octopus, lest they be partaken of. O'Rourke had a natural talent for coping with his prey. He, too, worked with a cool deliberation. After the octopus had got a fair purchase on him, he began to *pretend* resistance, with a series of squirmings and threshings, making as if to throw off the enfolding tentacles. All of these maneuvers were calculated to lead the octopus to tighten his hold. When O'Rourke thought that he was beginning to hear his own bones go crunch, he tugged at the signal cord and Vanderhoeven set to work hoisting bait and catch to the surface.

Once back aboard the raft and still in the grip of those tentacles, it was O'Rourke's assignment to stand quietly while his partner took a *schiavone*, a two-edged basket-hilted sword he had picked up in Italy, and methodically whacked off the arms of the octopus. Witnesses to this operation often spoke feelingly of the delicate touch Vanderhoeven had with that *schiavone*. He could take off a heavy tentacle with a single stroke and never once nick the skin of his bait. After the catch had been removed and butchered, O'Rourke was given a brief rest and then back he went to the floor of the sea.

It was such an original and efficient technique for snaring the succulent cephalopod that the two men were soon wallowing in money. They dried the octopus meat and sold it at fancy prices to Chinese merchants and restaurant-keepers from San Diego to Vancouver. And all this while O'Rourke was becoming perhaps the world's greatest authority on the thought processes and the personality of the octopus. He knew how to outmaneuver them, to outflank them, almost how to outthink them. He knew full well, many years ago, what today's octopus wrestlers are just beginning to learn—that it is impossible for a man with two arms to apply a full nelson on an octopus; he knew the futility of trying for a crotch hold on an opponent with eight crotches.

Eventually the work palled on both men. In Idwal Jones's opinion they grew bored with it after they grew prosperous. Neither O'Rourke nor Vanderhoeven could stand the thought of money in the bank and now they both had it and so they dissolved their partnership and scuttled their raft. Vanderhoeven disappeared into the East but O'Rourke stayed on in California, working as a stunt man in movies. He even listed himself in the talent catalogues as "Expert at Greeko-Roman Octopus Wrestling," and, in fact, he did work with octopuses in several films. It is said that Cecil B. De Mille admired O'Rourke's work and once engaged him to wrestle an octopus for three days when he knew quite well he would not be using the episode in the film he was shooting.

If we must know of what happened to this man O'Rourke, it is necessary that we touch upon romantic matters. He was still making ample money in movies, but he was an improvident man, with a hankering for the grape and an affinity for crap shooting. He often spoke of his beautiful fiancée back in Ohio, saying he intended bringing her out and marrying her so she could manage his affairs and keep him from spending more than he earned. One day the fiancée arrived, accompanied by about twenty relatives, all female. They moved in on O'Rourke and demanded T-bone steaks twice a day and he was compelled to sleep on a pallet on the back porch. He grew melancholy and restive over this state of affairs and probably had yearnings for the old days, the companionship of the debonair Vanderhoeven, and the deepwater embrace of a brunette octopus . . . but he married the girl nonetheless.

She was a big strapping cow-milking type of woman, constructed along the lines of the Powerful Katrinka, and she loved O'Rourke dearly.

To celebrate the marriage, O'Rourke's pals in the Coast Guard gave a party beside the municipal swimming pool at Manhattan Beach (California). There was considerable drinking and O'Rourke did his share. Quite frankly he was groaning beneath the incubus of those twenty female in-laws.

Finally he stepped to the edge of the big pool and delivered a poignant speech, which started out as a farewell to his bachelor days and ended up as a farewell to everything. He announced that he was going to leap into the pool, swim through the intake pipe to the Pacific, proceed out to sea (anticipating Fredric March in *A Star Is Born* by a good ten years), and disappear forever.

As he concluded his speech he shouted a stirring hail and farewell and launched himself through the air and the Powerful Katrinka, letting out a cry of anguish, leaped forward. She grabbed for her beloved O'Rourke and got hold of his swimming pants. His body shot out of the pants and as he clove the water he was more naked than he ever had been while prowling the octopus grounds. He went underwater and started to enter the intake pipe, and then he turned back and surfaced.

That is really the last view we have of O'Rourke—that moment of surfacing naked in the pool. He didn't make it through the intake pipe, but he did vanish through the overflow gutter of history, accompanied by his Powerful Katrinka. Neither Idwal Jones nor I acquired any knowledge of what became of him after that.

This I do know and gladly state: the Father of Octopus Wrestling, though possessed of all the normal instincts of the true bum, still retained certain admirable qualities of character. He had great physical courage, a fine sense of the dramatic, and, above all else, deep-seated personal modesty. I said deep-seated. Some years after that poolside party, Idwal Jones ran into a man who had been present. He said that O'Rourke told him he had changed his mind about going through the intake pipe because he could not abide the thought of arriving before the reception committee of heaven without pants on.

The game can indeed be proud of him.

CHAPTER 7

THE TALKING RAM OF FIJI

A common remark among travelers who have just returned from a journey through foreign climes is this: "I'm telling you, we had the best, the most marvelous god-damn guide in the whole wide world. We actually had to fight off the temptation to bring him home with us." Followed by interminable anecdotes about what this unexcelled guide did and what he said and how he said it.

I contend loudly and firmly that, during a dozen rambling journeys around the Republic of Mexico, I have had the best guide in the whole history of the world. Carlos Campo, of Mexico City. I have written about him at considerable length . . . about what he did and what he said and how he said it. And a couple of times I *have* brought him home with me.

We now come to the *second* best guide I ever had. My wife and I finished off an unforgettable winter in Tahiti, where I was gathering material for a book about the fabled isle, and before heading back home we took the long Matson Line cruise around the Pacific islands.

Our ship, the *Mariposa*, docked at Suva, the capital and principal port of the island of Fiji and we had one full and eventful day in and around the town. When we came down the *Mariposa* gangplank I asked somebody where I could lay hands on a competent guide. A gray-skinned man, a taxi driver, standing beside an elderly sedan, was pointed out to me as being quite adequate.

This was Ramresh, a Hindu who was once celebrated in Fiji soccer circles as The Ram. (Coincidence: My Number One guide, Carlos Campo, was a great soccer hero in Mexico and later was coach of championship teams.)

I am not able to furnish a detailed description of The Ram because I concentrated all of my attention on his manner of talk. He was a Buddhist Gatling gun. I scratched down notes feverishly but I couldn't keep up with him. I do recall that he was rather shabbily dressed in a business suit, wore a necktie, and had glittering, darting black eyes. Whenever I think of him I remember chiefly his passionate and unorthodox employment of the English language. New York taxi drivers are famous for their garrulousness (I always found them to be driveling boobs). The Ram was something else. I even suspect that he was a wise man. I'm not sure about it. I do know that while I was with him, he gave dash and color to just plain gibblegabble, vaguely in the tradition of Lardner and Mencken and Octavus Roy Cohen and Sou Chan.

The Ram discoursed at some length on the subject of Fijian shawker. It took a little time for me to realize that he sometimes used "sh" for plain "s" as in, "Now from these hill you shee the harbor and the *Maryposey*." He spoke English, I imagine, with influences taken from both the language of Gautama Buddha and the peculiar speech patterns of the Fijians . . . with just a smidgin of pidgin. The Fiji radio couches its broadcasts in Fijian, Indian, and English, and I suspect that The Ram acquired his cicerone style of talk via the airwaves. His radio offers no broadcasts in pidgin, but somewhere he had picked up fragments of that fascinating tongue as spoken in the vicinity of the Solomons and New Guinea.

As we toured Suva he often found himself at a momentary loss for a subject to talk about, when he would say either, "Don't worry!" (there was nothing whatever to worry about) or, "Thiss the main thing," with reference to nothing. He also used these two lines as a means of finishing off a sentence with a flourish.

He showed us many cockanuts trees, and a Cadillac church as well as a Meddadiss church. He had some kind of a graveyard fixation and took us to three, including a military cemetery. "Plenty Americans in," he said, waving a hand, "but not killing anywhere—only got sick and accidentals." He seemed to think that we'd enjoy knowing that many American troops were in Fiji during World War II. "American marings do practice here to invade Goddycanal," was the way he put it. "They make much good roads," he added. He said they used jips and jimseys and bulldozey. I got the jips and I got the bulldozey, but he lost me with the jimseys. Turned out to be GMCs.

He said, "I am old thirty-eight but look like twenty-two," a statement which demonstrated that The Ram's judgments were not infallible. He look like old thirty-eight. He spoke frequently about something called the Jippyaitch, and I finally had to ask him; he had reference to the famous Grand Pacific Hotel . . . only squares and tourists like me call it by its full name; in Suva it is known by its initials. It is a historic establishment and in its cool lobby British planters sit and drink their rum punches and say to each other, "Bugger you, Jack."

Once my wife asked The Ram if they had TV in Fiji. "We got much," he said, and added, "Many." He made a wild U-turn, drove three miles, and stopped in front of a TB sanitarium. He called the place the *housick* which is pidgin for hospital. They had no TV in Fiji.

I asked The Ram if he knew anything about the good old cannibal days in Fiji, the golden era before Progress came. He knew all about. Being a non-Fijian, or maybe even an anti-Fijian, he made his response with fervor, revealing that he had studied his local history. He spoke of a Ravrunt Baker. This Ravrunt Baker, a missionary, wasn't up on local customs. He gave the Fijian chief an ornamental comb and the chief poked it into his bushy, kinky hair. Ravrunt Baker decided the comb had not been placed properly, and reached out his hand to adjust it, and touched the chief's head. "Nobody," said The Ram, "allow to touch nambawan boss head only his Mama. So Ravrunt Baker they *kaikai* [eat] after cook up." Parenthetically let me say that the Indians do not love the Fijians and vice versa, and thus it may be said that the peoples of Fiji follow the course of peoples elsewhere in the world. There are today more Indians than there are native Fijians. The Ram smiled with smug satisfaction as he told how the *longlong* (idiot) Fijian cannibals consumed the Ravrunt Baker, then boiled his shoes and tried to eat them, thinking they were a physical part of the man, therefore meat. "Stoobid," said the Ram. "Many

Fiji veeples stoobid that time, many stoobid this very day." I agreed. The whole world is stoobid.

The Ram offered us another example of Fijian stoobiddity. "Always in these island is no metal dings," he said. "Always the Fiji veeples hungry for metal dings. So the ships come and trade nails and spikes to the veeples. What do the stoobid Fijians do? They go and plant nails and spikes, say they will grow up a good crop." A pause, then, "Thiss the main thing."

I urged him on to more cannibal lore and he told us of a chief who lived "inside Rickey Rackey (Rakiraki?) one hundred years long back, was well-know in Fiji as champion veeple-eating man. All time he eat one veeple he put one rock on his big pile rocks and he had nine hunded these rocks. Somebody count. Don't worry!" That Rickey Rackey chief sounded to me like a truly ferocious individual, and I have no doubt that eventually he *kaikai* all nine hundred of his rocks.

"How did they cook their veeples?" I asked. The Ram often used a "v" instead of a "p." I adapt quickly and found myself doing the same after a while.

"Stim," he said. "Stim, most time." I didn't gather it. "Stim come stimming out from oven," he said, and I got it. "But sometime boil."

"In a big black pot?"

"Yes. Thiss the main thing."

Did The Ram know why those noble old Fijians ate one another?

"In long back," he said, "everybody belonk to tribe. One *kokoruk*—mins chiggen, mins hen—one *kokoruk* from one tribe runs up the hill and down other side, and Fiji man from other tribe grabs this *kokoruk*, this chiggen, and kills and makes nice lunge. Now comes very bad war, all about one little chiggen. Comes to the end the war and many veeples with both sides are cook up and eat."

Seems a reasonable procedure by modern standards. Somebody hauls off and snatches my chiggen, my *kokoruk*, they're in bad trouble. My Mama didn't raise no stoobid children.

The Ram drove us out beyond the edge of town a couple of times so we could see the way the Fijians lived. At one point in our tour he took us into a thatched hut occupied by a native family. Two women, sitting on the earthen floor, looked up and spoke a word that sounded like "Gawrk." The Ram said to us, "Say Gawrk. Mins hello." We said Gawrk. There was a dish in the middle of the floor with two shillings in it. I dropped in some small coins. The two women said, "Tenkyu." The Ram said, "Say Tenkyu. Mins tenk you." We said it.

Thus a day with The Ram. Most educational. Back aboard the *Mariposa* (which had become almost a second home to us) I suddenly realized that I had seen very little of Fiji itself. I scarcely noticed the *sulus* and the *saris* worn by the natives, and the fantastic Fijian hair stylings which have been borrowed and adapted by our own splendid young people. Still, I had met and enjoyed my second favorite guide in all the world, and I can truthfully say I wish I could have taken The Ram home with me. Just for a little while. Thiss the main thing.

CHAPTER 8

MY BRIEF CAREER IN DUELING

This big envelope arrived from Polynesia and in it I found a copy of a French-language newspaper published on the island of Tahiti. Half the front page and all of the second were devoted to a wild and scurrilous attack on me.

I had spent a winter in Tahiti and written a book about my experiences and now the editor of this paper, M. Philippe Mazellier, was accusing me of gross inaccuracies, of vast and deliberate untruths, of malicious libels against the island which I happen to love more than any other.

I was furious. I had never before been accused of inept reporting, of deliberate falsification. I stewed. I steamed. I uttered wild oaths. What to do? In the United States it was once the custom to horsewhip an irresponsible newspaper editor. But this was a Frenchman in an alien land. Then I remembered the proper Gallic procedure. I would have to call him out. Fight him with pistol or rapier. Preferably rapier. Divide this Gaul into three parts.

I have never laid hand on a sword in my life and while I am adept with a rifle, I wouldn't be able to hit the Pentagon with a pistol at ten paces. Up until I was twenty-five years old I believed that swordsmen were accustomed to hollering "Tootchie!" at each other. Nevertheless, my honor had been despicably impugned and I must, forsooth, take action. But first I decided to go into training and study up on dueling—learn everything possible about the Code of Honor and its workings.

If I am nothing else, I am a thorough man. I am Agent 007+3 when I undertake an investigation. If I research a subject, that subject knows it has been researched. Almost immediately I found that men who indulge themselves in the serene pleasures of the code duello also are thorough men—thorough in perfecting their skills with sword and pistol. My foe was a Frenchman and I might assume him to be a capable swordsman. I was given momentary pause when I learned that Charles G. Bothner, winner of nine fencing titles around the turn of the century, could take a foil, an epee, or a saber and "slice a hair the long way with all three." Then I read about Cassius Marcellus Clay, Kentucky plantation owner and Lincoln's ambassador to Russia, whose name is perpetuated by the present heavyweight boxer—his antecedents were slaves on the Clay place.

Colonel Clay was a duelist of renown and a crack pistol shot. Better than Matt Dillon. As he lay on his deathbed, his favorite dueling pistol at his side, he felt life ebbing from his body. He opened his eyes and saw a fly crawling across the ceiling. He picked up his pistol, killed the fly with one shot, and then expired. For some reason I now caught myself thinking that my personal hinges are getting rusty and I cannot leap about and caracole the way Errol Flynn used to do it on the Spanish Main, running people through, one after another, faster than an Omaha pig-sticker sticks pigs.

There have been traditions of man-to-man combat since the time of the Neanderthal brute, when the boys stood nose to nose and whopped each other on their hippie-style noggins with large and jagged rocks. There came, too, the type of duel promoted by the Holy Roman emperors—the scuffles of the gladiators—and later on the rough play of King Arthur's boys. Then somewhere in Continental Europe the idea of the code duello developed, and it was believed that the man who was right always won, that Divine Wisdom had a hand in every duel. In 1371 the so-called Dog of Montargis incident gave emphasis to this point. The dog's master was murdered and the bereft animal began attacking a certain man of the town. Charles V ordered the man to fight the dog, using only a heavy stick; they fought, and the dog was about to kill the man when the battle was stopped. The victory of the dog was proof to the king that the murderer had been found, and he was forthwith hanged. By god, that's what I call justice.

Dueling was a rather debilitating affair in seventeenth-century France. The duelists began by firing arquebuses at each other. If nobody fell, they then resorted to swords. If one man lost his sword he was allowed to pick up his arquebus and try to brain his opponent with it. Both men then took off their metal helmets, which weighed as much as zinc washtubs, and began slashing at each other. If still on their feet, they next seized the wooden arquebus supports, shaped somewhat like large crutches, and walloped away with them until they were in splinters. Next came flogging each other with bandoliers and after that a resort to the nostalgic, old-fashioned custom of knock-down, eye-gouging, ear-biting combat, ending with the victor stripping every stitch of clothes off the vanquished. It wears me out just to write about it.

The French attitude toward the duello was summarized by Napoleon during his exile at St. Helena. "It is too bad," he said, "that death often results from dueling, for duels otherwise help keep up politeness in society." It is all but impossible to determine how many hundreds of thousands died at the altar of Napoleon's ambition—but, no matter; his observation on dueling shows he was a man of gentility, with a sensitive attitude toward life.

On the other hand Mark Twain, who was always keenly interested in the farcical aspects of European dueling, had a low opinion of the sincerity of Frenchmen in affairs of honor. Comparing Austrian dueling with the French variety, he wrote: "Here [in Austria] it is tragedy; in France it is comedy; here it is a solemnity, there it is monkey-shines; here the duellist risks his life, there he does not even risk his shirt. Here he fights with pistol or sabre, in France with a hairpin—a blunt one.

"Much as the modern French duel is ridiculed by certain smart people," Twain went on, "it is in reality one of the most dangerous institutions of our day. Since it is always fought in the open air the combatants are nearly sure to catch cold."

The celebrated dueling practices of German students, centered at Heidelberg, were very sensible. There was usually no actual animosity between the combatants; they were in there for the laudable purpose of getting slashed deeply on the cheek, thereby acquiring a ghastly scar that would last them a lifetime and serve as a badge of their manliness. It was the custom among these brilliant young intellects, after the doctor departed, to remove the bandages and rub salt in the wound or even to rip out the stitches. They wanted scars that were scars, scars that were hideous enough to attract lovely women to them. This student dueling in the Reich was outlawed immediately after World War II, but it has been slowly reviving and is now said to be widespread.

It may be that there has been a diminution in dueling in some parts of Europe because of the high cost of living. I mean high cost of killing. Count Ernesto Perrier, a temperamental Sicilian Monarchist, announced some years back that after fighting nine duels, he was finished. "It used to be," said the Count, "that you could fight a nice duel for two or three thousand lire. Now it costs at least 25,000 lire." He itemized duel expenses: rental of swords, 5,000; doctors, 5,000; dinner for seconds, 10,000; taxicabs and incidentals, 5,000. Concluded the Count: "I don't know anyone I dislike enough to pay out 25,000 lire to fight."

Some of this information might have been discouraging to an ordinary mortal, but my wrath toward that pip-squeak Polynesian penny-a-liner did not abate and I went on with my research . . . and ordered a sword. I felt that I was making progress; still, I needed more substantial data . . . so, back to the library.

The first duel fought in America was an encounter between Edward Doty and Edward Leicester, at Plymouth in 1621. Both were manservants and they fought with daggers. Each was wounded but not grievously, and the entire colony was scandalized by the event . . . not because a duel had been fought, but because these two lowly men had indulged in a social custom that was the prerogative of gentlemen, whereas they were only servants of gentlemen. They were severely punished for their effrontery.

Many duels have been fought from peculiar motives. Early in the nineteenth century a Virginia planter named Powell overheard a visiting Englishman say, "The Virginians are of no use to America—it requires one half of them to keep the other half in order." Powell called the scoundrel out and the Englishman killed him with his first shot. Thus Powell became, in the flicker of an eyelash, a truly useless Virginian.

My own favorite insult leading to a duel was a low-down slur cast against the Mississippi River. The Chevalier Tomasi, a distinguished French scientist with strong opinions on every known subject, was sojourning in New Orleans. He was consistently critical of American manners and mores, and one day, in a coffee house, he said to a Creole gentleman: "How little you know of the world! There are rivers in Europe so large that, compared to them, the Mississippi is a mere rivulet."

"Sir," said the Creole, "I will never allow the Mississippi to be insulted or disparaged in my presence. Take that!"

The glove-across-the-face bit. They met next dawning under The Oaks, and the French scientist got a bad slash across his river-deriding mouth. Did he learn restraint? For some time afterward he went around New Orleans saying that he would have surely killed his man but for the inferior metal in the American sword he had been compelled to use—he said the weapon buckled on him as if it were made of lead. This Frenchman, however, made no further snotty remarks about rivers. Or even ponds.

Related to the Tomasi incident is the story of an American naval officer who fought a duel with an English naval officer because the Britisher had referred to the American flagship as "a bunch of pine boards." A few years back Arthur Strange Kattendyke David Archibald Gore, eighth Earl of Arran, publicly called Sweden "a piddling sort of country." The Swedish ambassador challenged Artie who in turn named the weapons: "Motorcars in the Hyde Park Underpass." Duel cancelled.

At about this point in my researches, some of the romance, some of the derring-do, seemed to be slipping away from me. I felt constrained to remind Monsieur Mazellier of Tahiti that I had spoken favorably of coconut cream, Polynesian watermelons, the odor of white ginger, and the view from One Tree Hill. But then I turned my mind back to his knavish insults; and continued digging.

There have been many salty and sapient responses to challenges. Richard Steele, the great English essayist, as a young man nearly killed an opponent in a duel and thereafter campaigned against the practice. Once, to demonstrate the absurdity of dueling, he wrote this challenge:

"Sir: Your extraordinary behavior last night, and the liberty you were pleased to take with me, makes me this morning give you this, to tell you, because you are an ill-bred puppy, I will meet you in Hyde Park an hour hence . . . I would desire you would come with a pistol in your hand and endeavor to shoot me in the head, to teach you more manners."

Another type of response was sent by John Wilkes, English editor and politician, after he had been challenged by a man named Horne Tooke, who was under a charge of treason. Wilkes wrote: "Sir: I do not think it my business to cut the throat of every desperado that may be tired of life; but as I am at present the High Sheriff of the City of London, it may happen that I shall shortly have an opportunity of attending you in my official capacity."

Sam Houston, as President of Texas, received a steady flow of call-outs. One day a man arrived carrying a challenge. Houston handed it to his secretary and said, "Mark this Number 14 and file it." Then to the courier: "Your friend will have to wait his turn."

Patrick Henry, who was often embroiled in quarrels and challenges, once received a note from Governor Giles of Virginia, demanding satisfaction because, he said, Henry had called him "a bob-tail politician." He demanded to know what was meant by the phrase. Henry replied:

"Sir: I do not recollect having called you a bob-tail politician at any time, but think it probable I have. Not recollecting the time or occasion, I can't say what I did mean, but if you will tell me what you think I meant, I will say whether you are correct or not."

The challenged party, in many cases, has laid down some queer specifications. Sometimes the choice of weapons has been of a nature to set everybody howling with laughter, and bloodshed has been avoided. So it was with Abraham Lincoln, who was challenged at least twice in his Illinois days. In one instance he prescribed "cow dung at five paces" and there was no duel. In another, more serious affair, a man named Shields challenged Lincoln, who specified cavalry sabers. The party was being rowed to a sandbar in the Mississippi when Lincoln remarked that he felt somehow like a certain Kentucky boy who had been called to the colors in the War of 1812. The boy's sweetheart embroidered a bullet pouch with the words "Victory or Death." He looked at it questioningly and said, "Ain't that rayther too strong? Spose you just make it 'Victory or Crippled.'" The story put everyone in a pleasant frame of mind and at the sandbar the disagreement was patched up.

In 1819 General Armistead T. Mason, who was United States senator from Virginia, called out his cousin, Colonel John M. McCarty. They had quarreled over an election, and now McCarty proposed that they fight one of three ways: (1) standing on a barrel of gunpowder; (2) hand-to-hand with dirks, or (3) that they leap together from the dome of the capitol building and see which one survived. General Mason was not to be put off with jocosity, and they went to Washington's favorite dueling grounds at Bladensburg, Maryland. They used shotguns at four paces. General Mason was killed instantly and Colonel McCarty was shot to shreds, but survived. A story like this makes me a trifle queazy. I have been reconsidering this whole proposition. I do wish that Monsieur Mazellier would take into consideration the fact that I spoke glowingly of the Renault Dauphine, the no-tipping rule in Tahiti, and Lousie Chauvel's lovely chickens. I was almost ecstatic about Hinano beer. The only things I was severely critical about were minor matters, such as the government and the character of the people who live on the island, and the chickenshit newspapers. But no, I'll not back away from this thing. I'll not retreat an inch before this whoreson gulper of snails. No man shall get away with insulting a Smith! The lagoon off Papeete shall be incarnadined with the blood of this uncouth frog!

In Georgia, at the time of an infamous land grab, two judges got into a quarrel and there was a challenge. One judge called attention to the fact that his opponent had a wooden leg and demanded that, to equalize things, he be given a protective covering for one of his legs. The argument over this detail grew so comical that the whole thing was called off.

In the early years of this century Chicago had an oddball congressman named Billy Mason. He was known more widely than most congressmen because his picture appeared in advertisements for Nuxated Iron. This was a remarkable thing in itself, because Billy stood five feet two and was at least sixty inches around the diaphragm. During a junket to Paris, Billy made some slurring remark about the French and a Parisian editor published a challenge in his newspaper. Billy Mason had to answer it. He wrote:

> I will accept your challenge and meet you at 5 A.M. in the Bois de Boulogne. We will fight with pistols. According to the code duello, as the challenged party I will name the method of combat. I am short and wide and you are tall and thin. We will stand belly to belly. My second, with chalk, will mark your outline on me. We will then turn back to back, proceed fifteen paces, turn and fire. You will have to hit me between the chalk lines. Anything outside won't count.

The most famous incident out of the assorted duels fought by Andrew Jackson is the one involving the loose coat. Old Hickory's opponent, Charles Dickinson, was a dead shot. When they faced each other, Jackson let his pistol hang at his side, but wriggled himself around inside the coat so that Dickinson would misjudge the location of his heart. It worked. Jackson was hit, but he was able to stand and deliver a mortal wound to his opponent.

Possibly because of the Frenchified ambiance, the greatest town for dueling in the United States was, beyond all question, New Orleans. "Nowhere else in America," wrote Herbert Asbury, "and for that matter in few European cities, was the so-called Code of Honor regarded with such reverence and the duello so universally practiced as in New Orleans during the hundred years that preceded the Civil War."

Throughout that golden, gory era, the background music in New Orleans was the steady, rhythmic slap of fawnskin gloves across the faces of insolent men. There were intricate coded rules and there were unwritten laws, such as the one that said one ounce of whiskey was enough to throw in a foe's face to provoke a challenge—no need to be wasteful. At one time there were at least fifty fencing masters in New Orleans and many of them spent more time in actual dueling than in teaching. The most famous of their number was Joe "Pepe" Llulla; it was said of him that he maintained his own cemetery for the victims of his rapier.

The traditional dueling ground was a place known as The Oaks, now located in City Park. Here men fought with swords, squirrel rifles, Navy revolvers, double-barreled shotguns, double-bitted axes, and even Neanderthalian bludgeons. It is recorded that around 1810 two men fought with eight-foot sections of three-by-three cypress timber and knocked each other bowlegged.

The French gentlemen and the Creoles of the town were quick-tempered (like the oaf Mazellier) and eager to find an excuse to fight. One of the more steadily employed duelists was a man named Rosiere, from Bordeaux. He fought as many as seven duels in one week. One night he was at the opera, and a touching scene on the stage set him to sobbing. A man sitting nearby laughed. That man got a standing rib roast carved out of him the next morning at The Oaks.

Bernard Marigny, from the most illustrious family in Louisiana, was a great pistol shot. In 1817 he became embroiled with a state legislator named Humble, a former blacksmith, seven feet tall with biceps the size of Carolina hams. Eventually Marigny challenged Humble who, true to his name, at first said he would not fight. A friend told him that he had to fight, that no gentleman could refuse. "I am not a gentleman," said Humble. "I am only a black-smith." They then told him he would have the choice of weapons and so, after pondering the matter, he sent Marigny this reply: "I accept, and in the exercise of my privilege I stipulate that the duel shall take place in Lake Ponchartrain in six feet of water, sledge hammers to be used for weapons." Marigny, who was five feet eight inches tall, read the note, burst into laughter, and there was no duel.

There is more, much more, in the way of history and folklore touching on the gallant institution of the duello—but it all has a rather discouraging effect on me. I have begun to weaken. I feel somewhat in the mood of Mark Twain, who said: "I think I could wipe out a dishonor by crippling the other man, but I don't see how I could do it by letting him cripple me." As regards Monsieur Mazellier, I am now more inclined to employ the technique used by another Frenchman, Anatole France, responding to an insulting and challenging letter he received from Joris-Karl Huysmans. M. France scribbled a note and handed it to the courier. It said: "To M. Huysmans my compliments, and tell him M. France suggests he have his water examined."

No, I won't even go that far—I'm not going to antagonize M.

Mazellier any further. I have been reading a book, *A Planet Called Earth*, by Dr. George Gamow. He advises us that about five billion years hence the sun is going to explode and turn into a tiny star that nobody will notice. "The heat developed by the explosion," Dr. Gamow writes, "will no doubt melt all the planets which had been living peacefully with the sun for ten billion years and streams of hot gases may even throw molten planets clear out of the solar system. When the force of the explosion is spent, what is left of the sun and its planets will gradually cool to the temperature of interstellar space, which is hundreds of degrees below freezing."

What's the use? Who wants to defend his honor with swords or pistols or double-bitted axes or Lincolnian cow-flops or cypress timbers when a thing like that is coming at us? In my own heart I know that I spoke favorably of Polynesian buried pig, and I saluted the glories of steak *au poivre* as served up at the Hotel Taaone. I am reconciled to a career of sitting before a log fire and contemplating the eternal verities. I find myself now with strong feelings of amity and comity toward M. Mazellier of Papeete. I want him for my friend. I have sent him a letter of abject apology.

CHAPTER 9

MY TWO HEROES—SAM AND HARRY

Cuteness bugs me almost beyond endurance. It is my opinion that people who talk baby talk (other than babies) belong in a hospital for the criminally insane. There are moments when I'd dearly love to belt Smokey the Bear a good one right in the chops. I would happily adjust the noose around the necks of those who say "brunch" and "bye now" and "anyhoo" and "all righty." I support the belief of Samuel Johnson that children, until they attain the age of eighteen, should be raised in a barrel and fed through the bunghole. On the evidence of modern times, I despair of them after they have been released from their barrels. In short, I am cynical (in moderation) and lacking in sentimentality.

Yet I frequently find myself grown saccharine and almost simpering over two figures in American literature, and I describe them unhesitatingly as my heroes. Their names: Mark Twain and Henry Louis Mencken. I sometimes catch myself indulging in the ridiculous conceit of being thrilled that I was alive in this world at the same time Mark Twain lived. And I am almost psychopathically proud of the fact that I knew Mencken and had the privilege of personal relationship with him over a period of thirty years.

I often bore people to the edge of distraction by talking about these two men. An unfeeling friend of mine has remarked: "Any day now he'll start calling them Sam and Harry."

I became a Mencken nut first and a Mark Twain buff shortly afterward. In time I learned that Mencken was himself a devoted admirer of Mark Twain, but I never suspected the full extent of the connection between the two until a day in the late 1930s when I was visiting Mencken in Hollins Street. I got Harry to talking about Sam and he took me into the dining room and stood me before a massive secretary that had belonged to his father. Among the books on an upper shelf were half a dozen first editions of Mark Twain, who was a favorite of Mencken's father.

When Mencken was nine years old he discovered that shelf. He had developed an appetite for reading but the available fare had been meager and mediocre, and then one day he dragged a chair over to the secretary and climbed up to have a prowl. By superb chance (I sometimes think it borders on the supernatural, to which I am not addicted) his hand fell upon a greenish volume titled *The Adventures of Huckleberry Finn*. The boy took it down and read it with mounting excitement and then went on to the other Twain books.

"When I was twenty," Henry Mencken said, "I had a column going in the Baltimore *Herald*. I wrote in it that the critics were all lunatics for failing to recognize that *Huck Finn* was the greatest novel ever produced by an American. I wrote that in 1900. I have never changed my mind. Up until my forties I read it at least once a year, and I still drag it down and read it again from time to time."

In one of his books Mencken said that his discovery of Huck was "probably the most stupendous event in my whole life." He had been destined, by his father's decree, for the family tobacco business. He was eighteen and working in the Mencken cigar factory when his father died. Three days later Henry put on his best suit of clothes and made his way to the city room of the *Herald* and applied for a job.

"It was an inevitable sort of thing," he told me. "It went straight as an arrow back to that day I climbed up here and plucked out *Huckleberry Finn*. I was no more than fifty pages into it when I decided I was going to be a writer when I grew up. I never faltered in that resolution."

Old Harry! And old Sam! What a pair! Kindly pardon me, folks, while I brush a sentimental tear from my eye.

CHAPTER 10

MY FINAL VOYAGE—BY DEMIJOHN

A young fellow came up to me the other day, right in front of City Drug, and says, there seems to be a lot of talk lately about the high cost of dying and malfeasance in our mortuaries and the profit motive amongst body-style undertakers, not to mention land grabs in our cemeteries. Have you, he says, made any special provisions respecting the disposal of your remains when you up and coil off this mortal shuffle?

So I says, who the hell are you? And he says, I am doing some man-in-the-street interviews for the *Weekly Blat* on this subject because it is a subject of interest to a great many people. They indentify with it.

So I says, happy to oblige the press at any time, and it so happens I do have some arrangements which I intended keeping secret from the world until the fate accumply, but now that you've asked about them in such a demure way, I'm willing to make them public.

Then I told him as follows:

They talk about all these world problems that give a man goose bumps in the night, but nobody seems to be aware of the graveyard explosion. Has it ever occurred to you, *Blat* man, that the day will come eventually when all the land masses of the earth, plus every archipelago and island and atoll, all of this will be one vast graveyard? That there won't be any place any more for anybody to live? Well, it *has* occurred to me, and the spectral portent has motivated me, to some extent, in the drawing up and the setting down of my own arrangements. There is nothing very special about them, but I'll be most happy to furnish the details for your esteemed gazette.

As you must know, young man, it has become most unlawful in various parts of the country to scatter human ashes indiscriminately over populated areas and upon public waterways. There is already enough junk drifting around in the atmosphere that embraces our planet without adding disintegrated people—and it is true that things of this nature were getting a bit out of hand for a while. So many people were scattering ashes out of airplanes that the remnants of folks were getting all mixed up together and amalgamated before they ever hit the ground. Togetherness, you might call it. I happen to be of the firm belief that, in spite of the interdiction, many citizens are going up in small planes and scattering their loved ones secretly. I frown on this practice and I might add that I have no desire to be bootlegged to earth.

In any case (I went on), I began my funereal document by specifying that I wanted members of my immediate family to take my urn on board a handsome ocean liner and somewhere at sea, either in the Atlantic or the Pacific, consign it to the deeps. My motives were simple and somewhat paternalistic. I consider sailing aboard a modern luxury liner to be one of the major pleasures of life, and so I thought that it would be nice to take my final journey on such a ship. Moreover, I would be, in a small way, calling public attention to the dangers inherent in the graveyard explosion. Finally, I would be giving members of my family a farewell gift of a luxury cruise to foreign climes.

That last point, *Blat* man, is more important than it sounds. A man likes to bequeath something of consequence other than good will to his heirs, and it is not in my scheme of things to leave an estate of any consequence for them to squander or quarrel over. So here we have the single prospect of an all-expenses-paid ocean voyage and the tantalizing question, to wit: who gets it? I can keep them on tenterhooks the rest of my life, and while I can't intimidate them by threatening to disinherit them out of a bundle of cash money, I can always glower and say to them: "By god you better mend your ways or you won't get to go on that trip with my ashes!" Believe you me, they'll think twice before they take advantage of my benevolent nature in my fading years.

Now, newspaper guy, after I got these details fairly well settled, I turned back to my scheme for attracting public attention to the grave matter of the graveyard explosion. In this present-day world of promotion by holler-and-howl, where advertising is shrieked at us in our living rooms, I concluded that it would be necessary for me to dramatize and ceremony-up the casting overboard of my urn. A distasteful task it was, but I revised that part of the plan.

For a while I thought of having my ashes sealed not in the customary bronze urn, but instead in an old-fashioned earthenware jug, of the type Southerners are said to use for sorghum molasses and corn liquor and for blowing into musically. Still not quite spectacular enough.

Then I got it. I finalized. My ashes are to be placed in a large glass bottle and I have prepared a note to be inserted just before the bottle is securely corked. When it is hurled overboard by my loved ones it will float and drift possibly for months before it finally bobs its way up to some distant shore. The person who picks it off the beach will be perplexed over its contents until he fishes out my note, which will read somewhat as follows:

To the Finder of This Bottle—

They may not look like it, but these are my mortal remains. I must explain to you Sir, Madam, or Little Kid, that in the latter part of my life I became a dedicated and almost impassioned traveler to distant lands. Whenever I could get the money together, I would journey off to faraway places and enjoy myself more than anyone can imagine; later on I would usually write and publish a report on my pleasures and adventures in Europe or the Pacific Islands or Latin America or even in the various quarters of the United States. As you, Bottle Finder, stand on this lonely (thickly populated) (choose one) beach, you are witness to the culmination of my final voyage. Unhappily, I don't know where I went, or am. I will have no inkling whether the last of my trips took me to Europe or Africa or New Zealand or St. Kitts or Chile or the Azores or Luzon or Catalina. But wherever it is, or I am, or what's left of me, I would have enjoyed it if I could have lived on a little longer. No, actually I wouldn't've. If I had lived on a little longer I'd never have made it here, wherever I am, though I'd have wanted to, I think. So, Finder of My Bottle, please scatter my ashes on the water in front of you, even if they happen to be in a fjord or the Bay of Fundy, where they have all those goofy tides. After that, please communicate with my children and advise them: "Your dear father finally made it to the Canary Islands (Cape of Good Hope), (Tasmania), (Dingle Bay), (Oregon), (Pitcairn), (Atlantic City), where he always wanted to go."

So I says, there it is, Mr. *Weekly Blat*. That what you had in mind? And he says, well, to tell the truth, it runs a little long. And I says, in that case, maybe I ought to try to make my own small contribution to the avant-garde literature of passing away; so why don't you just leave it lay and I'll make a nice cheerful magazine article out of it, and if I sell it, I'll add the proceeds to the fund for that wonderful ocean voyage they're going to get if they keep their noses clean and accord me the respect I'm entitled to as undisputed head of the family.

And he shrugs and says, suit yourself, my friend, I can make it without your somewhat bizarre scheme, and he says, So long Daddio, and then he wandered off toward the Safeway in quest of another man-in-the-street.

As for me, I just stood there a few minutes in thought, wondering what size bottle I would need to make it all the way to Tristan da Cunha or wherever I make it to. This I know —I want something out of the ordinary and quite expensive, something on the order of a Pitkin bottle, blown about 1790 by a craftsman employing the German double-dipped method.

Or, better yet, a handsome demijohn made of rare Sandwich pressed glass. That's the ticket. That's what I want—a real expensive antique demijohn, because in all my years of pleasurable travel, I stuck to one guiding motto:

I go first class or I don't go at all.

CHAPTER 11

HEY DOC, WHAT YOU GOT
IN THAT LITTLE BAG?

Fella I know, interesting sort of fella, came up to me last Wednesday afternoon at 2:23 by the clock, right near the Methodist Church on East Main, and said:

"Know what-all a doctor's got in that little bag he carries around?"

"No," I said. "What?"

"Morphine sulfate," he said, "codeine phosphate, stethoscope, acetylsalicylic acid, sphygmomanometer, percussion hammer, analgesic ear drops, phenobarbital, otoscope-ophthalmoscope, paraldehyde, procaine penicillin, streptomycin, sulfonamide preparation, tourniquet, measuring tape, water for injection U.S.P. whatever the hell that means, two thermometers, two syringes, antihistaminic, nitroglycerin for sublingual use, needles, tongue depressors, cotton applicators, amyl nitrate, a synthetic antispasmodic, quinidine sulfate, scissors for bandages, adhesive tape, sterile gauze pads, gauze bandage, elastic bandage, digitalis preparation, mercurial diuretic, caffeine and soldium benzoate, aromatic spirits of ammonia, rubber gloves, analeptic, atropine sulfate, epinephrine, flashlight for dark nights, aminophylline, dihydroergotamine, rubber drain, splinter forceps, apomorphine, obstetrical pituitrin, wide-mouthed specimen bottle, prescription pad, tetanus antitoxin, catheter, scalpel, and this don't count what he's got in his pockets. How *about* that?"

I had to say something. I said, "Who'd a thought!"

CHAPTER 12

DECLINE AND COLLAPSE OF A CHAMPION

If proximity has anything to do with the ordering of human affairs, with special reference to golf, then I should be a champion in the game.

The proximity involved here lies in the fact that I am a close neighbor of Lee Trevino. He lives in El Paso and I live in a lesser (in size only) community called Alpine. We are 220 miles apart, but in West Texas 220 miles means no more than "just up the street a piece." A West Texas cattle rancher, standing treetop tall, can spit 220 miles. Out of the side of his mouth. In this area if you have a neighbor living as close as Lee Trevino lives to me, you begin complaining bitterly about the population explosion.

Nonetheless, as I said, this close proximity ought to have some extrasensory, or osmotic, effect upon me and make me a golfer of championship caliber. My god, what am I saying? I have *been* a champion golfer.

Leave us go back to Denver in the year of 1928, when I was a young reporter on the fabulous Denver *Post*. We had a fine, two-story, elegantly fitted Press Club occupying its own building, which stood off a good distance from all other buildings so people wouldn't hear the noise. One evening in the summer of 1928 some of the gallant knights of the press were disputing about their individual golfing talents. It was a typical Press Club debate, even-tempered and serene, and only a few pool cues were swung. I wasn't there. It was my night to be home.

At the height of the cyclonic disputation somebody suggested that a Press Club tournament be organized, with each contestant putting up five bucks and the winner taking the pot. There was only one dissenting vote: a sports writer who said it would mean giving up a week's sugar-moon money. Sugar moon was the staple swill in Denver, deriving from the sugar beet, and was dispensed by a Mr. Nowatney who kept his old horse and wagon parked across the street from the south entrance to the courthouse. A bottle of Nowatney's sugar moon had to be consumed within six hours of purchase, else it would rot glass. I speak of it at some length because it will pop up again in this *feuilleton.*

I owned a set of Sears Roebuck clubs, a pair of full-blown white linen knickers, some spiked shoes, and a dozen golf balls that looked as if they had been trampled by a herd of slovenly water buffalo. About once a week I played a round with Joe Alex Morris, Walden Sweet, and Morris Watson. And so, feeling qualified, I scraped together *my* sugar-moon money and entered the tournament. Meanwhile a committee of the more forceful Press Club members went to the Cherry Hills Country Club and induced (strong-armed) the management into giving us access to their course free of charge and in addition putting up a handsome silver trophy.

Too bad there was no television in those days. That tournament would have kept the entire nation enthralled for hours. One of the unprecedented novelties was the presence of three comely girl reporters pushing a two-wheeled cart over the grounds. In the cart were glass jugs of Mr. Nowatney's sugar moon, plus assorted chasers and a half bushel of Sen-Sen. I do not remember my final score. I do not remember playing the second nine. Yet when I emerged from the Nowatney smog I found myself holding a hatful of money and a trophy, the smallest trophy in the history of athletics. (My small daughter used to carry it around as her "hard doll" and eventually lost it down a catch basin.)

It was reported later that the tee shots during the final half of the tournament were somewhat erratic and Lee Taylor Casey, the top columnist of the town, remarked that the safest place for a spectator to stand was directly in front of the man about to drive. I was told that during the last six holes I simply sparkled, even though my eyes crossed from time to time as I addressed the ball.

I went on from Denver to New York City and continued in the newspapering trade and played golf occasionally with Joe Alex Morris and Morris Watson, who also had moved East. Eventually I became a book author and bought a nice country house in North Westchester, and now I began golfing with a couple of my neighbors at Waccabuc Country Club. There were three of us: my neighbor Avery, my lawyer Bonesteel, and me. One evening Lawyer Bonesteel came to my house.

"I'm fed up with Avery," he said.

"How come?"

"He's the biggest cheat I've ever seen on a golf course. You mean you've never noticed? Keep an eye on him Saturday."

I did. To begin with, Avery was not ept. He seldom took less than eight strokes on a hole, but whenever he had eight strokes he would quietly write down "4." And he was forever nudging his ball out of unpleasant lies.

Having got in the habit of watching one partner, I began keeping an eye on Lawyer Bonesteel. Damned if *he* wasn't cheating, too. I was beginning to get discouraged. I sat one whole evening brooding over it. And I thought of the temperamental outbursts of these two dishonest partners. They were club-throwers. They threw clubs into water hazards and over the tops of trees. With little provocation they would snatch off their hats, hurl them to the ground, and leap up and down on them. On missing a short putt, they'd leap around, screaming curses that would have curdled the universal alkahest.

I myself didn't throw clubs (except maybe once) but I could outcuss the both of them. It was said one night on a TV talk show that there have been only four truly great cussers in American history, viz., Huck Finn's pap, Eugene Gant's old man in *Look Homeward, Angel*, my old man, and me. I acquired my great talent for violent language at my revered father's knee.

I considered the matter of exercise. I had four acres of property and a Dutch colonial house. There were a dozen chores to do every day. There was a vegetable garden to keep up. I decided that this work was better exercise than golf. When I finished with a chore and turned around and looked at it, I could feel a sense of accomplishment. After a golf game with Avery and Lawyer Bonesteel, we almost always rode home full of sullenness and anger, cussing and growling quietly. Now that I think back, I did have occasional earth-shaking tantrums in my garden. The mere sight of one of those prehistoric monsters, a tomato hornworm, turned me blue all over and set me to destroying foliage with gardening implements and screaming curses that unhinged chipmunks and sent woodchucks scrambling for the deep woods.

Adding it all up eventually, I handed my set of clubs to my college-joe son and said, "Don't ever let me take them back."

I have not played a round of golf in twenty-odd years since Waccabuc. Nowadays I live in a house on the side of a mountain (next door to Lee Trevino) and I sit on my front terrace and look down on a golf course. I'm a long way up and the players in and out of their little go-carts are Lilliputian figures. I am acquainted with some of them and there are times when I feel as if I'd like to go down and walk around with them. Thus far I have fought off such temptation.

It is an insidious and a virulent disease, golf. Any day I may suffer a mental collapse and rush down to Sears and buy me a set of clubs. I might even yell over to my neighbor Lee Trevino and ask him to pop around and join me in playing a few holes. I could lick that guy easily if somebody would dig me up a crock of sugar moon.

CHAPTER 13

VAGUELY ABOUT VOLKSWAGEN

When VW asked me to write a story for a joke book they were publishing (*think small*), I had to confess that all I knew about Volkswagen was the relative advantage of their four-passenger convertible over their bus.

My daughter has four young sons, wilder (then) than the wildest Comanches. Her husband bought a Volkswagen bus for her to use in hauling them from here to there and back to here. Each of her four boys has a friend or two, and often some of these friends would come along for the ride, and some of them had dogs, and the dogs enjoyed shunpike tours. My daughter finally set up a holler. "This bus," she said, "has become a combination football field, basketball court, boy scout camp, and zoo." She solved her problem neatly; turned in the bus and got a Volkswagen convertible bug. Four boys, maybe one dog, sometimes one friend, plus my daughter as driver . . . and there is no space for Comanche shenanigans.

Let us proceed.

The late Fred Allen never learned to drive. He said there was no room for such foolishness in his life, but I knew him quite well, and it is my conviction that he was a-scairt of anything with a motor in it. Back in his radio days Fred wrote a line for his rustic character Titus Moody who, when asked what he thought about television, replied: "I don't hold with furniture that lights up."

Once when I was working in Hollywood Mr. Allen came out to make a picture at Paramount. There was a scene in the picture wherein he was supposed to emerge from a restaurant, get into a big car, and drive away. He had to move a mere thirty feet—just far enough to get out of camera. After some minimal directions, they tried him on the set, where he came close to slaughtering a motley assortment of grips, dinkies, actors, juicers, button-dusters, and associate producers. Clearly he needed additional instruction.

A guy took him to the desert where he couldn't hit anything but cactus and worked with him for two days. Fred flunked door-opening, couldn't find the starter button, and broke out in a sweat when he was told to put his hand on the gearshift lever. He cussed some, too.

So how did they manage it in the end? They hooked wires onto the car; he came out of the restaurant and got into the driver's seat, with ample aplomb and authority; then he waggled the gearshift lever meaningfully and a tractor pulled the car out of camera range.

I once knew a mildly irascible man who was manager of a New York theater just a couple of blocks from the building where car-shy Fred Allen lived. Every afternoon around five this man's wife arrived and drove him home to Central Park West. He was always frightened by her driving, which he considered to be slipshod, unlawful, and clumsy. He often spoke harshly to her, saying he fully expected to die at her hands, any day. Yet for some reason she went merrily along unmangled, day after day and year after year. She never got tickets, she never had accidents, cops never chewed her out. This aggravated her husband almost beyond endurance.

Then came The Day. She had picked him up and was driving him up Sixth Avenue. At Central Park South she stopped until the cop at the intersection gave the go-signal. She moved forward and swung into her left turn. Midway in the turn a whistle sounded. Her husband looked back and saw the cop waving . . . at *them*. "Now you've done it!" he said to his beloved. "I knew your damn-fool driving would get you in trouble!" He was burbling with inner joy and exultation. He could tell by the look on the approaching cop's face that she was finally gonna get it—a tongue-lashing at the very least, and maybe even a ticket. He just sat with a slight smirk, smug in the knowledge that he lived in a well-ordered world.

The cop arrived and spoke forthrightly to the wife. "Lady," he said, "I want to have a good close look at you. I have been standing on this corner three years, three hideous years, the worst years of my life, and you are the first person I ever seen who made this left turn the way God meant it oughta be made. Lady, if I had a medal on me, I'd give it to you." With which he stepped back, executed a low bow, and waved her on her way. My friend the theater manager slid lower in his seat, grinding his teeth. He muttered something about cornball cops under the heel of Tammany. And he quit speaking to his treacherous helpmeet for three long days.

Next let us consider my own wife. When I moved to the country quite a long time ago, she had never driven a car (or even a nail). It was now obvious that she had to learn. I didn't know about the basic rule in modern civilization that goes: No husband should ever attempt to teach his wife how to drive, unless his aim is to lay down grounds for a divorce. I took her out twice. I showed her how to drive. Then I said to her, "X%※&Z!@X¢!!? +Y!!!" over and over. For some reason she resented this type of conversation, so she fired me as her instructor and sought assistance at the garage where we did business. The owner of the place took her out to a flat meadow and spent an hour with her. He told her that the best way to teach a woman to drive is to have her drive backward. In reverse. All the time. Anbody, he said, who can drive expertly in reverse can surely drive expertly in the other direction. He brought her home and told her to practice on our driveway (which was as long as a city block and steep as the Matterhorn) for a few days before venturing onto the public highways.

What followed was one of the most harrowing weeks of my life. Backward was the only way she wanted to drive. She had to go forward at times in order to get into position to go backward, but she was genuinely frightened of obstacles lying ahead of her. She backed into our rock garden. She backed into trees. She bashed in the front of my tool shed. She got the car hung up on a stone wall and the garage people had to come and derrick it off. They didn't make any critical remarks, but I noticed them shaking their heads in dismay.

Our son came home from engineering school and I assigned him the job of giving her driving lessons. He went out with her for two days and then came to me and said, "Dad, I can't take this. I'm beginning to forget that she's my mother."

I wanted to abandon the whole project, but she wouldn't agree. And I still wanted desperately for her to learn to drive so she could go downtown and buy the groceries and the chinchilla stoles and refills for my ballpoints.

Then on a Sunday afternoon the matter was resolved. The garage owner who advocated backward-driving came to my house with a friend. The friend turned out to be one of the most famous automobile drivers in the history of the carburetor. Ralph DePalma. Anyone of my generation will remember him—he was the Ty Cobb, the Pudge Heffelfinger, the Jack Dempsey of automobile racing. We sat on the terrace for a while and talked of the Indianapolis 500 and other internal combustion topics, and then a thought crossed my mind.

"Mr. DePalma," I said, "my wife here has been trying to learn to drive and she's having a little trouble. I wonder if you might be willing to take her out and give her a few pointers."

"Be happy to," he said, and off they went. They were gone a couple of hours and when they came back my wife was driving her car—frontward. She turned it around, almost expertly. The next day she drove alone to the village and got back alive and undented.

I have never quite trusted her. When it is necessary for me to ride with her, which isn't often, I sit in a nervous crouch with one hand on the door handle, so I can make an emergency escape. I complain continually—she scooches the driver's seat up too close to the steering wheel which in turn scooches me up too close to the dashboard; she doesn't sound her horn at dangerous curves; she doesn't angle correctly getting into the garage. But she only smiles and rolls bravely on her way, content in the knowledge that she's never had an accident, never been given a ticket. Her only response to my . . . well, to my nagging, is to say, "You forget that I studied under Ralph DePalma."

It would only seem equitable for me to bring myself into this gallery of drivers. I am one of those rare motorists who exercise caution far beyond the demands of duty whenever he is at the wheel. I give the business of driving my steady, alert, undivided attention at all times. I never take my eyes off the road except for brief scannings of hidden driveways and fallen-rock zones. I carry a trunkful of emergency equipment—ropes, flares, first-aid kits, hunting knives, claw hammers, K-rations, wading boots, and a bottle of No Doz.

In short, folks, I'm a drivin' man from way back. Just give me time to get muh revs reckoned, jiggle muh gear ratios a trifle, file down muh intake manifold, and saturate muh sump, and . . . Zzzzwoooooooooooooosh! Ah'm ready for Clermont-Ferrand and the French Grand Prix. Driving what? Muh daughter's VW bug . . . fully equipped with all my gear plus four kids and a dog.

CHAPTER 14

THE ADVANCEMENT OF SCIENCE
AT FIDGETS' RETREAT

Some people said he was an illiterate and indolent man. Others said he wasn't worth the powder that would be needed to blow him up. In short, a bum. I have reference to my father.

Offhand I would say that he enjoyed to fish. In the later years of his life he lived alone, by strong preference, on the shore of Diascund Creek, a tributary of the Chickahominy in Virginia. The site where he anchored his trailer home was called Fidgets' Retreat, for the reason that he and his cronies were inclined, on occasion, to twitch. It is about fifteen miles from Colonial Williamsburg.

I doubt if he knew it, but he was a man of science. He always tried to put into practice what he used to preach in his younger days. He led a most precise and orderly life, except when he was drinking, which was about half the time. In the years when he had a house swarming with unruly kids he would sometimes fling up his arms and cry out, "God damn it! What we need around here is a little *system!*" In a voice freighted with both anger and anguish he uttered this exhortation so often that it grew to be a sort of sentimental thing in the family and was adopted by his sons and his various sons-in-law; even today all of them employ it in bellowing against the inefficiencies of their respective wives. Including, of course, me.

He bequeathed still another charming idiosyncrasy to his children—his obstinate inability to spell the word "hope." He always spelled it "hoap." He'd write, "Hoap to see you soon," or, "Hoap the G. D. Govt drops dead." Today his children in their intramural correspondence always spell the word Pop's way.

There at Fidgets' Retreat my father divided his time between (1), fishing; (2), reading; (3), cooking and keeping his house in scrupulous order; and (4), the advancement of science.

He effected a dietary revolution among the native Virginians who frequently dropped in to visit him and listen to him talk. A Virginian, when he catches a catfish, speaks a few heavily accented cusswords and hurls the whiskered varmint back into the crick. A catfish to a Virginian is fit only to be eaten by Yankees. In fact just a few miles upstream from Fidgets' Retreat there was, and still may be, a "catfish house" where the despised creatures were packed for shipment into the crumbling Nawth.

My father, however, grew up in the Mississippi Valley and he'd rather eat catfish than pompano or rainbow trout or *huachinango veracruzana*. He took them small and rolled them in flour and fried them just exactly right. In lard. Lard out of a lard bucket. For a while he served them up to his Secesh friends without identifying the breed, and he always got the same reaction: "Harry, that's the best 'y god fish I ever laid a fork to." Eventually Pop let the catfish out of the bag, and the Virginians he had been feeding were converted. Today they eat catfish and love it.

He was an old-fashioned fisherman, steadfastly opposed to new-fangled methods and devices. He'd have nothing to do with flies and lures and spoons and other kinds of artificial bait. He used worms. On occasion he'd fish with minnows, if they happened to be readily available, but he preferred worms. If he had been able to make his own fishhooks he'd have done it. As it was, he took the hooks he got from the store and, using a pair of pliers, spent hours bending and twisting them until he felt he'd got them shaped exactly right for taking catfish, bass, bream, perch, or eel.

His only close neighbors were Frank Driscoll and Booster Hodges, who occupied a cabin within whooping distance of Pop's trailer. Sometimes when they didn't feel like fishing the three men would play Scrabble, and it is said that their "discussions" concerning the legitimacy of certain words could be heard halfway to Richmond. There was always, in fact, a good-natured antagonism between the three men.

Pop read mountains of books and magazines and accumulated facts which he enjoyed tossing around in the soft Virginia air. "Fish don't ever sleep," he'd say to Frank and Booster. "They only stop and rest a little." He'd tell them how the age of a fish could be determined by examination of its ear stones; he'd describe a fish in India that squirts a jet of water at an insect, knocking the bug into the water where it could be captured; he'd tell them about an Egyptian catfish that turns over and swims upside down when it's frightened—it thinks nobody can see it when it's in that position.

In time Frank and Booster got a little fed up with this unremitting flow of facts. Sometimes they would scheme up ways of striking back. One springtime Frank Driscoll got hold of a gadget known as a worm-shocker. It was a metal rod at the end of an electric wire. When the rod was shoved into the ground and the juice turned on, the fishworms came wriggling out of the earth like streams of hamburger out of a butcher's meat grinder.

Frank and Booster buried the rod in the ground near their cabin, concealing the wire, and then summoned Pop from the crick.

"Harry," said Frank, "I've learned a new way to get worms without digging for them. Watch this."

He took two flat rocks and began rubbing them together, tilting his head back, closing his eyes, and muttering jungle gibberish. Inside the cabin Booster hooked the wire onto a storage battery. In a few moments the worms began squirming out of the ground. Pop was impressed, but he tried not to show it.

"Yeh," he said, with Edisonian composure, "I know all about that rock-rubbin' system. Read an article about it once. It's not as good a system as the one where you rub sticks together. You poke one stick in the ground and you take another stick that's got rozzum on it, and you rub 'em together, and up comes the worms. You *grunt* 'em up. That's what they call it. Sounds just like gruntin'. Place down in Florida, a whole town, makes a business outa gruntin' up worms." He let this encyclopedic information sink in, and then hit his enemy with: "I remember in the old days how we used to stick a pitchfork in the ground and hit it on the handle with a broomstick and the worms would come leapin' through the sod by the hundreds." He thought for a moment, then polished off his antagonists with: "A fella didn't have to go to all that trouble, though. Just scatter coffee grounds all over your yard and the next morning you'll have plenty of worms."

He held with no kind of voodoo, no magic, no miracles. He was a rationalist and believed that it is possible to be superstitious without being superstitious. Elsewhere I have told about how I was walking with him once and saw him sweep wide around a ladder and I asked him if it was an act of superstition. "Nawp," he said. "Not a bit. I ain't got a superstitious bone in my body. All I say is it don't pay a man to take chances." On another occasion I saw him heave a rock at a black cat and again I challenged him. "It so happens," he said, "that I got no use fer black cats."

He was a stubborn man, recalcitrant as a sandy-land mule. He often quoted an uncle named Dicker Smith back in Southern Illinois. In the early years of this century, Dicker Smith observed that "mottomobiles is ruinin' the country." While I hold that Dicker Smith was a major prophet, I mention him only to suggest that my father came by his contrariness through family. He, too, believed that mottomobiles was ruinin' the country but even more he believed that 'lectricity was ruinin' the country. When he finally found out that the worm-shocker was an electrical device he wouldn't have any truck with it and argued that fish wouldn't bite on worms it enticed out of the ground. "Them worms are all sick," Pop said. "Kill a robin if he bit into one."

Eventually, over his protests, a power line was run into Fidgets' Retreat. He submitted when it was pointed out to him that he could have an electric refrigerator and get rid of his coal-oil lamps. He balked, however, when his children offered to get him a television set.

Visiting one winter at the home of his daughter in Maryland, he spent half a day studiously looking at television programs. Finally he got up and walked away from the set and delivered his verdict.

"That," he said, "ain't the way people are."

Some time later his daughter said to him, "Pop, I've often wondered what you people did for fun back in the days when you were a teen-ager, back when there wasn't any TV, and no radio, and not even movies. What on earth did you do with your time?"

"Oh, we found plenty to do," he said defensively.

"For example."

Pop cast his thoughts back to Paleozoic times.

"I recollect," he said, "one day when the lady next door—I forget her name—she come home from the store with a new spool of thread. I happened to be over there and picked up the spool and it said on the end, '120 Yards.' So the whole family, and me included, we took 'er out in the alley and unwound 'er and stretched 'er out and measured 'er. And by god she was fourteen inches short."

He fathered nine children and he commanded strong affection from every one of them, which is a bit strange considering his materialistic approach to corporal punishment; he walloped us, boy and girl alike, during all our tender formative years. On account of my undeviating orneriness, he whipped me till I almost bled—regularly and on schedule. It had a good effect on me. I won't go so far as to say it made me any better. But I never got appreciably meaner. I remained sort of static. Consequently I have never been in any of our major prisons. Only small jails.

I said Pop was a scientific man, yet he could be deeply sentimental about some things. He had what almost amounted to a passion for new trusses. One corner of his trailer was piled with so many discarded trusses that it had the look of a barbed wire entanglement. One day his daughter Martha made him an elegant model (she called it a Schiaparelli) with red and white ribbon spiraled around the belt part; the pad was white satin, with ecru lace gathered at the edges. Tiny blue satin bows were placed discreetly here and there, and there was a small frilly pocket with a dollar bill in it—emergency saloon money. Pop loved it, and said it was the way a truss ought to be, and never bought another.

When he arrived in his mid-seventies we installed him in a nursing home in the Virginia countryside. At the very beginning my sisters went to the owners and said, "We don't want him to know he has cancer. Please don't even hint at it." They agreed to keep him in the dark about the horror that was killing him. And then after a few short months he was dead. My sisters went back to the nursing home to gather up his few belongings, and to thank the people for taking such good care of him, and for not letting him know. They smiled—the people who ran the place.

"The second day he was here," they said, "your father called us in and said we were never to tell his children that he had cancer. He knew it all the while."

CHAPTER 15

GRAPPLING WITH ESPAÑOL

Recently I was back in Mexico, a country I have visited frequently
and where I speak the language with fluency and aplomb.

One afternoon a Mexican journalist came to our room in Mexico City's Hotel Reforma. My wife and I and the newspaperman
decided we wanted refreshments and I picked up the phone.
When the room-service man answered I said, *"Por favor, dos
cervezas y una . . ."* and then I broke off the sentence. I
wouldn't go through that Sidral thing again. So I started over in
English, "Two beers, please, and one Pepsi." I changed my wife's
order from Sidral to Pepsi because I couldn't face up to the language barrier.

Several years earlier in a room in the same hotel, two men came
visiting. I wanted beer, the two guests wanted beer, and my wife
wanted Sidral, which is an apple drink much favored by Mexicans.
With mucho confidence I told room service, *"Por favor, tres
cervezas y una Sidral."* The room-service guy said in English,
"What was that last?" and I repeated una Sidral. After a while the
door buzzer sounded and I opened up and there stood a waiter
with a rolling table. He wheeled it into the room and then I saw
the *tres cervezas* and a small plate in the center of which rested
one sweet roll.

I held my tongue but after the waiter had gone I began to
grow a trifle testy. I am proud of my expertise with Español.

Twenty minutes later I phoned down for a repeat, specifying

Sidral. Once again I had to repeat the word. I pronounced it See-*drawl* although I have noticed that some people, including Mexicans, say See-*dral*, the second syllable rhyming with pal. That is the wrong way to say it, the way the Mexicans say it. Indubitably. So this time the waiter arrived with a tray and on it stood *tres cervezas* and a small plate and in the middle of the plate, wrapped in cellophane, una big cigar.

And so it came about that, on this most recent visit, I chose to speak flat-out Gringo to room service. They simply couldn't understand the correct pronunciation of Sidral. The thought crossed my mind that those tin-eared Latins might send up a he-fowl or a tea towel or even a B-gal. In any case I did not utter the word "Sidral" over the phone and my wife drank Pepsi.

I admire the Mexican people no end. Always have. Still, I have to admit that they are not too conversant with the Spanish tongue. They talk it well, and beautifully, but somehow they just don't listen to it right.

CHAPTER 16

HOW STRONG THE TOES?

An international research organization, aware of the fact that I have a professional interest in eccentric aspects of the human body, has sent me the following item:

> *Nanette Fabray has stronger toes than those of an average-toed human.*

This flat-footed declaration had been clipped from a national journal where it was set down without quibble and without any qualification other than the statement that Miss Fabray counted ballet among her accomplishments.

One of the major faults of our present civilization is the tendency of uniformed people to issue stern and illogical pronouncements of this nature. The instant I read it, my hackles rose. I was more than a little indignant. I know toes. I know them almost as well as I know fingers and it may be remembered that my opus, A Short History of Fingers (Lib. Cong. Cat. Cd. 63–17425), was saluted as "the first really thorough study of ten long-neglected subjects." I am a finger man but also, I repeat, I know toes.

With some tolerance I concluded that the published description of Nanette Fabray's toes had been one of those little rhetorical embellishments that a writer tosses in without a period of reflection. I never would say, even on impulse, that I have stronger toes than the average-toed human. I don't even contend that my toes are more powerful than the toes of Nanette Fabray. I only *suspect* that they are. For me to declare it outright would be speculative as well as fatuous.

Nevertheless, in the interest of scientific probity, I challenge the proposition. I consider myself to be an average-toed human. I will pit my toes against the toes of Nanette Fabray any time, any place, strengthwise. I challenge her with confidence, in spite of the fact that my toes are considerably older than hers and have had more wear.

Who knows the strength of other toes? I mean *all* other toes? When I was young I knew a boy in the Middle West who could shoot marbles with his toes. He was no carnival freak. He was just a kid who lived down on Division Street with his shoes full of adroit and virile toes. I can remember that I once compared toes with him and there was no appreciable difference in their looks, although I'm confident that his were wirier. Inside, that is.

From time to time each of us in that youthful gang had a go at his specialty, tried to grasp a marble in our toes and knuckle down, or metatarsus down, but our toes were simply not up to it. One or two of the kids got so they could clutch a marble and hold it above the ground, but it required almost superhuman effort and concentration. There was one boy who'd get his big toe and his index toe wrapped over a taw or a steelie and then contort his features into such an expression of agony that the rest of us feared he was on the verge of throwing a fit. I speak of his ordeal merely to point up the genius of the boy who could shoot a marble ten or twelve feet with his toes. To this day I believe it is a thing you have to be born with.

When we first watched that Division Street boy shoot marbles, it was a little sickening; but after we grew accustomed to the novelty of the performance, it became a wonderful experience to watch him work. Now and then I grow nostalgic and sentimental about it. That boy shot marbles with his toes the way Nureyev dances, the way Willie Mays catches flies.

I've long since lost track of him, and I can't even remember his name. I would like to renew my acquaintance with him and I've thought of advertising, but I am shy and I hesitate about approaching a clerk in a newspaper office with: "Wanted—Information re boy who lived on Division Street, Decatur, Ill., around 1916, could shoot marbles with his toes. Box F188."

I'm curious about how life dealt with him. He would be my age, if he's alive, and I would assume that he has a set of toes worth looking into. Or at. It may be that in time he developed an opposable big toe—he couldn't have been too far from it in the time when I knew him. I imagine that by this late date he has given up marbles. But he might be doing something else constructive with his toes, such as playing the steel guitar or picking strawberries. Those marvelous toes of his childhood could conceivably be as well known as the toes that Ben Agajanian doesn't have on his kicking foot. On the other hand, life being what it is, it is quite possible that he let his toes go all to hell, neglected them, and that he's limping around somewhere today in obscurity, with a set of gnarled and graceless digits of no earthly use to him, even for picking up his socks.

I would like to inject an additional personal note into this toe affair, with special reference to the toes of Nanette Fabray. I believe, with many other romantics, that it is sometimes possible to look deep in a person's eyes and tell many hidden things about that person. I once spent a couple of hours with this same Miss Fabray on the terrace of a Manhattan penthouse and, because they were there, I looked deep into her eyes. I saw nothing that would suggest that she was a girl with stronger toes than the average-toed human. Toes were the farthest thing from my mind. Nor did Miss Fabray say a word about the strength concealed within her slippers. I have an idea that if her toes were all *that* strong, she herself would have known about it and she would have, girl-like, managed to drop a hint about it. Indirectly, perhaps, with some airy and subtle remark such as, "Did you happen to know that I have toes on me like a buffalo?" Or by some unostentatious gesture, such as slipping off her shoe and casually cracking a macadamia nut with her toes. Or even just holding them aloft, absently, and snapping them to the rhythm of the music that was coming from a nearby radio.

She did nothing, and said nothing, respecting her toes. It is therefore my judgment that there are toes hidden within the vamps of tens of thousands of American shoes that are, ounce-for-ounce, infinitely stronger than the toes of Nanette Fabray.

This need not sadden her. Those eyes . . . well, there on that penthouse terrace her eyes were a good deal more powerful than those of an average-eyed human. She had no need of special toes.

CHAPTER 17

THE ILLEGITIMATE SON
OF BUFFALO BILL

The thing we remember best about Gene Fowler was his laughter.
I've known other men of Jovian mirth—Robert Benchley and
Buddy DeSylva among them—but none with anything quite approaching that rich, explosive, and resonant laughter with which
he seemed to infect whole civilizations of his fellow men. Rafael
Sabatini unwittingly described Fowler in a famous line: "Born
with the gift of laughter and the sense that the world was mad."

Gene owned a remarkable speaking voice, cavernous in its
depth, a cello voice, rich and vibrant and warm. It never changed
up to the day of his death in the summer of 1960. At three-
score-and-ten there was no old-man cackle from Fowler; his talk
and his laughter were as the sound of a cathedral organ.

He'd sit, in those last years, on his California terrace and talk
about the glorious decades, the Fowler years, the era of his
fabulous cronies—John Barrymore, Ben Hecht, W. C. Fields,
John Decker, Thomas Mitchell, Jack Dempsey, Damon Runyon,
Jimmy Walker, Leo McCarey, Red Skelton, Nunnally Johnson,
Jimmy Durante, Charlie MacArthur . . . Every one of them
worshiped him. And as he sat and talked of them, his laughter
would go rolling and booming down the slopes of "St. Agnes
Memorial Park" and up the far canyon wall to titillate the house-
holders along Tigertail Road.

St. Agnes Memorial Park! Gene Fowler built it with his own
hands, wrestling thirteen tons of boulders into place, plus a chunk

off the Rock of Gibraltar and a massive bone from a Colorado dinosaur—"the only thing on earth that's older than I am." A mere corner of a hillside rock garden, you might say, but it was adequately dedicated by Fowler's friends, Interior Secretary Fred A. Seaton and Labor Secretary James P. Mitchell. Quietly in attendance, of course, was Agnes Fowler, who married Gene in 1916 and for whom he named his "National Park."

The Silurians, an organization of old-time New York journalists, has dubbed Fowler "easily the most colorful and adventurous newspaperman of our time." He achieved this reputation in eleven rollicking years of working for New York newspapers, following on a historic apprenticeship in Denver. He stood tall and handsome, and gave the impression of slenderness in spite of his two hundred pounds of hard bone and muscle; he was graceful in his movements and charming enough to lead visiting Queen Marie of Romania, and a galaxy of glamorous actresses, to fall wildly in love with him.

Does all this sound implausible? There is no exaggeration—ask anyone who knew him, and tens of thousands knew him: actors, newspapermen, heiresses, gangsters, editors, wrestlers, poets, fighters, tavernkeepers, cops, novelists, statesmen on all levels, whores, printers, fliers, press agents, bartenders . . . surely bartenders.

It was remarked that a stroll with Fowler through the arroyos of midtown Manhattan was akin to a triumphal procession, somewhat like the St. Patrick's Day parade minus band music. Helen Hayes said, after her first meeting with him, that she always thought Gene Fowler was a fictional character, a legend invented by her husband, Charlie MacArthur. And there he was, in the flesh, precisely as Charlie had always described him. Ben Hecht's wife, Rose Caylor, encountered Gene for the first time in the middle of a night when he entered the Hecht house mistakenly through a greenhouse door and arrived in her bedroom with one shoe in his hand. He bowed slightly and said, "You need have no qualms about me as a house guest. I always sleep with one shoe in my hand to put out any fires I may accidentally ignite."

Consider, too, the California morning when Leo McCarey's young daughter Mary informed her director-father that a man who said he was Gene Fowler was in the living room and wanted to see him.

"So early?" said McCarey. "Does he look as if he's been drinking?"

"I don't know," said Mary. "He has a bat in his hand and is wearing the uniform of the New York Giants."

Fowler was like the Brooklyn baseball magnate described as "a man of many facets, all turned on." Ben Hecht considered Fowler's *Illusion in Java* to be one of the most sensitive and skillfully written romantic novels of modern times. John K. Hutchens, the percipient literary critic, holds that Gene's novels deserve far greater recognition, on merit, than they ever received. Yet Gene's fame was made not with his novels but with biographies of his friends.

When Gene was first coming into view as an author, his publisher asked him to compose an autobiographical booklet. It remains today a minor classic and the opening words are: "Gene Fowler, an American peasant, was born March 8, 1891, on the west bank of Mullen's Mill Ditch in Denver, Colorado."

And so he was, though his true name was Eugene Devlan. His father, a timid patternmaker in a locomotive works, couldn't abide the adamantine opinions of his mother-in-law and ran away to become a mountain hermit before Gene was born. Thirty years later Charles Devlan rang the doorbell at the Fowler apartment in New York City. It was the first time the two men had ever seen each other. Gene looked at his father a moment, took note of the fine set of whiskers, and exclaimed: "So *that's* where you've been hiding all these years!" Thenceforward they were good friends.

Gene lived his first four years under the name of Wheeler, which his strong-willed grandmother bestowed upon him; then his mother married a man named Frank Fowler, who adopted the boy and gave him *his* name. All his life Gene was famous for his inability to remember names, and he justified his failing by saying that frequently he couldn't even remember his own.

He worked at boy-jobs around Denver and got through high school and then went to the University of Colorado with the intention of working his way through medical school. He was on his way across the campus to enroll when his eye fell upon the building where journalism was taught. He turned and walked in and registered there.

"It occurred to me," he said years later, "that I wouldn't be able to bear up under college life for more than a year." So, one year at Boulder and he headed back home. A railroad conductor, sharing his sandwich with the boy, heard him speak a mighty ambition: "I'm going back to Denver and some day I'll be making thirty dollars a week! You just wait!"

Gene was a man of erudition in spite of his unimpressive scholastic history. He studied the classics. He read the great books because he found pleasure in them. In his New York days, he once told me, he set himself the task of reading every word of Shakespeare. He made it, and acknowledged that he reaped great benefit from it, but he confessed that "there were times when I earnestly wished that the Bard had been trampled by Stratford oxen while quite young."

He wolfed down Tolstoy and Aristotle and Darwin and Karl Marx and Ibsen and Voltaire and in prosperous times bought first editions of Mark Twain. He would frequently startle his raffish friends by quoting from Herodotus.

He had a special facility when it came to book titles. His novels were called *Trumpet in the Dust*, *Shoe the Wild Mare*, *Salute to Yesterday*, and *Illusion in Java*. His first biography, the story of a New York criminal lawyer, William J. Fallon, bore the title *The Great Mouthpiece*. The saga of Bonfils and Tammen and the Denver *Post* became *Timberline*. Mack Sennett's life was chronicled under the title *Father Goose*. There could have been no other title for his book on Barrymore than *Good Night, Sweet Prince*. The last two biographies were *Beau James* (Jimmy Walker) and *Schnozzola* (Durante).

Gene's account of his own Denver days was contained in *A Solo in Tom-Toms* and his unfinished final book, *Skyline*, was a reminiscence of his life in the New York of the twenties. He spoke of that period as "a carnival spin of mass make-believe —the world's last brief holiday from fear."

He often wrote poetry and at times his prose grew a bit voluptuous. His city editor once cautioned him to soft-pedal the flowery prose and "get straight to the essential facts immediately." On the next assignment, a murder in the Bronx, Gene began his story: "Dead! That's what he was when they found him."

He never had much faith in the quality of his work. He is responsible for a line that is dear to the heart of every author who has had to face up to a deadline. "A book is never finished," he said. "It is abandoned."

He took no pride in the work he did for the movie studios. Still, he wrote his scenarios with the same exuberance of style that went into his books, a style described as an admixture of Swift, Addison, Mark Twain, and Walt Whitman. Once he told me that he would work diligently in the Hollywood script sheds until he began to hear flutes. "When the sound of flutes came," he said, "and there *were* no flutes, I knew it was time to leave the studios and go to work on another book."

He never let himself be impressed by the big salaries and the splendor of the movie industry. On his first working day in Hollywood he arrived at the studio gate wearing striped pants, cutaway coat, high silk hat, gates-ajar collar, and riding a bicycle. Summoned to his first story conference, he arrived ten minutes late with his trousers in his hand. He flung them onto the conference table and ordered, "Have these cleaned and pressed by tomorrow morning!" and quickly took his departure. They gave him an office expensively and tastefully furnished; he had everything hauled away and brought in a small battered desk and a hall tree. On the mantel, where there had been a golden clock out of the Empire period, he substituted a head of cabbage. The only assignment his gorgeous secretary had was to go, each afternoon, to the head of the studio and say, "Mr. Fowler sends his compliments and wants to know what time it is."

There are some who say that Fowler was indifferent toward women. They base this foul canard on a single episode out of his life. In Denver Gene once attended a high school dance where a ravishing young creature, daughter of the rich, made a bold play for him. As she soft-talked him, Gene sat in a pensive, dreamlike state, and the Colorado Lorelei believed she had him firmly in hand. She offered him a penny for his thoughts. "I was just wondering," said young Fowler, "if a horse's legs ever go to sleep on him."

When Gene's eyes first lit on Agnes Hubbard in Denver, back in 1916, he told her firmly that she was to be his wife. She demurred. She worked at City Hall where he began systematically pursuing her through the corridors, calling out loudly for all to hear, "Whether you like it or not, you are going to be the mother of my children!" When at last Agnes consented to an elopement, Gene's flair for the subdued detail led the party to the majestic Red Rocks Park, then an undeveloped natural amphitheater.

Agnes and Gene rode to the wedding in a racing car borrowed from a saloonkeeper and driven by a gambler known as Cincinnati (later slain in a Detroit gang war). Gene's best man was a prize-fight promoter and there was a clergyman at hand, though the groom sat down on a rock and did a complete rewrite job on the customary ritual. The minister complained, but Gene and his genteel friends ordered, "Read!" and he read. It should be noted that the bridegroom's wedding cloak was one he borrowed from Jack Dempsey; it was a cinnamon-brown job with pearl buttons the size of silver dollars.

Many years later Gene took Agnes back to Red Rocks and when they saw the great stadium that had been erected there, Fowler pretended astonishment that such a monument should be built in his honor. Back in Denver he continued this pretense so convincingly that some people believed him. He even issued a public statement saying he felt there were more deserving men who could have been honored with the stadium. "I think," observed one stout citizen, "that we'd better rig some sort of a curtain over the State Capitol before he claims it as a cottage we built for him."

The children of Agnes and Gene Fowler are Gene, Jr., a film editor whose wife is the daughter of Nunnally Johnson; Jane, also married and also a film editor; and Will, former newspaperman and author of an affectionate biography of his father. W. C. Fields once wrote a friend about having dined "with Fowler's unholy family." He reported that Gene's youngest son, Will, smoked black cigars and drank whiskey until it ran out of his ears, that little Jane spit tobacco juice all over Fields' shirt front, and that Gene Junior "tried to roll me for my poke."

Gene's best-remembered caper as a New York newspaperman, often written about, concerns the expense voucher he handed in after an expedition to interview three naval balloonists forced down in the frozen tundra of Saskatchewan. When the Fowler voucher was turned in, it included several odd charges involving the rental of a dog-sled team. There was a touching mention of a heroic lead dog's death in the line of duty—$350. Marble head-stone for same valiant husky—$100. The newspaper auditor informed Gene that he had not quite accounted for all expenditures and back came the final item: "Wreath for bereft bitch—$1.50." Gene claimed to be the author of Fowler's Law of Expense Accounts, which commands: "Bring no money home."

All his life, in fact, he retained a cavalier approach to economics. On the jacket of Lucius Beebe's last book, *The Big Spenders*, is a Fowlerism done in his own hand: "Money is something to be thrown off the back end of trains."

Will Fowler remembers being with his father one day shortly after Los Angeles had decreed a ban on trash burning. Gene was building a final fire in his incinerator and he asked Will to fetch a carton of papers from his study. Will had an opportunity to examine the contents of the box before they were destroyed—fat packets of cancelled checks made out to destitute friends (and friends of friends), dating back as far as 1925 and totaling, at a rough estimate, more than half a million dollars.

Gene didn't die broke, but neither did he die wealthy. If he was disrespectful toward money, he was even more contemptuous of pomposity. Back in his New York days his superior in the Hearst organization was Arthur Brisbane, whose vastly popular column, larded with somber pontifications, was often spoken into a dictating machine in the Brisbane limousine. One evening Fowler spotted the big car parked on the street, crept inside, imitated Brisbane's voice and recorded a dreadful editorial warning against an impending catastrophe—an attack on America from airplanes piloted by intelligent apes. Brisbane's secretary transcribed the column on the following day and it had been set in type before the ruse was discovered. Fowler survived this prank as he survived many others, including his famous rendition of *The Last Rose of Summer* on the accordion, played into a transcontinental telephone for the edification of William Randolph Hearst himself. Hearst liked him.

In the many years that I knew Fowler I never asked him a question without getting a response bristling with dramatic implications and comic overtones. Offhand I remember the time I sought from him some evidence of genius or at least of notability among his forebears. Wasn't there, somewhere in his family tree, an ancestor of distinction? "Certainly," he responded. "My grand-mother's hair was once admired by General Lew Wallace."

There are actually no incidents in the life story of Gene Fowler; "incident" is too trifling a word to describe the monumental and cataclysmic events that characterized everything that happened to him. Consider his first trip to New York at the invitation of Damon Runyon. An undertaker friend in Denver was shipping the body of an elderly lady east to Albany and it was necessary to buy two passages on the train. Young Fowler traveled on one of the tickets as escort to the body, which he referred to as "Nellie." Arriving in Chicago he was seized and thrown in jail for transport-ing a female person across state lines for immoral purposes—a charge trumped up by certain playful Chicago newspapermen, alerted by Fowler's pals in Denver. Somewhere he lost Nellie and showered her Albany kinfolks with telegrams saying, "Mother is well and will be with you shortly." He never found her.

When he reached New York, where Runyon had been thinking that the brash young man was ready for the Big Time, Fowler decked himself in an outfit which he believed to be the latest in citified style—pince-nez on a black ribbon, a walking stick, and a flowing Byronic tie. Damon Runyon closed his eyes, shuddered slightly, took the visitor to a ball game and then sent him back to the Rockies. A few months later he relented and got Gene a job in New York.

Always astonishing conduct from Fowler. In 1924 he engaged Pat Crowe as an occasional baby-sitter for the Fowler children—the same Pat Crowe who in 1900 kidnaped Edward Cudahy, Jr., and collected $25,000 ransom. Who else but Fowler, on becom-ing managing editor of the New York *Morning Telegraph*, would pomptly hire for his staff such writers as Lardner, Hecht, Winchell, MacArthur, Pegler, and even the silent movie idol Lew Cody?

When Henry Ford told him, during an interview, that some day men would wear a little gadget on their wrists and get messages through it, Gene responded: "God sake, Mr. Ford, don't invent such a thing—I'm already being driven crazy by plain telegrams." And when Sir Thomas Lipton, standing amidst a distinguished group of yachtsmen, asked, "Gentlemen, did I ever tell you about the time we were standing off Cowes and the Queen of Spain was——" Fowler interrupted with, "Sir Thomas, if you've told it once, you've told it a dozen times!"

Shortly after Pearl Harbor was bombed, there was a patriotic gathering at the home of W. C. Fields. Present with Fields and Fowler were John and Lionel Barrymore and the artist John Decker. Fields showed off the forty cases of gin he had laid by, remarking in passing that he figured it for a short war. There was some sampling of the hoard. By midafternoon feeling against Japan was running high and the group left for downtown Los Angeles to enlist in the armed forces. Lionel's wheel chair was taken along in case he was given an immediate overseas assignment. At the recruiting center John Barrymore solemnly stated his age as nineteen, Fields demanded duty as a commando, and Fowler outlined his previous military experience in terms that ranked him above Bonaparte and Pershing. The recruiting officer merely inquired: "Who sent you, the enemy?"

I saw him last in 1959, the year before he died. After a long visit at his house, he drove my wife and me down to Hollywood. Something happened on that ride that seemed to pinpoint his galactic zest for living, his genius in finding pleasure in things that were troublesome to other people. We were on one of the freeways, and all around us were two and a half million Angelenos, all cursing these superhighways with hate and bitterness.

Just to be making noise, I said, "Pretty frightful, these freeways."

"I love 'em," said Gene. "Almost every time you get on one, you're in for adventure. A few days ago I missed my exit again— I do it about half the time—and so I was stuck. You can't turn around. You have to keep rolling. So I kept rolling and wound up in the Valley, and there I was, close to my son Bill's house, and I hadn't seen him and his family for a week or more, and so I just dropped in and we all had a swell time."

He worshiped his grandchildren. Correction: he worshiped *all* children. And he loved animals. A catalogue of the Fowler pets over the years includes a honey bear that hanged himself, a frog called Mister Zukor, a parrot that talked to Gene on the phone coast-to-coast, and the duck Montmorency that would unnerve the neighbors with his feverish quackings if he didn't get his daily ration of whiskey.

In 1948 Will Fowler was converted to Catholicism, along with his wife and three children. On receiving the news Gene remarked: "When the Pope hears of this there'll be a red alert over the Vatican." He attended the baptismal ceremony during which little Michael Fowler swung a tiny fist and hit Father O'Shea in the face. Gene grinned and whispered to Will: "A natural-born Mohammedan." And he told Will: "If one of your sons should become a priest, please do not expect me to address him as 'Father.'"

Then two years later, much to the astonishment of his iconoclastic pals, Gene Fowler became a Catholic.

For the remaining years of his life he was deeply devoted to the Church, though he seldom talked of his religion. "I'm not a roof-top Catholic," he said. But the Fowler wit and gaiety prevailed whenever he did speak of it. He told Lucius Beebe that he had been marked for Catholicism because of his Grandmother Wheeler. She had been dead wrong about everything. "For example," said Gene, "she contended that there were three classes of people who can't drink: first, the Indians; second, the Irish; and third, everybody else. She was loudly against all Catholics, so the Catholics had to be right."

Gene's friends always were aware of his preoccupation with death. Will Fowler says that his father began to dwell on death as early as 1925. "I'll never live to be fifty," he'd say. Then it would be sixty, and finally seventy, and he made seventy. In almost every case where death entered his field of vision, his gift of laughter would intervene.

In the 1920s he was standing one day at the corner of Forty-second Street and Broadway. He had been sleeping only a few hours a night and now he suddenly grew faint and sank to his knees. Agnes leaped to his side and Gene said, "I knew it. I knew it would be something ridiculous—dying right on the corner of Forty-second and Broadway!" Then he started laughing, and Agnes laughed with him, and he was soon all right.

Again, in 1939 he and Leo McCarey were gravely injured in an auto smashup. Gene was unconscious when he arrived at the hospital, but he soon revived. A day or so later he phoned his secretary and asked her to pick him up in front of the hospital. She found him there, bandaged and wavering on his feet. He told her he was a dying man and that he wanted the end to come in a saloon with sawdust on the floor. Please, he said, head for East Sixth Street. The girl compromised by taking him to a nearby hotel cocktail lounge where, after some drinks, he agreed to return to his bed of pain. She let him out at the hospital emergency entrance and, as she drove away, heard him yelling at some interns, "Can't you fools see that I'm an expectant mother!"

The death of his warmest friend, John Barrymore, was a great blow to Gene, and the actor, who loved Fowler more than any other person, seemed to sense it and leavened the blow with wit, speaking his last words to his friend. "Come closer," he murmured, and Gene came closer. "Tell me, Gene," said Barrymore, "is it true that you are the illegitimate son of Buffalo Bill?"

Gene was a title-holding hypochondriac. He complained unceasingly about his liver which he said was scarred like the face of a Heidelberg extra in *The Student Prince*. He wrote me once that upon attaining the ancient age of sixty, his bones were popping so that "when I clamber out of bed each morning I sound like a castanet solo."

One of the last interviews with Gene was by Jack Smith of the Los Angeles *Times*. Describing his sensations at being in the Fowler presence, Smith wrote: "I felt strongly the sense of being, for the moment, a member of that princely company. I was among that enchanted cast of characters from The Era of Wonderful Nonsense."

He, Gene Fowler, was the sum and the substance of that Era.

CHAPTER 18

A USEFUL WORD

I feel quite certain that there are people mixed up in my little personal world who speak with perplexity of me, as follows: "He's a strange one—he just stands around and keeps saying a word that sounds like Twupguttem."

It's true. I do stand around and say Twupguttem a lot. I say it at social gatherings and I also say it on the streets of New York City and McLeansboro, Illinois, and Yucca Valley, California, and Atlanta, Georgia, and Odessa, Texas. I utter the word frequently and sometimes bitterly when I'm looking at people on television, and I bellow it forth during periods in which I'm reading the newspapers.

Twupguttem is the pronounceable form of TWPGTM, and TWPGTM is federalese for "The wrong people got the money." It used to be that I would murmur the sentence in its full-blown entirety whenever I found myself in the presence of people I thought it suited. Then I waxed chicken and rendered it into cabalistic form, for fear the wrong people who've got the money would overhear what I thought about them and shatter my bridgework.

Let me illustrate how it works. Not long ago I read that a celebrated (and rich) playwright had gone to Tiffany's or Cartier's and had them make a cast of his hip, from which they fashioned a golden cigarette case that would snuggle up to the countours of his outer hind end, or ass. I said Twupguttem.

Later someone told me about a draggle-tailed comedian who had suddenly hit it big and built himself a mansion. In this mansion he installed a pub, every stick of which was imported from England. Then he all but outdid William Randolph Hearst by installing a second pub in his house, so he and his cronies could crawl from one to the other. I said Twupguttem. I think I added an extra word, less esoteric, to cover the second pub.

I say Twupguttem a lot when I hear or read about the heavily heeled people who jerk themselves about on the dance floor in such establishments as the White House, sometimes keeping it up till dawn. I say it when I contemplate the Beautiful People of the so-called Jet Set. I say it when I witness the hairy death-rattle songbirds at their work, together with the mule-jawed little girls who sell two million records without opening their mouths very wide.

It is really astonishing, once you take up saying Twupguttem, how often you'll find it comes trippingly on the tongue. At the beginning I didn't say it more than half a dozen times a week, but now . . . well, you know the frequent remark, "Sure is a lot of money around these days."

It has occurred to me that saying Twupguttem is consuming too much of my time, and so I'm giving it up altogether. I have to give it up. I have two important projects cooking in television, either of which might put me in the chips. If it happens, there are plenty of character assassins around who would glory at the chance to look at me and say Twupguttem.

I don't want that to happen. I don't want my own petard hoisted at me. I prefer things the way they are, with people speaking pleasant sentiments about me, such as, "He writes for the *Reader's Digest* but I hear he's a Commie."

That's all right, but please! Not Twupguttem!

CHAPTER 19

CARRY ME BACK TO
COCKAROUSE COCKTIMUS

A few months before Lindbergh flew the Atlantic, another boy
and I were driving through Arkansas in a Model T (with side
curtains) pretending to look for work. We were approaching the
town of Smackover and we got into a scholarly discussion of how
the name may have originated. It was my theory that a couple
of the first settlers had a fight and one of them flattened the
other—smacked him over. My companion had some kind of a
ridiculous notion that one of the early settlers tried to nuzzle a
saloon filly and *she* smacked *him* over.

Arriving in Smackover we entered a drugstore and approached
the proprietor and asked him for the answer. He told us we were
both wrong. He said the first settlers arrived by muleback and
in order to reach the site of their proposed town, they had to
ford a deep stream. The intrepid leader of the group rode his
mule into the creek, hit a deep spot, "and the water went smack
over his head."

I was happy with that explication for a long time, and I still
am, in spite of what the books say. They assert that the French
explorers called the place *Chemin Couvert*, or covered road, and
this in time was slurred into Smackover. Covered road? Covered
with what? Sorghum molasses? Asafittidy bags? I'm sticking with
the druggist and that man on the mule.

My Arkansas experience made a lasting impression, and down

through the years I have retained an abiding interest in the origin of place names in the United States, especially town names. It may be that this interest goes back to an earlier time when I got to investigating the name of the community where I was born: McLeansboro in Southern Illinois. The metropolis of my nativity was named for a Dr. McLean, an early squatter who donated the land for the townsite. When it came time to pick a name, one man produced a book on Greek mythology and proposed Penelope, which he pronounced Penna-lope. Then another citizen struggled to his feet, a man who, in the words of a local historian, "had partaken too freely of tanglefoot." I don't think the historian meant that the old guy had been eating flypaper. What he said was: "Boys, 'y god, less call 'er after Ole Doc McLean here!" And so they did.

In later years another historian told how the town had grown "from the darkest and vilest pit, where the slime of the serpents would pour, to a thriving temperance town of two thousand." McLeansboro, a bone-dry town throughout most of its history, was given its name by a drunk. In passing I would like to say that a nearby hamlet, a sort of suburb of McLeansboro, was called Goosenibble, but it disappeared from the map and I was never able to find out where it got its name.

Somebody once wrote that McLeansboro's chief brag was this: "Our town is the only town on the face of the earth named McLeansboro." A long time after my residence there, I lived twenty-three years midway between the towns of Mount Kisco and Chappaqua in the New York suburbs. And where did those two places get their names?

The only history of Mount Kisco I was ever able to get my hands on opened with these lines:

ORIGIN OF THE NAME KISCO
The name Kisco is an Indian word, the particular meaning of which has never yet been ascertained.

Unsatisfactory. Some people said that Kisco was the name of an Indian chief who reigned over the neighborhood. I undertook some digging and found out that the chief of the tribe in my part of Westchester County was actually Cockarouse Cocktimus. The Indians of Westchester were Mohegans and were divided into sub-tribes, and Cockarouse Cocktimus ruled over one of them. Another local sachem had the name of No Name. Frankly, I would have enjoyed telling people that I lived at Cockarouse Cocktimus, New York, or having my mail addressed to No Name, New York. Just as I would have been pleased to give *Who's Who in America* my birthplace as Goosenibble, Illinois, or even Penna-lope.

Nobody will believe this, but the chief brag of the people in Mount Kisco was: "Our town is the only town on the face of the earth named Mount Kisco."

Now, as to nearby Chappaqua. This is a town where the quality lives, where commuters out of Wall Street and Madison Avenue make their homes. They think well of themselves, at least on weekends. In 1954 a group of Chappaqua clubladies announced that they had discovered the meaning of the Indian word *chappaqua*. They said it meant "Land of the Laughing Waters." They had it almost right. A few years earlier I had consulted an old history of the county and found that Chappaqua means "The Place of the Drunks."

You may readily see that my fascination with place names could develop into an absorbing hobby. During my roamings around the United States it sometimes turned into a sort of game, fully as entertaining as license-plate poker and less costly. I still play it from time to time with my traveling companions, trying to guess the origin of town names that lie up ahead.

Today there are whole gaggles of college professors and graduate students scouring the country, seeking the origin of place names, putting out books containing their findings. I doubt if they come up with anything quite as tenderly lyrical as the derivation of Spitting Rock as explained by Abe Burrows: "On this spot an Indian maid once spit all over her lover." Or Jim Street's discovery that Stephen Foster's song, as originally written, started off: " 'Way down upon the Yazoo River, far, far away." After the lyric had been written that way, someone told Foster that Yazoo means "waters of the dead" and he hurriedly got out the atlas and switched to Suwannee.

I no longer live between Cockarouse Cocktimus and The Place of the Drunks. For five years I have been a citizen of Texas (from an Indian word meaning friends) and I have driven over large portions of the state, which is composed of many large portions. There are more cities and towns in Texas than a man can count. We have a community called Comfort, not far from San Antonio. I have a friend in Oaxaca, Mexico, whose ambition is to ride a train into that town just so he can hear the conductor call out, "Comfort station!" We have another town called Arp. Arp is in strawberry country and, in fact, was originally called Strawberry. In the early days the shippers had to label their crates by hand and they complained that printing out "Strawberry" was too dern much work; they decided on a shorter name and chose Arp in honor of their local editor.

So many fine towns have disappeared. There used to be a place in Texas called Bankersmith, after a kindly and altruistic old banker named Smith. And one named Grayback, from *Pediculus humanus humanus*, the body louse. Still another called Pancake; you might spend an eternity trying to guess the origin of that one. It was named for a kindly old rancher, J. R. Pancake. And what could you make out of a town called Hemaruka? It was a whistle-stop on a railroad and a vice-president of the line christened it as a tribute to his four daughters, Helen, Margaret, Ruth, and Kathleen.

Driving toward the splendid city of Corpus Christi, Texas, not long ago in the company of a friend named Ken McCaleb, I noted that we were approaching a town called Odem. I asked Mr. McCaleb to play my little game with me and after a while he said: "The man who founded this town came to Texas from New York and when they asked the reason for his migration, he said, 'Everybody back East—I owed 'em.' Get it? Owed 'em. Odem." I suggested gently that the McCaleb theory was hogwash blended with sheep dip. I then gave him my explanation. When the settlers arrived on the scene they found a black man sitting on a stump playing a banjo and singing "Odem Golden Slippers!" Mr. McCaleb glanced around the car, looking for a blunt instrument, but found none. Then we arrived in the town and found out that it got its name from a sheriff, Dave Odem.

While Odem exists today, Tesnus has vanished from the map of Texas. It is Sunset spelled backwards. There is no longer a Ti in Oklahoma—it got its name from the initials of Indian

Territory, turned wrongside out. Once there were towns named Rat and Damifino in Missouri, but folks thought they lacked poetic feeling and either changed them or abandoned them. The same for Total Wreck, Arizona. It's mentioned in the books but try to find it out there amongst the red rocks and the cactus. Lousy Deal vanished from Nevada, and Knockemstiff from Ohio, not to mention a town in South Dakota where the early citizens called in a mining man they liked and told him he could name the place for his wife if he so desired. He named it Holy Terror and Holy Terror it remained throughout its existence.

There is a bump in the road up near the city of Abilene, Texas, which was once a thriving little community called Scranton, after the city in Pennsylvania. What the people in the Texas Scranton didn't know was that the eastern Scranton was formerly known as Skunk's Misery. Maybe that's why the Texans gave up.

One of the most celebrated towns in Indiana is Santa Claus, which acquired its name from a quip, a sarcastic remark. The town was laid out in 1846 and the folks decided to call it Santa Fe. A Post Office Department man told them they couldn't do it because there was already a Santa Fe in Indiana. This angered the people of the new town and one man got so mad that he yelled at the postal official: "All right, you lah-de-dah bureaucrat, how'd you like it if we called it Santa *Claus?*" Be-danged if it didn't stick.

One note of warning if you decide to take up my little hobby. Be cautious about your sources. David Snell, a writer friend of mine, once asked me if I knew how Staten Island got its name. I didn't. He said that when Henry Hudson sailed the *Half Moon* up the Lower Bay of New York he pointed to the shoreline on the west and said to his spyglass-holder: "'s dat an island?" I am not a violent man in matters of nomenclature, else I would have strangled this Snell where he stood.

In the event I attain any academic standing for my work in this field, it will be because of the final item in this compendium. For many years parlor comics and vaudeville comedians loved to poke fun at an imaginary town called Podunk. At least they thought it was imaginary, and the place-name books thought the same. I am prepared to state that it was not imaginary at all.

Once while thumbing through a book about Upstate New York

(perhaps by Carl Carmer) I found Podunk described as a hamlet nestled up against a brisk-flowing stream not too far from Albany. And how did Podunk get its name? From its sole industry, a gristmill, powered by an undershot water wheel. As the big wooden wheel turned in the stream, the sound made by its vanes or paddles was: "Po-dunk, po-dunk, po-dunk!"

Man, that's history!

CHAPTER 20

THE ROMANCE OF COUNTRY JOURNALISM

Fella who runs one of these journalism schools out in the South-west part of the country approached me recently and asked me if I would make a talk in front of his students, an inspirational lecture about my years as a newspaper hand in various cities, towns, and villages. I said no. I said that if I did, it wouldn't be inspirational.

Afterward I got to thinking about my glorious achievements in journalism and just for kicks I sat down to see if I were capable of composing such a speech as the perfesser suggested. I cast my thoughts back over the years and then, out of the deeps of memory, there came to me the details of the Bowling Green Adventure.

It used to be (before the New Journalism struck an already help-less country) that among the staff of every big city newspaper there would be one or two reporters or desk men who yearned for the simple, relaxing, independent life of owning and editing a country weekly. I'm told that the tradition is not altogether dead today. I have known quite a few who wanted to make the break and who did it—bought the Dogtown *Gazette* and took up suffering for a profession. The savants of the journalistic world were not of much help, offered little in the way of discouragement —even old Horace Greeley put together some purple prose cele-brating the worth and the romance of country journalism. If I seem to speak with a slight bitterness, please do not consider it slight.

A trifle more than forty years ago I was a certified beachcomber in Florida, functioning on a strip of sand attached to a lake in Sebring, a town since become famous for its automobile races. In one respect it was an ideal beach for combing because nothing ever drifted ashore, except an occasional human being, and human beings were a drug on the market at that time, as they are today.

The great land boom of the early 1920s had disintegrated and I, an ingenuous unemployed newspaperman of nineteen, had been reduced to caulking rowboats and dinghys in order to earn a few dimes for eating money.

Then along came two guys who had been printers on the Sebring newspaper when I had been its editor. They were now trying to survive by operating a small printing shop and, like me, they were beginning to get lean and stringy. These two printers asked me if I would like to be co-founder and editor-in-chief of a newspaper in the town of Bowling Green, Florida, forty miles westward in the direction of Tampa.

Would I! I was so tired of my diet of grapefruit, picked off the tree, that I would have accepted a job as editorial director of the telephone book in Shafter, Texas, a town bereft of citizens. So we formed a three-way partnership, with the printers putting up the money (I think they had to go clean to Threadneedle Street to get it) and handling all mechanical operations. I would do the rest. I still ache all over when I reflect on it.

We rented a one-room wooden building two blocks from the heart of downtown Bowling Green. The heart of downtown Bowling Green could be distinguished only by the presence of a brick building which housed the town bank.

The structure in which we launched the Bowling Green *News* had an appearance of age; it sagged at the corners and in the areas between the corners. I judged that it had been put up during the Tyler administration.

Next door to it, with a grubby vacant lot between us, stood a similar edifice, aged and infirm and unpainted. This was a little grocery store run by a Mr. Gosspaugh, whose britches hadn't been ironed since his store building was erected, who believed that shaving brought on blood poisoning, who changed his undershirt once a month if it suited his whim, and who wore galluses over the undershirt.

Mr. Gosspaugh was a Florida cracker and spoke with the gift of tongues. I had a notion, at the time, that he was the originator of Southern dialect. Sometimes I couldn't understand what he was saying, but his customers could. His customers were mainly people buying chewing tobacco. By the plug or by the sack. On time.

I engaged a room in the home of the banker who, as I remember, was a widower. The room smelled like eight-foot-deep in the Okefenokee Swamp, but this stagnation was complemented by the town's drinking water, a rich sulfuric potable that tasted like clabbered benzine. There was one crumbling ruin of a cafe in town. I had to eat there, though the food was of uncertain quality; I would not have slopped a hog with it. I might add that it was summertime in lovely, bucolic Hardee County, and hot as a witch's tit, day and night.

(Some of my readers have a habit of giving me hell over my use of the expression *witch's tit*. The correct thing, they assure me, is *cold* as a witch's tit, not hot. I use them both. Depends on the witch.)

It is needful that I outline the procedures by which we produced a newspaper each Friday morning. My two associates lived in Sebring and ran their print shop. In Bowling Green I worked from twelve to fifteen hours a day, selling advertising, or trying to sell it, gathering news items, confusing the pages of a large ledger which was our bookkeeping system, cleaning house, and performing many lesser chores. I had no automobile and two or three times a week one of the printers made the eighty-mile round trip to pick up such copy as I had prepared. All the type was set in the Sebring shop and locked into forms. At noon on each Thursday those forms were hauled to Bowling Green in a panel truck and the real work—the bewitchingly beautiful and heavenly hours of going to press—the *real* work began.

We had a Treadwell press, a great iron monster which I still dream about after I have eaten a banana cheese soufflé. At one end of this monster, when it was functioning, a row of long wooden fingers rose and fell, flapping large sheets of printed matter onto a flat surface. The Treadwell could be operated effectively, it was rumored, by two men and a boy. I was the boy. I stood beneath those flapping fingers and snatched the pages away and stacked them off to one side.

We usually began the press run just before the dinner hour so that none of us would have an opportunity to eat and thereby waste money. I am sorry that I never kept a fever chart on that Treadwell press, a performance record showing the number of times it broke down during the production of a single issue of the Bowling Green *News*, and the approximate time span between each breakdown. I know that the printers spent more time trying to fix that machine than they spent running it. If you think those intervals of repair work represented rest periods for me, you are mistaken. As soon as the press groaned and wheezed and clanked and quit, I turned to other pursuits such as getting the printed pages arranged into the accepted form of a six- or eight-page newspaper.

We were never finished with the press run before daylight, but eventually the two printers, smeared with ink and grease and sweat, would load their type back into the truck and head out for Sebring, too weary to even wave farewell to me. It was now time for me to wrap and address the papers and get them to the post office. After that I would go to the Flyspeck Grill for a breakfast of hard grease. Then out on the town to endure the insults of prospective advertisers and to gather news items for next Friday's issue.

I can't remember how long this nightmare went on. Not more than three months, during which time advertising revenue fell off steadily and the skinflint banker began asking for my room rent in advance. He said the town was in some kind of a recession. Something had happened to the Hardee County strawberry crop —the snout beetles and the spittlebugs had moved in, devouring the runners in the fields from Plant City to Wauchula.

Came another Thursday afternoon and the boys arrived from Sebring. They didn't seem to possess the usual zest and exuberance that characterizes the proprietors of great public journals. They were out of sorts and I heard one of them call the other a son-of-a-bitchin' dumbhead.

We pitched in. By this time getting out that miserable rag had become a matter of rote and the only variety and novelty we experienced was in the Treadwell's capability of finding altogether new ways to collapse.

This night it broke down more than was its habit, and I sprained my thumb, and the printers cussed a good deal, but at last the job was finished. The boys set out for Sebring and I looked at the rolled copies of the *News* that had to be taken to the post office. It was around 9 A.M., and I wandered through the back door and into the Florida sunshine. I sat down in the dust and leaned my back against the unpainted wall of the newspaper shop. I remember wondering whether I'd ever be able to get to my feet again.

I grew up in small towns in the Middle West, where barnyard humor was prevalent. At an early age I knew most of the jokes and "risky" situations. And so now we encounter a rather remarkable occurrence. In a way it is a case of life imitating art. It was an incident straight out of American folklore and, I think, a turning point in my life.

I heard a door slam. I was too bone-weary to turn my head but I cut my eyes to the left and saw Mr. Gosspaugh hustling down the path to his outdoor convenience, a loose-jointed two-holer. Mr. Gosspaugh entered this structure and closed the door and for a few moments I forgot about him. I was about to fall asleep in the warming sunshine when I heard a maniacal shriek, followed immediately by another, and still another, and then the door of the privy burst open and out came Mr. Gosspaugh, making Comanche noises. He was leaping around much like a kangaroo, for his britches were around his ankles and his legs were tangled in his suspenders. Then down he went, still howling, threshing about on the ground and raising clouds of dust. The only word I could make out in all that screeching was "Wasps! Wasps!" And I remember thinking, without much emotion, "Wye, my goodness, this is a re-enactment of an Indiana incident I heard about when I was in my early teens."

Mr. Gosspaugh's wife came slamming out of her kitchen door and went to the aid of her fallen mate. His howling did not diminish by so much as one decibel unit as she got him to his feet and led him into the house. I did not move a muscle. I did not even call out a word of sympathy.

Mr. Gosspaugh remained inside the house no more than two minutes, then the kitchen door flew open and out he came, grasping again at the seat of his suffering, screaming louder than ever, dancing up and down, galloping around in circles. I found out later what his secondary trouble was. Once in the house he had shoved his wife to one side, grabbed a bottle of Sloan's Liniment, poured a goodly quantity into his cupped hand, and sloshed it into the affected area. It was the same as setting fire to his crotch, and now he was outdoors again and on the ground, crying out for the Lord to put him out of his misery.

I didn't move.

I said to myself, "No matter how bad he feels, he's still better off than I am."

Eventually Mrs. Gosspaugh got her husband back into the house and after a while even his moaning ended. I continued to sit in the dust and the sun for a while. I recall that an unpleasant thought crossed my mind: I had the privilege of sharing that outhouse with the Gosspaughs because our newspaper had no facility of its own. Squatter's rights, you might say. I resolved that I would never cross its threshold again.

I got the mail sacks to the post office and soon thereafter had one of the printers on the phone.

"I quit," I said.

"Good," he responded. "You make me happy. I quit, too."

There were no more issues of the Bowling Green News. I visited the town for an hour recently and recognized not a single street or structure, and I could not locate the site of the News building. I talked to a few mature citizens and they said they seemed to remember that the town had some kind of a newspaper a long way back. "It didn't last," one codger told me. "I understand it warn't much of a paper."

The death of a newspaper is usually the occasion for great sorrow, especially among members of its editorial staff. The death of the Bowling Green News wrought no sadness in its editorial staff—me. Shortly afterward I found myself employed on a weekly newspaper in the town of Lake Wales, Florida. The publisher had a pup tent in his back yard and told me that I could sleep in it and save the expense of room rent. I slept in it for two or three weeks and then resigned.

That Lake Wales paper was the last weekly I ever worked on. I decided the bigger newspapers, the dailies, were for me. I still think that Mr. Gosspaugh and his wasps helped take all the romance out of country journalism, and pointed me straight toward the big cities.

CHAPTER 21

LOOSE TALK IN
THE DENTIST'S OFFICE

A committee from the Society of Paid American Humorists has recently called on me and threatened to lift my franchise, cancel my license, strip me of my shoulder things, and read me out of the service. They are sore. I said, "What's the matter you guys?" They glowered at me and I noticed that they all wore side arms. Then their spokesman stepped forward and said: "Just what the hell kind of a rotten humorist are you anyways?"

I demanded a bill of particulars and got one. They said I have committed an offense that is close to unpardonable: I have not done a scathingly humorous piece about dentists.

"But," I cried, "I have *too* done such a piece! I wrote amusingly about my dentist years ago. A Dr. Adorjan who had a dog that served as his receptionist. Surely you must remember *that* brilliant piece!"

"We remember it," said the spokesman for the committee. "That one didn't count. You were *nice* to your dentist. You were nice to his dog. You spoke kindly of Dr. Adorjan and made him out to be an ordinary mortal, without a streak of sadistic villainy in him. We repeat: what the hell kind of a rotten no-good humorist are you anyways? You neglected to be scathing. You didn't *scathe*. You failed to say a word about the crushing, shuddering fear that descends on a person bound for the dentist's office. You didn't talk about the unbridled horrors of drilling and the sawmill whine and roar that goes with it. You didn't even mention the frightful stab of the novocaine needle, and . . ."

I fell to my knees, my hands clasped together in earnest supplication, and begged them for another chance, begged them not to take away the only livelihood I know, such as it is, and I said I'd go right downtown and bust my dentist one in the snoot if they wanted proof of my fidelity. I said that this very day I would rectify my apostasy and write a piece blasting the miserable ass off of all dentists; and those who have dogs, I'll blast their miserable dogs.

"Do it in twenty-four hours," they said, "or get out of town." So . . .

For a great many years now I have considered myself to be an earnest advocate and sincere apologist for dentists. Christ knows they could use a few. I'm acquainted with people who, if they happen to see their dentist approaching on the street, will duck quickly into an alley or a doorway and stand there and tremble. They behave in the manner of those quiet and kindly heretics who took down with the jerks whenever they espied Old Torquemada strolling in the marketplace at Seville.

Sad to say, my attitude is changing. I am beginning to find fault with dentists. First, I am disgruntled over the matter of the little mirror on the end of the steel stick. And second, I think it is time that the dentists and their helpers tidy up their language.

Let us consider the little mirror. For years I have been trying to get dentists to order me one. I want to be able, in the privacy of my own home, to inspect the back of my teeth from time to time, to see what's secretly going on back there, to see what's developing or, more likely, what's disintegrating.

The dentists have always put me off or merely smiled and nodded and then failed to come through. It has become pretty clear to me that the dental code ordains that no patient shall be allowed to have his own little mirror on the end of a steel stick. The dentists have decided, probably at one of their national conventions, that it would be bad policy to start handing out the little mirrors indiscriminately. They reason, I assume, that if a person starts yawning open his mouth and looking at conditions from the inside outward, it won't be long before he'll begin scaling and cleaning his own teeth. He might even try his hand at simple fillings, using Portland cement or spackle or sodder (with a borax flux). I am gradually approaching the opinion that the dentists, normally considerate and compassionate men, are being just a trifle selfish in this mirror proposition.

My second and principal complaint, however, is aesthetic and concerns the spoken word. A dentist's office, I've discovered, is a hotbed of loose and irresponsible talk. This talk falls into three main categories, as follows:

1.   Politics.
2.   X-ray analysis.
3.   "Discomfort."

Barbers were the original dentists and barbers have traditionally been gabby and so it is that dentists, through atavistic retrogression, are usually quite articulate while they work. There is an important difference, however, between the garrulous dentist and the verbose barber. A customer in the barber's chair can answer back.

I have always, it seems, had dentists with strong political opinions—all of them muleheaded and wrong. I go in for a simple filling. He crams my mouth full of machinery, plus wads of folded gauze, plus that thing that hangs over my lower lip and goes zurrrk . . . zlp zlp . . . urk urk urk . . . zurk glk glk zurk . . . ssszzzzz . . . guzzzzurk . . . all during the halcyon time of drilling and filling. At the same time the man in white is delivering a long harangue, often on a subject of a partisan political nature. He states his views with force and conviction and they are always antigodlin to my own position, but *I can't say a word in rebuttal.* I am the world's most captive captive audience. The only way I could refute the bounder would be to spit out a couple of pounds of stainless steel and gauze and oil of cloves, rise up in the chair, and declare: "Now, you just listen to *me* for one god-damned minute, you ill-informed snollygoster!" But of course I would never actually do such a pugnacious thing, being a gentleman, and so he has me in his power, and he knows it. Or does he know it? Sometimes I wonder, especially when he persists in asking me questions about where I stand on this issue or that, knowing that I cannot give him one intelligible word in response.

A tape recording of my part in the conversation would have me saying: "Glawg yunh . . . yawr uh uh huh kakaka glilg nahr . . . ummmmmm blerf gurg yawr puhhhh." That is not the sort of political reasoning that would likely make a favorable impression on the electorate.

Now, about the X-rays. There is a thing called the Wolf Viewing Box. It is not for looking at wolves. It is a box manufactured by some people named Wolf. It is recessed into a wall and has a glass front and it is for viewing X-rays. Lately I have had extensive traffic with an oral surgeon who, week after week, has performed on me with such appalling thoroughness that when I finally got my mouth in the clear I said to him, "Why don't you just get a bucksaw and cut off my whole head and cure everything at once?" My franchise as a humorist requires that I make comical remarks of this nature in all contingencies—comments that are great yocks to everyone except oral surgeons (and oral dentists).

Usually the dentists and the oral surgeons like to show X-rays to their patients and so they have a Wolf Viewing Box installed near the chair, and the girl brings in the film and it is hung up with a little metal clothespin and the light is switched on and the doctor takes a ballpoint pen and ballpoints at things and says:

"Notice that little dark area right in here? Shows an occlusal laud is causing an alveolar bone loss in the periodontal ligaments, where the pattern of bone resorption and apposition is fouled, much like a fishing line gets fouled, against the gingival third of the coping. Can you see it?"

"Sure," I say.

I can't see it. I can't even see any teeth. I have never in my life been able to make out anything on an X-ray except once when a doctor showed me one of a bobby pin in a baby's stomach. Nevertheless, I always tell him that I can see bone resorption fouled up on the periodontal fishing line; I don't want him to go through the whole recital again. It is not stimulating talk. And so he proceeds:

"I believe we'll have to remove, right in this area here, well, I think we'll have to take out these deposits of supragingival calculus in order to gain access to the gingival sulci, and drench it in sassatate. Right here. See it?"

"Yep."

I don't see it. But I see something else.

"Hey," I speak out excitedly, "look at that big black thing there. Great ballsa fire, look at it! Don't tell me it's——"

"That," says the doctor, "is an old filling. Now, right in this area here we have a——"

"A filling!" I cry out. "My God, I don't have any filling the size of *that* thing. It looks like the Matterhorn . . . with sprockets on it!"

"It's a filling," he says firmly, and he proceeds to that other area where there is a decreased osteoblastic activity, related to cartilage resorption by chondroclasts, and then he speaks suddenly in emotional tones, as follows:

"Hmmmmmmmm. Hmnh! What an endentulous lower mandible!"

This observation does me little earthly good and so I just close my eyes and yearn for a stiff shot of chlordiazepoxide which is either for steadying the nerves or eliminating beetle grubs from the lawn.

Finally, and most important of all, there is the gross misuse of a single English word, not alone by plain dentists and journeyman oral surgeons, but by all their smiling helpers. I have incorporated this complaint in a letter. It is not directed to my own dentist, for he is six feet and a half tall and has strong hands. It is addressed to all practitioners and reads as follows:

Dear Doctor:

Your business is teeth, my business is words. I allow you to advise me about teeth, so I trust that you and all members of your staff will accept my advice about the way in which you employ a single word. It is used with great and distressing frequency around your office. It is the word *discomfort*.

You say to me, "When you get home there may be, later on, a bit of discomfort. If that should occur, there will be some pills for you to take. Miss Z. will give them to you. If the discomfort continues tonight, call me tomorrow morning, and we'll see if we can do something about easing the . . . uh . . . discomfort."

Kindly don't use that word any more, Doctor. Kindly say it this way: "When you get home there may be, later on, stabbing, piercing, excruciating, screaming, screeching pain, as if molten metal were being ladled into your head. If that should occur, Miss Z. will give you some pills to take. If the raging, unbearable, screaming pain continues tonight, call me tomorrow morning, and we'll see if we can do something about easing the . . . the frightful and hideous torture."

I realize, Doctor, that there is not much real difference between the two descriptive techniques, but I think I prefer my own as being just a trifle more accurate than yours. I hope, therefore, that you and your people will employ my terminology in the future and, by the way, could you get me one of those little mirrors on the end of a steel stick?

Respectfully,

Recently I've heard of a publication called the *Glossary of Prosthodontic Terms*, which is described as the Webster of the dental profession. It is put together by erudite tooth people who are members of the Nomenclature Committee of the Academy of Denture Prosthetics. One of the journal's purposes, I judge, is to choose words that will fall softly on a patient's ear. Dentists are urged not to say *bite*, but *occlusion*; don't say *gums*, say *gingiva*.

I don't know if I've squared myself with the Society of Paid American Humorists, but I do believe that I have made a substantial contribution to dental semantics. I offer the above observations, including my negative analysis of the word *discomfort*, to the Nomenclature Committee of the Academy of Denture Phonetics, free and clear.

Perhaps, as a gesture of appreciation, they will vote me a little mirror on the end of a steel stick. No. On the end of a *solid silver* stick. It shall be my very own Academy Award, and I promise that I'll never put it in my mouth.

NOTE: After the foregoing dissertation appeared in *Family Weekly* magazine, the mail brought in dozens of little mirrors

on the end of steel sticks. And one other item. From the Institute
of Dental Research, Walter Reed Army Medical Center, Washington, D.C. 20012, came a larger package. It contained a flashlight and two mirrors, one of which was shaped like a kidney.
There was no note, no letter, included in the package. I fussed
with it for an hour, trying to figure out how it could be used
by me in examining affairs inside my mouth. At last I took it
to my dentist and laid the stuff out before him and asked for
advice. He said: "That stuff's not for examining your teeth. It's
for looking up your ass."

CHAPTER 22

THE VIRGIN OF TAXCO

In Mexico a woman's costume often tells more about her than her letters to the folks back home. Depending on the way it is worn, a *rebozo* can provide enough communication to bring Marshall McLuhan up short.

In Taxco, where I have been a frequent visitor, the Mexican women as well as the *gringa* expatriates and even some of the tourist ladies wear *rebozos*, but they also affect a capelike garment which conveys an important message to the world. It is called a *quexquemetl*, though not by me.

This *quexquemetl* is similar in design to the more familiar *poncho*. It is a squarish piece of fabric with a hole in the center. It is placed over the head and worn so that it hangs with the edges squared across the front and back or with the corners pointing downward. This is not an adequate description, but I am no Yves Saint Laurent.

If a woman is married, she wears the garment squared across. If she is a virgin (or wants to give that impression), she turns it so the corners are pointing downward, fore and aft.

Once in Taxco my wife bought a *quexquemetl* and though there were only two messages to convey with it, she remained confused about its use as an important medium in the communications arts. She could never remember which way to turn it to identify her condition. Most of the time she was walking the cobblestone streets of Taxco, at her age, with the cape telegraphing word to the entire town that she was unplucked. A source of embarrassment to me.

I finally gave up trying to teach her the proper way for her to wear it. I simply had to say, "For all I'm concerned, you can just let your reputation go to hell."

CHAPTER 23

AN ENCOUNTER WITH CAVE BECK

A little serendipity is a dangerous thing. A couple of weeks ago, while working on an article about Fiji, I was trying to find out the word for *chicken* in pidgin English, and I was looking in a book called *The Story of Language* by Mario Pei. I didn't find the chicken-word but on Page 440 I stumbled upon the name of Cave Beck, a seventeenth-century scholar who invented a language for universal use. When put on paper it employed a combination of letters and numbers; in actual speech the numbers became spoken sounds. Crazy? Wait.

Dr. Pei set down a sampling of this language. "Honor thy father and thy mother" becomes, in Cave Beck prose, "leb2314 p2477 pf2477." When you want to speak the line you don't say it the way it looks. You say, "Lebtorconfo peetofosensen piftofosensen." God damn it, I'm *not* making it up. If you can't believe me this early in the year, kindly consult *The Story of Language*.

I was so impressed by Cavebeckian language that I sent off a letter to my old friend Fred Beck, a wise and witty Californian, suggesting that he ought to undertake a genealogical investigation to determine if old Cave Beck was an ancestor of his, so he'd have something to be proud of.

Fred Beck wrote back that Cave Beck was his uncle "so far removed that it is sickening." He also said that some of Cave Beck's linguistical blood courses through his own veins, for he himself has lately been working up a universal language, some-what similar to his Uncle Cave's. Then Fred Beck wrote, at the end of his letter:

$$848$$

I knew at once that he was trying to communicate with me in the language he was inventing. So I applied my algorithmic mind to "848"—my skill in binomial theorem, spherical trigonometry, addin', subtractin', and multiplyin'—and in eleven days flat I came up with:

$$801 = \text{gin}$$
$$45 = \text{vermouth}$$
$$2 = \text{olive}$$

Thus: $801 + 45 + 2 = 848$
And $848 = $ a martini

I now wrote to Fred Beck and told him there was something haywire with his formula, that I hadn't been able to make any-thing out of it but a martini. He replied that 848 *is* a martini, but not a martini to his taste. He had rechecked his equation and discovered that he had made a significant miscalculation.

"What we have in 848," he said, "is a frightful thing to con-template—equal parts of 801 and 45. Slop with an olive in it." So he furnished me with a revision:

$$\frac{801 + 45 + 2}{5} = 812$$

I threw that one into my home computer and it came out a dry martini with a maraschino cherry in it. I didn't think that was what Fred Beck meant, so I gave it a whirl with pencil and paper, and got a glass of buttermilk with a stove bolt in it. Most discouraging.

I went back to Dr. Pei's book and immediately got serendipped into another universal language, called Interglossa and invented by Lancelot Hogben, an English savant who writes books about arithmetic, about internal secretions, and about comic strips. Dr. Pei said that Interglossa contains elements of Greek, Latin, and Chinese, and he gives us a sampling as follows: "Mi pre kine top tendo un acte re." Now, get ahold of something solid. That translates (Dr. Pei says this) into: "I past go place purpose a do thing."

If someone has popped his cork, it is not me; it is Lancelot Hogben or Dr. Mario Pei. I past go place purpose a do something else, such as get back to work.

And at long last I can now tell you that the pidgin word for chicken is "kokoruk." It just had to be.

CHAPTER 24

OOFTY GOOFTY, RONLY BONLY, AND 5/8

In the Golden Age of the hideous pterodactyl and the dagger-toothed tyrannosaurus, back around 1930, I went on a cruise to Panama and aboard ship made the acquaintance of a man who said his name was Sallard. I told him I had never encountered that patronymic before and he agreed that it was rare.

"Know what my nickname was in college?" he asked.

"No, what?"

"Potato."

Ever since then I have been interested in the peculiar folklore of nicknames. Twenty years ago the American Name Society invited me to join their club on the strength of a book I wrote called *People Named Smith*. They charged money for being a member and so I declined. What I'm after is something more on the order of the Nobel Prize for Literature, where they bestow a fond accolade on you and at the same time give you something like seventy or eighty thousand dollars. Further than that, I didn't think my book on the Smiths really qualified me for membership in the Name Society. It was vulgar in spots. My book, not the society. Still, I may join up eventually, on the strength of my researches into the subject of nicknames.

I have tried to confine my investigations to the United States and this has precluded my mentioning some excellent nickname lore in, for example, England, where Sarah Churchill was called Mule by her father Winnie, where the villagers of Ayot St.

Lawrence, on perceiving the majestic approach of George Bernard Shaw, were accustomed to saying, "Yon comes Old Hair-and-Teeth." Where Actor Rex Harrison has long been known as Sexy Rexy, for reasons that escape me.

Among the generality of human creatures there appears to be a great yearning for dignity, as witness our Shriner and Legion and political conventions, the restrained behavior of the ladies in the bargain basements, the United States Senate in the throes of a filibuster, the heart-warming sound of hammering as spite fences are flung up all over the countryside. In the light of this great itch for dignity, many people consider their nicknames to be humiliatingly hateful and try desperately to shuck them off, usually without success.

A nickname, said William Hazlitt, is the heaviest stone that the devil can throw at a man. Billy the Hazz was only partly correct. Let us consider two men in the world of sports who seem to have suffered under heavy stoning.

Up to 1950 Willie Jones had been a good third baseman in big-league baseball and he was known to the world as Puddin'head Jones. In 1950 the Philadelphia Phillies were the sensation of the baseball world and were called the Whiz Kids as they whisked to the pennant. In that year, with himself and his team the talk of the country, Puddin'head Jones grew dissatisfied with his nickname, feeling it to be somewhat *infra dig* for a fellow of his prominence. At his urgent request, I'm told, the sportswriters quit calling him Puddin'head; one newspaperman, however, aggravated by Puddin'head's flush of pride, referred to Mr. Jones thereafter as Willyum.

I have a friend in Washington who has sent me a report on a similar situation. Byron White was once a great football hero at the University of Colorado and such was his speed and dexterity that he became known as Whizzer White. People forgot that his name was Byron. Whizzer remained Whizzer when he was appointed an Assistant Attorney General by President Kennedy. But the day he was named to the Supreme Court of the United States, he whizzed no longer—in the newspapers and on the airwaves he became Justice Byron White. Except to one capital wag who said that the group formerly known as The Nine Old Men was now Eight Old Men and a Whizzer.

There are many individuals who travel through life with fairly ridiculous nicknames which somehow acquire luster and charm and sometimes even dignity from the character and personality of their owners. Bing Crosby, for example. Ike Eisenhower, Bugs Baer, Pee Wee Reese, Buffalo Bill Cody, Satchmo Armstrong, Dizzy Dean, Bernie Baruch. Or the many Reds—Smith and Lewis and Barber and Skelton and Grange, among others.

As for Ike, the mother of the Eisenhowers had a strong distaste for nicknames bestowed upon her boys, as do most mothers. Josef Berger has written in the New York *Times* of a woman who gave her boy the name Eric, feeling that if he had to have a nickname, Rick wouldn't be too hard to take. The child's playmates foxed her, however, and the boy became known far and wide as Earache. Mrs. Eisenhower named her third son Dwight in the belief that it would not lend itself to a diminutive. "She was right," her famous son said many years later. "Nobody could shorten it, so I became Ike." After he had been elected President Mr. Eisenhower was asked in a television interview: "Would you prefer to be addressed as General or as Mr. President?" To the surprise of all he replied: "I think as long as I live I will answer most readily to the name of Ike."

Some years ago in Racine, Wisconsin, there lived a shipping clerk whose name appeared in the phone book as Oofty Goofty Bowman. Reporters, happening on the name, went to see its owner, assuming that it was a case of an odd nickname that stuck. Oofty Goofty told them that he was named Oofty Goofty after an old-time vaudeville actor who had been a close friend of his parents. "By gosh," said Oofty G. Bowman, "it's my name and I'm gonna stick by it."

There have been many such instances of people having strange names that sound like nicknames but are not. A census taker once asked a piney-woods woman her first name and she said it was Pishie. How did she spell it? She wasn't rightly sho, but she took him in her cabin and pointed to a faded calendar from which it had been taken—a lithograph of Psyche, the mythological Greek sexpot. Stepin Fetchit, the languid Negro actor (himself named for a racehorse), had a son named Jemajo. People thought it was a nickname until Mr. Fetchit told Joseph Mitchell it was the boy's true baptismal name, standing for the first two letters of Jesus,

Mary, and Joseph. There was a man in North Carolina some years back called Pism C. Jackson. It was not a nickname. His folks got it out of the Bible—Psm. C. (for Psalm 100).

There are many prominent individuals whose names are susceptible to nicking but who somehow seem to have escaped the onus. The point is emphasized in a story told by Jack McPhaul, a Chicago newspaperman who wrote a book under the name he was accustomed to use as a by-line. His publishers urged that he call himself John J. McPhaul by reason of its being more *distingué* than Jack McPhaul. Mr. McPhaul later told the *Saturday Review*: "Maybe they're right. Now that I think about it, authors under the name of Chuck Dickens, Hank James, Hank Thoreau, Wally Emerson, Andy Gide, or Jackie Keats probably would never have gotten off the ground." He might have added Bobbie Lou Stevenson, Puddin'head Shakespeare, Manny Kant, and Bobbie Frost.

Recalling our kickoff boy, Potato Sallard, let us look at some other nicknames that blossom out of their owners' surnames. The classic example, of course, is the man named Rhodes or Rhoades, who is inevitably and unconditionally called Dusty from the cradle to the ultimate twitch, save in one single instance: it is nowhere recorded that the austere Cecil Rhodes, diamond king, dictator of South Africa, and angel to all Rhodes Scholars, ever was called Dusty. In passing I must mention a dog bearing the nickname Dusty—he was born on Christmas Day and his owner, Stephen Huguenot, named him Adeste Fideles, which was later abbreviated to Dusty.

My friend James Street, historical novelist and short story writer, went through life having weisenheimers address him as Forty-second and One-Way and Dead-End. (Another friend, Mel Heimer, with whom I once worked on a New York newspaper, for a while was saluted in the city room with, "Hey, Weisen!" although he was not one.) A man named Garrison, though he weighs 280 pounds, is apt to be called Snapper, after the famous jockey. Drummonds, such as Roscoe, the erudite Washington journalist, respond to the name of Bulldog. People named Newton, to be sure, must learn to live with the nickname Fig, and I have heard that the late Oscar Hammerstein had a friend who always addressed him as Ball Peen.

As unofficial historian of the vast and briskly cumulative tribe of Smiths I have for years been collecting nicknames acquired by people of that denomination. A Smith often needs a good substantial and distinctive nickname if for no other reason than to escape the distasteful Smitty. There is evidence to suggest that the most colorful nicknames on earth belong to Smiths. All my life I have been Bud to my family, though for a while I was called Slanthead by my newspaper cronies who, under the spell of tavern dizziness, embraced the ridiculous notion that my head had a slant to it.

The late General Walter Bedell Smith, who was Eisenhower's chief of staff, was called Beetle by his comrades, but he once wrote me: "When I was a small boy I was inclined to be sensitive about the wide distribution of the name [Smith]. Then I started to school and other boys immediately gave me a nickname, Fishface, and everything was all right—I had acquired distinction."

Perhaps the most bizarre Smith given name was that of 5/8 Smith, a respected businessman and civic leader of Pearson, Georgia. His father was named Frank Smith and was beset by multiple confusions; there were five other Frank Smiths in the town and so when his son was born he sat himself down and said, 'y doggies he'd concoct a name that no other Smith in history ever had, and he did, and entered his offspring in the books as little 5/8. Not Five-eighths, but 5/8. It wouldn't seem likely that a man with such a lovely name would ever suffer having it nicked, but 5/8 did. To his wife he was Willie, to his friends simply 5. They shortened it.

There was a prison guard in Arkansas years ago called Pick Handle Smith, for the reason that he once slaughtered six convicts with a single sweep of a pick handle. Cotton Ed Smith of South Carolina was, in the words of John Gunther, "probably the worst senator who ever lived, no mean honor." Erastus Smith was called Deaf (pronounced Deef) and gave his name to Deaf (Deef) Smith County in the Texas Panhandle. He was one of the most skillful of the Southwest's frontier scouts—a real accomplishment for a man who couldn't hear a mule bray if it was in bed with him. John Lardner once told me of three war correspondents on Guam who were distinguishable one from another by their nicknames: Wonderful Smith, Horrible Smith, and Pack Rat

Smith. In Albany, Georgia, a lawyer and former mayor was known universally as Taxi Smith though his true name was James. In college he was required to run in the freshman marathon, an assignment he disliked for the reason that he had flat feet which ached all the way up to his knees if he ran so much as four yards. He started off the race, trotted till he was out of sight of the other runners, then hailed a taxi which dropped him near the finish line. His deception was soon exposed and he became known as Taxi Smith from there on out.

In Philadelphia there was a beekeeper named Euphonius Smith, who was known all his life as Phony Smith. I have records of a Negro child called Bust Smith who was born during a flood and whose full name was William McKinley Louisiana Levee Bust Smith, and of a boy born in Oklahoma in 1901, later to be called Loy Smith, who was christened Loyal Lodge No. 269 Knights of Pythias Ponca City Oklahoma Smith.

There are people, of course, with nicknames whose origin no one would ever be able to guess. Tables Davis, for example. He was a dancer in vaudeville and as part of his act he would crouch down, seize a kitchen table in his teeth, and lift it high off the floor. Elia Kazan, the director, is known far and wide as Gadge. "When I was in college," explains Mr. Kazan, "I was like a gadget—small, compact, and eccentric." Burgess Meredith is called Buzz by many people, though to his wife and very close friends he is Sedgerub, which is Burgess spelled sorta backward. I have heard of one Mabry, city editor of a Texas newspaper, who was famous for his cyclonic cussing; he could say "It's a nice day" and manage to work in at least three obscenities with a profanity or two for punctuation. One day a reporter aimed a wad of paper at a wastebasket and hit Mabry in the head, causing him to knock over an ink bottle and saturate his britches blue. He leaped to his feet and screamed: "Who . . . the . . . BLAZES . . . threw . . . that?" He was known as Blazes Mabry from then on.

There is in New York City today a prominent businessman who is called Albie by his friends though his name is neither Albert nor Alben. When he was an undergraduate at Cornell he took a physical examination. The school medics mailed their report on a postcard to his fraternity house. It said they had found albumen in his specimen. His fraternity brothers got hold of the card first and pinned it to the bulletin board and he immediately became Albie and is Albie today, and his associates have no inkling of the nickname's true origin.

Westbrook Pegler was always Bud to his friends and his family and the explanation is obvious: Destiny marked him from infancy as everybody's ever-lovin' buddy. There was once a gangster called Fingy Walzer, so denominated because he had a finger missing. Mack Grey, a Hollywood character, once was steady companion to George Raft and was named Killer. People assumed that he was an ex-hoodlum with notches on his gun and that he was Raft's bodyguard. The truth was more romantic. Grey had originally been called Killah, which is the Yiddish word for hernia, one of which he had.

In Pennsylvania there was a man known as Hungry Sam Miller —he once ate 144 fried eggs, 48 pies, and 200 oysters at a sitting. H. L. Mencken, remarking on the custom in men's service clubs of wearing nicknames on saucer-sized lapel buttons, added that, "The first Rotarian was the first man to call John the Baptist 'Jack.'" Mr. Mencken also enjoyed telling about the family named Zass, who had difficulty finding acceptable first names for their two daughters; they finally solved their considerable dilemma by calling them Alice and Clarice.

Dick Bradford, the Santa Fe author, tells me that he once knew a girl in a Southern city whose nickname was Teet. When she was a baby someone having a first look at her exclaimed: "Land sakes, isn't she petite!" So they started calling her Petite, and then shortened it down to Teet. It was inevitable that she would grow up to flaunt an impressive chest and she tried for years to get people to call her Mary Lou. But Teet she was and Teet she remained.

Gene Fowler's lusty son Will is sometimes called Spike. In his newspapering days Will was built like a wrestler, with huge biceps. Once while somewhat orry-eyed he made his way to a Los Angeles tattoo parlor and set the man to work on one bicep. A crucifix, a scroll with his wife's name worked in, a salute to his Pop, and various other adornments. In the end, ginfully admiring the decorations, Will told the artist that he deserved a by-line, and the man signed his name, Spike, to the endermic mural. Will still has his kaleidoscopic bicep and some of his old friends still salute him as Spike. He has told me, too, of a character in New York named Pitzy Katz, who was a friend of Gene Fowler's. As a kid this Katz boy was adept at pitching pennies and acquired the name of Pitchy, which his Lithuanian mother corrupted to Pitzy. A loverly, loverly name, Pitzy Katz.

Irvin S. Cobb always regretted that he had not been named for his father, Joshua Cobb, for if he had been so christened, he would unquestionably have been called Josh Cobb—a perfect by-line for a country-style humorist. My friend J. G. Gude of radio and television, Jim Thurber's closest friend, was George as a boy and one day he took down with the yellow janders, and the yellow shading stayed on quite a while, and his pals began calling him Jap. He is today Jap Gude to the communications industry.

Dizzy Dean once said: "Most ballplayers got nicknames and Birdie Tebbetts's is Birdie because he's always a-hollerin' like a little ole kinairy bird." I once heard a woman on a TV quiz show respond to the question, "What was Babe Ruth's real name?" She said, "Wye, Babe Ruth." They told her no, that it was George Herman Ruth. "That's insane," she snapped. "Everybody knows his name was Babe Ruth." George Ruth had nicknames other than Babe; Bob (Piano Legs) Smith, the baseball historian, says his teammates called him Jidge and sometimes Two-Head. Lou Gehrig was known to his colleagues as Biscuit Pants. Umpire Brick Owens got his nickname from the fact that a fan once threw one at him. I have heard that the stalwart pro football lineman Hawg Hanner took pleasure from his nickname, though if I had the doing of it, I'd have called him Sohelpme. Pitcher Elwin Roe, as an infant in an Ozark crib, was inclined to flap his arms around wildly and yammer unintelligible prose poems at the world. One day a neighbor lady, observing this performance, exclaimed: "Derned if he don't act jis like a preacher!" And so he became Preacher Roe, even unto the day when he was as famous as Mary William Ethelbert Appleton Burke, nicknamed Billie.

I've read of an R. B. Jones whose initials stood for nothing and who went to work on a government job. He handed in his name to the payroll office as "R (only) B (only) Jones." His first paycheck was made out to Ronly Bonly Jones and it is to be supposed that his friends still call him Ronly Bonly.

Finally, another Jones. The late Hugh Troy told me about him. This man lived years ago in a small city in Idaho. He early became conscious of the fact that there were many creeks in the mountainous area surrounding the town and each creek had been given the name of the man who had discovered it . . . such as Blair Creek and Miles Creek and MacMillan Creek and Sheehan Creek. This man Jones decided that it would be a splendid way to preserve his name on earth for all time to come—to discover an unnamed stream or rivulet and call it Jones Creek. So he went exploring and spent all his spare time at it, and the quest became almost an obsession . . . yet he could find no creek without a name. Still, he kept searching and in time the people of the town began calling him No Creek Jones.

When No Creek Jones was about seventy-five years old he located the end of his rainbow and found a little creek that had never been given a name.

To this day that stream has always been called No Creek Jones Creek.

CHAPTER 25

OUR BEAUTEOUS AUTHORS

This being my day to dwell on American Literature, permit me to consider the physical aspect of the average author. It is both disconcerting and humiliating for me to do so.

Within the vast body of my published work I have remarked several times that a composite picture of all American authors would be sufficient evidence to refute any claim that God created man. I do not, necessarily, have reference to the Hairy Things of the New Day. I speak of the genteel writers of my own generation and perhaps the generation before me. I met and sometimes fraternized with a great many of them and man-oh-man! They weren't hidin' behind the door when the ugly pills were passed around.

In Southern Illinois (as I have remarked before) my grandfather Cad Allen is remembered for a number of sage observations, including this: "Generly speakin', ugly people are nicer people than good-lookin' people." I'll buy that. But not alone because it was spoken by my grandfather. I'd give it a switch and say that generly speakin', ugly people are *smarter* people than good-lookin' people. And that's a fact. Generly speakin'.

Consider Bernard De Voto and Sinclair Lewis and Damon Runyon and Franklin P. Adams and Booth Tarkington and Theodore Dreiser. I stood in the presence of each of these and I can assure you they would have given a dromedary pause. Think of George S. Kaufman and Joseph Hergesheimer and Irvin S. Cobb (whew!) and Ring Lardner and Alexander Woollcott and Hendrik Willem Van Loon. Little children would have taken cover. Even the greatest of them all, H. L. Mencken, looked like a sausage maker with erysipelas and usually dressed like an umpire.

You think I'm being too severe? Possibly a trifle unfair? Listen, Buster, I'm a critic. And I haven't even mentioned the lady authors. God help us every one!

I'm willing to make a concession. Certainly there were strikingly handsome men named Richard Harding Davis and Scott Fitzgerald and Gene Fowler. Also me.

I'm a fair man. I even strive for a positive approach and in the striving find myself considering poets. For years I have been pondering the question: Why do our leading poets have such nice-sounding names? Consider Robert Frost, Carl Sandburg, Stephen Vincent Benét, Robert Hillyer, Walt Whitman, Robinson Jeffers, Edna St. Vincent Millay, Robert Penn Warren, Richard Armour, Sidney Lanier, Marianne Moore, Henry Wadsworth Longfellow, Nick Kenny, Mark Van Doren, Ogden Nash, Bayard Taylor, Edgar Guest. All real pretty. Their names, I mean.

On second thought, forget it. I refuse to be taken in by anything so affirmative as beauty in nomenclature. I call your attention to three other American poets of note: Michael Wigglesworth, W. D. Snodgrass, and Adelaide Crapsey. If I can lay hands on any of Adelaide Crapsey's work I am going to read it. She rose above her name.

As for pulchritude among the New Crop, let me compliment these eager young people, all hip to the needs of the day. I have been noticing their photographs in the literary journals. Such things as sideburns down to the area of the clavicle; upper parts of their faces framed in an explosion of three and a half pounds of untended hair. *Too good-lookin' to let live.*

CHAPTER 26

DUCK CALLS IN THE DINING CAR

Most tourists, both domestic and international, think that the principal pleasures to be obtained from travel are sightseeing and the chance to purchase gimcracks, kickshaws, and fribbles. The major attraction for me, however, is people-listening. Strangers who would never dream of striking up a conversation with me in a department store or a washroom will talk me purple on a ship, a plane, or a train.

I've noticed that many traveling Americans are suspicious and wary of strangers who try to be friendly. I take my chances and welcome their company. I've written whole sections of books about weird and fabulous conversations I have had with weird and fabulous people on shipboard. I've set down conversations I've had with people on planes, and I've often been accused of making it all up. "How do you manage," I am asked, "to dream up all those insane characters?" I don't have to dream them up. It isn't necessary to invent them. Never. Like Mount Everest, they are there.

It is now my pleasure (and anguish) to call back the golden days of railway travel. I nourish the fervent hope that the Amtrak project succeeds far beyond the wildest expectations and that high-class passenger service returns to the railroads. I don't think that it will. In the years when I lived in New York I almost supported the New York Central and the Santa Fe with my trips to and from California. Whenever I got bored with thumping a typewriter (and whenever I could afford it) I would say to my wife, "Time to ride the Century and the Super Chief." And off we'd go. Many times there would be no particular reason for us to visit Los Angeles—it was simply a compelling urge to ride those superb extra-fare trains.

On one of the last such journeys I took I was traveling alone, and during the round trip I had fourteen meals in the diners, each with a different companion or companions. I can testify from that experience alone that, given half a chance, granted the smallest encouragement, the average railway passenger will not only strike up a conversation with a stranger—he'll describe the business he's in and show you his bridgework and cuss his partner for a low-life crook and lie about how much money he makes and tell you what he honestly believes as concerns the efficacy of prayer. He'll expound his personal political theories and tell you how many times he has quit smoking and discuss his sleeping habits and give you his recipe for spaghetti sauce and tell you how he goes about getting things wholesale. He'll speak of a new loophole his attorney has found in the tax laws and of the unreasonable attitude his wife takes toward his drinking and what he said to his neighbor about that ferocious beast that passes by the name of dog and how he doesn't believe Hell has real fire going in it. In other words, and for reasons I cannot fathom, he'll tell you things that he'd never tell his analyst or his next of kin.

When I had those fourteen successive meals with strangers, I talked to all of them and all of them talked to me. Some, I'll admit, had to be primed like a pump but then, like a pump, they gushed.

Several times the steward escorted me to a table for two and placed me opposite middle-aged or elderly women. Given this circumstance, almost invariably a common behavior pattern evolves.

The lady gives me a quick suspicious glance and then bends to her soup, or stares out the window, or begins studying the menu as if it were a gripping spy novel. She studies that menu intently even though she has already ordered her meal. Her whole attitude tells me that she is thinking: "What terrible luck I have. I'd better watch my pocketbook." The little wordless drama, following its rigid pattern, continues for a while. She spends considerable time rearranging the silverware, playing a nervous game of checkers with knife and fork and spoon and napkin. And I, of course, will be doing much the same sort of thing. Four or five minutes of this bilateral discomfort, and then I might say, "Nice sandy desert out there." Or she might say, "We're running a little behind time."

If I am the one to break the steely silence, she might simply grunt unpleasantly, or she might unbend and say, "We'll be in the desert for quite a spell yet." This is her way of informing me that the travel dodge is old stuff to her and that she considers me to be an equilateral, rectangular plane area, or square.

I take a sip of water and rearrange my silverware and hum a few bars of "Twuz Just a Garden in the Rain," which throws her into an even grimmer mood, for she has believed all her life that singing or whistling at table is nigh to a penitentiary offense. In my mind I am collecting my thoughts, trying to figure out some way of letting her know that I've outtraveled her maybe three to one and that I don't need any guidance from *her* about the length of time we'll be in the desert. The best I can come up with is, "I ordered the baked beans with brown bread—it's usually very good on this train."

"Oh, yes," she responds. "I know. I was just dying to order the same, but it don't agree with me. I've *always* known how good they are on this train." I murmur to myself, "Lord deliver me from a knowing woman!"

By now, however, under the firmly established rules of the game, the time has come to cease hostilities.

"Do you happen to live in Chicago?" I ask.

"Just outside," she says agreeably. "Winnetka. You from Chicago?"

"No. I'm from New York. That is, just outside of New York."

"You may not believe it, but I *like* New York."

"You do? What do you like about it?"

By the time the meal is finished I could write a novel as long as *Les Misérables* about that woman's life and times. We two, who regarded each other with distrust and suspicion at the beginning, have become boon companions, sharing our innermost secrets, even distorting our individual prejudices in order to avoid conflict of any kind.

The behavior of the train traveler is usually the same at the first encounter, no matter what his type, be he safecracker or suffragan bishop; thereafter the mutations of the game are wonderful. You meet all kinds. I had lunch with a man who was a fire engine salesman, who said he hadn't shot a game of pool in thirty years but that he could still remember and reel off the color combinations for each of the fifteen balls. Did it, too. I broke bread with a man who hated the sight of me for the first five minutes, exhibiting that distaste clearly, and within an hour he was urging me to get off the train with him in New Mexico and spend a week as a guest at his ranch where he had his own golf course and *frontón* court. A lady who gave me icy glares when I sat down opposite her spent the remainder of the day following me around the train, imploring me to write a letter to that stubborn mule of a husband of hers, telling him she was one hundred and ten per cent right in wanting him to move the family from Kansas City to Pasadena.

There was a story of sorts in every one of my table companions. I ate with a man who said he had been a world's champion duck caller. He pulled a wooden gismo out of his pocket, a thing with a reed in it, and offered to demonstrate duck calls for me right there in the dining car. I asked him not to. As a long-time friend to ducks, a student of duckdom, as well as something of an authority on the printing of unprintable noises, I am aware of the fact that there are established sounds and noises customarily made by ducks and certified in the bird books. Certain ducks, or drakes, go yeeb-yeeb and whee-whee-whew, and the Old Squaw duck goes onk-a-lik, ow-owdle-ow. I didn't care to have these sounds coming from my table. This man, however, kept moving his duck-deceiver toward his mouth, being most eager to demonstrate an assortment of calls, which he described as: mama's eatin'-time call, the come-back call, and ever'body's favor-rite, the mama duck hollerin' hot fer the drake. I told him that if he sounded these duck calls, it might attract undue attention, might even panic the other people in the car, possibly fetch a brace of half-plucked ducks winging out of the galley. I stayed away from this man for the duration of the trip, though now and then I thought I heard yeeb-yeebs and onk-a-liks in the distance.

There was an elderly chemist with a sense of humor who got to telling me things about moths. He said that a moth needs a lot of Vitamin B to survive, and he gets it from the perspiration stains on clothing. The chemist and I went from the diner to the club car, where he helped me work out a plot for a science-fiction story called *Vengeance of the Moths*. The climax of this spine-tingling tale comes when several armies of powerful warrior moths storm the nation's largest factories where underarm deodorants are manufactured and gnaw the buildings down to their very foundations.

Finally, on that one transcontinental adventure, there was a gaudy woman of uncertain vintage, freighted with blue jewelry and a peck and a half of cosmetics, who had breakfast across from me and told me I was an admirably "quiet" eater. She then said that her husband was a very noisy eater.

"I can't stay in the same room with him," she said, "when he's chompin' away at the Grape Nuts. And when he goes to work on a stalk of celery, the thrashing machines and the jackhammers take to the hills."

I asked her how she accounted for the fact that some people make more noise than others when they are eating.

"I've thought about it," she said. "I got an idea that my husband has bones in his head that are built wrong. What I mean is, they got no marrow in them. Hollow."

She heaved a great sigh and closed her eyes in thought.

"I should be married," she said, "to a jerk with no marrow in his head bones!"

I tell you, there is more than adventure and romance in the dining car. There's knowledge. Yeeb-yeeb. Ow-owdle-ow.

CHAPTER 27

WHAT'S THIS ABOUT THE THIRTIES?

I'm glad Bertrand Russell turned out well. Or am I, really? There was a time when I thought . . .

I arrived in New York in 1929 as a young newspaper reporter full of beans and downright sick with an overweening and childish interest in people who wrote books. I spent my days chasing after authors, both foreign and domestic, with all the drooling enthusiasm of today's more intelligent young people shagging down Mongoloid musicians and stutter-singers. I pestered such people as Sinclair Lewis and Carl Van Doren and Fannie Hurst and H. G. Wells and Thomas Wolfe with such persistence that I know most of them would have enjoyed belting me to the sod. I have noted, in the last few years, a steadily developing interest in the literary folklore of the 1930s and since this was the period of my author-chasing, I may have a small contribution to make to the picture. Louis Sherwin says I have.

Louis Sherwin was the top writer on the New York *Post* in those days and I admired him no end and considered it a great day when I encountered him around Park Row or out on assignments. It may be that he had written a book or two.

There came a day when I went to interview a visiting British author named Bertrand Russell. There was a large gap in my knowledge of contemporary literature, for this little guy with the look of a startled pullet meant nothing to me, except that he had written some books. Books that some people thought good.

The interview took place in the home of Russell's publisher. W. W. Norton, I think it was. Louis Sherwin was there and half a dozen other newspaper people, and each of us was handed on arrival a copy of the Englishman's current book—a volume that had something to do with mathematics for Christ's sake.

So here we were, sitting around and drinking contraband booze and asking questions like do you write with a pen or on the typewriter and how does it feel to be accused of mortal turbitood and what do you think about William Seabrook eating that human flesh and what do you favor for breakfast and explain free love.

It wasn't very exciting and then it came time for the gentlemen of the press to pick up their things and go, and Sherwin stood up and approached Bertrand Russell, book in hand, and asked if he might have it autographed. Russell (I didn't know he was a blinkin' Earl) requested Sherwin's name and then inscribed something in the book. I considered stepping up and getting my copy autographed and then decided against it. I thought to myself, Sherwin is the kindly type, a gentleman, and is just doing the polite and thoughtful thing. He's making this limey chipmunk feel important, sorta. One gesture of international comity would seem to be sufficient.

Since that day I have had a tendency to cringe whenever I've thought of my country-jake ignorance. And to cleanse my soul I recently decided to confess all, to tell the story of my bumpkin behavior in the presence of one of the great men of our era. I wasn't able to find anyone who knew of the interview, I couldn't locate a clipping of anything I might have written about it, and I was about to forget the whole thing when I remembered Louis Sherwin. I inquired around and finally located him. He is now associated with Nelson Rockefeller in the governor's office in Albany. So I wrote him a letter and asked if he could remember the incident in the W. W. Norton home. The next thing I knew Sherwin was on the phone, and he said:

"Forget that Bertrand Russell thing. The hell with him. I have only a vague recollection of the interview and anyway, you survive in my memory of those years for another performance. Do you remember the time J. David Stern gave a stag dinner for that old goat Dreiser, and you . . ."

Sherwin now recalled for me what happened at that dinner, which was attended by twelve or fifteen men including Ben Hecht and Burton Rascoe and other prominent writers. Louis said that I occupied a chair directly across the table from Theodore Dreiser and I sat like a statue all through the dinner with my eyes fastened on the famous novelist. Not a worshipful look, Louis assured me, but more of a glare. This made Dreiser much more nervous and twitchy than he was ordinarily and before long he had hauled out that god-damn handkerchief and was indulging in his most celebrated fidget—folding it and unfolding it and then folding it again and shifting about in his chair.

"This went on for two solid hours," Louis continued, "and had everyone at the table fascinated, everyone except J. David Stern. He was getting sore as hell about it and he was glaring at you the way you were glaring at Dreiser. You didn't eat anything—just sat and stared at Dreiser unrelentingly, and the sweat was standing out on the old goat's forehead . . . and then at last you broke it off in him."

The way I broke it off in him, according to Louis, was to speak at last in a loud, resounding voice.

"Dreiser," I said, "they tell me you are a man of stature." I emphasized the final word in the sentence, then paused, and finally added: "Anybody asks *me*, you got about as much stature as an Indiana fire plug."

That was all. It sorrows me that I remember the incident in the same vague and uncertain way that Sherwin remembers the Bertrand Russell affair. I know that I was handed my hat and coat and told to leave. Probably by J. David Stern. Still, it is most heartening to hear Sherwin's final judgment on the matter.

"In my book," he told me, "it was the greatest single god-damn incident in the literary history of that lunatic period. It should be chronicled in detail and spread upon the record. Son, you were far ahead of your time."

And I didn't even know it.

CHAPTER 28

FURDSLEY'S READING LIST

Waite Furdsley, the eminent American novelist, slept late on this snowy Saturday morning in early December. He had been up half the night reading a Western titled *The Lawless Border*, by Allan V. Elston.

He carried the book downstairs and before breakfast placed it on the ledge by the bay window where he kept those volumes that were next in line for his reading pleasure. *The Lawless Border* would be given to a neighbor later. Furdsley glanced over the dozen titles, trying to decide which one he'd take to bed with him tonight.

There was *The Twisted Thing*, by Mickey Spillane, and *A Time for Astrology*, by Jess Stearn. Also *The Sensuous Dirty Old Man*, by Dr. "A"; mysteries by MacDonald and Macdonald; *The Wit and Wisdom of Billy Graham*; *Sock It to Her: The Art and Science of Female Seduction*, by Stanley J. Conner; *The Bank Shot and Other Great Robberies*, by Minnesota Fats; *Playboy's Complete Book of Party Jokes*; and *The Pictorial History of Astrology*, by Sybil Leek.

While he was having his eggs, Mrs. Furdsley brought him his mail. Monthly bills, for the most part, but there was a letter from Cato Black, editor of the *Sunday Gazette Book Review*. It said:

> Dear Mr. Furdsley:
>
> As is our custom each year, when we bring out our Christmas issue, we are asking prominent American au-

thors to cite the five books they most enjoyed reading during the last year. The books need not have been published during the year. Could we have your five?

Immediately after breakfast, then, Waite Furdsley went to his study and sat down at his typewriter and made up his list. This is the way it went:

Dear Cato Black:
    The five books I've most enjoyed reading during the past twelvemonth were:
    T. S. Eliot: A Memoir, by Robert Sencourt.
    Paris Journal, by Janet Flanner.
    The Tenants, by Bernard Malamud.
    Letters of Louis D. Brandeis, Vol. I.
    Louise Agassiz Fuertes and the Singular Beauty of Birds
    Much thanks for asking me in. In passing I would like to remark that your book section improves in tone and quality with each successive issue.

                                        Sincerely yours,

                                        Ole Furd.

Mr. Furdsley put the list into an envelope and sealed it, stamped it, and then settled down to Chapter XI of his work-in-progress, a novel called *Brazen in the Back Seat.* He hoped he'd be able to polish off the chapter by mid-afternoon. There were a couple of television shows he wanted to watch. And he had decided to take *Sock It to Her* to bed later on.

CHAPTER 29

SHAKE HANDS WITH MY YAFNEY

Sometimes when I sit bemused at my typewriter I gaze at the big
Webster Third, which occupies a stand fourteen inches from my
right elbow, and I say to myself, "There it is. The whole thing.
We've got it all. Every single dad-blamed word a human American
could possibly need to communicate with other human Americans."

And then the disturbing moment comes when I realize that we
haven't got it all, that it is *not* all in the book. There are words
we need that do not exist. A word, for example, to designate an
in-law who is not, under the rigid rules of heraldry, consanguinity
and kissin'-kinship, actually an in-law.

I have reference to such a person as Donnell Van Noppen, Sr.,
of North Carolina. He is my daughter's father-in-law. He and I
visit back and forth from time to time, the same as it is with my
son's father-in-law, Al Miller of Michigan. (It is not my intention
to slight the women in-laws who are involved in this labyrinthine
puzzle—I'm just trying to keep an overly complicated matter as
simple as possible.) There are times during visits with these in-
laws of my children when we encounter a third person, and introductions are in order. I grope for a word—a word that doesn't
exist. There is a certain clumsiness, almost a coldness, to: "This is
Mr. Van Noppen, who is my daughter's father-in-law." Or, striving
for clarity: "Shake hands with Al Miller, the father-in-law of my
son Allen—he is married to Al's daughter Barbara, and this makes

my son Al's son-in-law, if you know what I mean." It happens that I have a genuine affection for these people and I insist that there ought to be a more lyrical way of describing them.

Another aspect of our proposition concerns the fathers-in-law or the mothers-in-law of my sisters and brothers. These constitute a multitude, but there is no apt word to describe them. "Oh yes," I might say, "I know Mrs. J—— quite well. In fact she is a relative of mine. That is, sort of. She is the former mother-in-law of my sister."

"Former?"

"That's right. Her son was my sister's husband, but they are divorced, and Mrs. J—— is, technically speaking, no longer, officially you might say, no longer a mother-in-law."

"So what is she?"

"She's . . . well, she's nothing."

Is that a nice thing to say about a respectable woman? I've struggled with the problem from time to time, but never with any appreciable success. It can become even more complex than the attempt to designate my divorced sister's former mother-in-law. Quite clearly, I was related to this lady—at least I *felt* as if I were kin to her; she was a witty and handsome person and the hell with what the genealogists might say. But what *was* our precise relationship? I finally concluded that she was my mother-in-law-in-law-by-marriage, and almost in a whisper (because of that divorce) I added the word "distant." And then came a real snarl: one day I was introduced to this mother-in-law-in-law-by-marriage's sister-in-law. I *had* to think of her as my . . . No! I won't undertake it!

I submit that new coinages are urgently needed, wholly new and original words. Not long ago I heard a neighbor say to my wife, "My roommate at college was my father's brother's wife's sister's daughter." There simply had to be a better way to describe that roommate. A single word should suffice. Cuzlug, perhaps. Think how much better it would sound if our neighbor said: "Just imagine my surprise when I got to college and found that my roommate was my very own cuzlug."

For the time being, until more scholarly men can take over, I would like to propose *cuzlug*, as well as the words that follow, to fill some of the gaps in our lexicon:

Nannymam: The mother-in-law of one's son or daughter.

Patricarp: The father-in-law of one's son or daughter. Thus, the Messrs. Van Noppen and Miller, whom we met earlier, would be my patricarps, as I would be theirs.

Transpappy: The father-in-law of one's brother-in-law's sister.

Lawdylaw: The father-in-law or mother-in-law of one's sister or brother, whether living together or divorced. I still feel that Mrs. J——, cited above, remains my lawdylaw even after her son and my sister are put asunder.

Yafney: The mother-in-law of my brother-in-law, meaning my wife's brother's wife's mother, or my own sister's husband's mother, or my brother's wife's mother.

Yifyafney: The sister-in-law or brother-in-law of my yafney.

That should do for openers. Later on I may go deeper into this matter. If, by odd chance, my new words should prove acceptable to the dictionary-makers and are admitted to the language, I shall be a proud and happy man; I'll celebrate by throwing a dinner party to be attended by all my nannymams, patricarps, cuzlugs, lawdylaws, yafneys, and yifyafneys. We should have a real swingin' time, because I truly love my kinfolks.

CHAPTER 30

THE DEBRIEFING OF MAJOR VEBLEY

Being a man who had little formal education, who knows five rules of grammar and isn't too certain about those, I am, quite naturally, a purist in regard to the English language. Misusages that I can recognize as misusages bug and bother me. I can't stand bum coinages. And I now have one in mind that I suspect is fairly bum. It concerns our involvement in the exploration of space, an area where you would think people ought to talk sensibly and with precision.

Before any of our astronauts are flung into orbit or hurled at the moon they are given a long and painstaking *briefing*. The same is true of the Soviet spacecraft riders.

In the secret briefing room they say to the astronaut:

"Now, Orville, you know that little lever two and a half, three inches long, over to the left, about level with your eyebrows? What's that lever for, Orville?"

"Turn on the air-conditioning?" suggests Orville.

"Nope."

"Is that the one that activates the sassatate tank?"

"Negative. It's the one you pull down on if you want to make a sharp right. Now, repeat after me . . ."

There follows a recitation on the location and purpose of the little sharp-right-turn lever.

Then on to the next lever, or push button, or twitching needle, exact location of the spark plugs, how to extinguish a grease fire with salt, the correct method for shortening a rope by tying a sheepshank, malfunction of the magneto, shooting pictures with a wide-angle lens.

So, we know what is meant by the word *briefing*. But there is a variation of the word that is used later and that sometimes gets me to talking to myself in the night. Each time I hear Ole Cronk speak of an astronaut's being *de*briefed at the conclusion of his flight, I begin to set up imaginary scenes and invent imaginary dialogues in an effort to get at the precise nature of the operation.

The astronaut takes his prescribed walk on the moon and then descends to his home planet and splashes into the sea and he and his iron gazebo are hoisted onto the deck of a naval vessel. He is taken below immediately and given a quick physical check and a ham on rye. Then he is . . . but let the newspaper writer or the newscaster take it away . . .

"After that, Major Vebley was flown by helicopter to an unannounced destination, a few hundred miles distant, for the customary debriefing."

There it is. Every one of them has to go through it. Every one of them, including even that Soviet boy-and-girl team, had to be *de*briefed before returning to the cities for ticker-tape parades and mammoth press conferences and, in the case of Russian astronauts, wet kisses from the Head of State.

This is the thing that has bothered me: what on earth happens when they get Major Orville Vebley into that debriefing room? I have pondered the question for hours and now, at last, I have arrived at the only possible answer. There can be no other. There is only one conceivable way in which an astronaut can be *de*briefed.

He is taken into the room. He stands before the debriefing team. The head of the team speaks.

"Orville," he says, "you remember all that stuff we told you during the three months of briefing at Cape Kennedy?"

"Yes, sir . . . I remember it very well."

"Okay. Now . . . *forget it!*"

"Yes, sir."

What was done before has now been undone. Major Orville Vebley has been *de*briefed.

CHAPTER 31

A FRIEND OF OURS NAMED HARRY

(written in 1964)

When in years to come the folklore of our time is assembled, the self-styled Old Farm Boy from Jackson County will surely have a substantial position in its pages. The reference is, of course, to Harry S. Truman. A whole body of lore and legend has grown up around his Missouri contrariety and his country-jake forthrightness, and this is the stuff that appeals to many of us who stem from the same migrational strain as Give-'em-Hell Harry. I personally evolved out of that strain and I know something of the Missouri Syndrome; I've been living with it (under the name of Nelle) for thirty-seven strenuous years. And as they say in the Ozarks, I jist love and ad-marr it.

Harry Truman belongs to a part of the nation sometimes spoken of derisively as the Bible Belt. He himself has called it that. Those who are inclined to put a better face on it, call it The Heartland. Mr. Truman wouldn't likely flinch if you called him a clodhopper, or even a rube, but he might wince if you spoke of him as a grass-roots agrarian. It would be typical of him to snap out that there are a lot of grass roots in Central Park where the wild muggerbeast roams.

He has always gloried in being a country boy, scornful of the pretensions of the stuck-up sassiety folks in the East. Every time he has put on soup-and-fish he has somehow had the appearance of a man playing the clown. Back home whenever someone got gussied up in a boiled shirt, Harry and his cronies had a standard taunt: "You look like a jackass peerin' over a whitewashed fence." Once when he was being given a degree he tripped over his academic gown. "Woops!" he exclaimed. "Forgot to pull up my dress!" At the time of his daughter's wedding a reporter asked him what he thought was the proper attire for the father-of-the-bride. "Well, sir," said Mr. Truman, "you wear the best pair of pants you've got and just so long as you're covered up, you'll be in style."

In his book *Who Killed Society?* Cleveland Amory listed Truman as among the murderers and told how the Old Farm Boy horrified some of Washington's most fastidious hostesses with his flouting of the rules. He once gave a celebrated party-thrower a case of the deep vapors by arriving without Mrs. Truman, thus throwing the seating arrangements out of kilter. "Bess's feet hurt her," Mr. Truman blandly explained, "so I told her to stay home." An indignant dowager in Palm Beach once approached Warren Austin, ambassador to the United Nations, and seriously asked him to do something about those gaudy shirts the President was wearing at Key West. It has been said that Mr. Truman never quite knew whether to salute, stand still, or shake hands with somebody when a band played *Hail to the Chief*.

He was often called "Mister Average" and his own recent estimate of himself goes: "Missouri has produced three notorious characters—Mark Twain, Jesse James, and me." At the time of his nomination at Chicago in 1948 he was sitting on a folding chair, munching a hot dog with mustard, and swigging at a bottle of pop. Four years earlier, when he came out of nowhere as the nominee for Vice-President, reporters asked him to describe himself and he said, simply: "I'm a workhorse." At the time of the Great Upset, when he astonished the world by beating Dewey, many investigators tried to find out why it had happened. Said a citizen of New Lebanon, Ohio: "Running around and yipping and falling all over his feet—I had the feeling he could understand the kind of fixes I get into."

When he was born his father celebrated the event by nailing a horseshoe over the barn door and planting a tree. When he dies he says he wants to be buried in a coffin made of mulberry wood, because "I want to go through hell a-crackin' and a-poppin'."

He has always been inclined to speak his mind, to answer questions with straightforward statements of fact. A pompous reporter, hoping to get for himself a little footnote to history, asked Mr. Truman, on his return to Independence after nearly eight years in the White House: "What was the very first thing you did after you arrived home?" Said Mr. Truman: "I took the suitcases up to the attic." He gave reporters the same style of answer when he arrived in Washington for the funeral of John F. Kennedy. What did he plan to do first? "I'm going to the hotel and sit down a while."

Other Presidents have lapsed into "country ways" on occasion. Cal Coolidge had his rustic moments and used to fetch a rocker out to the porch of the White House and sit and rock in full view of traffic on Pennsylvania Avenue. At his first State Dinner a waiter asked Abraham Lincoln if he'd take the red wine or the white. "I don't know," said Abe. "Which one would *you* take?"

Here is an excerpt from President Truman's diary for November 1, 1949:

Had dinner by myself tonight. Worked in the Lee House office until dinner time. A butler came in very formally and said, "Mr. President, dinner is served." I walk into the dining room in the Blair House. Barnett in tails and white tie pulls out my chair, pushes me up to the table. John in tails and white tie brings me a fruit cup, Barnett takes away the empty cup. John brings me a plate, Barnett brings me a tenderloin, John brings me asparagus, Barnett brings me carrots and beets. I have to eat alone and in silence in candle-lit room. I ring. Barnett takes the plate and butter plates. John comes in with a napkin and silver tray—there are no crumbs but John has to brush them off the table anyway. Barnett brings me a plate with a finger bowl and doily on it. I remove the finger bowl and doily and John puts a glass saucer and a little bowl on the plate. Barnett brings me some chocolate custard. John brings me a demitasse (at home a little cup of coffee—about two gulps) and my dinner is over. I take a hand bath in the finger bowl and go back to work. What a life!

For their part the Johns and the Barnetts and other servants were unaccustomed to the punctuality of the Trumans. On the dot of seven they marched into the dining room—a thing without precedent in Presidential families.

Coming as he did from the middle of the country, the ocean held a deep fascination for Mr. Truman and he spent a lot of time on the Presidential yacht. They could never get him, however, to embrace the language of the sea. To him the deck was the floor, the companionways were staircases, the head was the bathroom, topside was upstairs. "Let's go out and sit on the back porch," he'd say, and doughty salts would gnash their teeth, as is their wont.

Nobody relished a "Truman story" any more than Truman himself, and long after his departure from the White House he enjoyed retelling them. Here are two that met with his favor:

A Catholic priest stopped at the cabin of an anti-Catholic farmer in the South and asked for a drink of water. The farmer took one look at the swing-around collar and shook his head no. The priest, glimpsing a picture of Pius XIII hanging on the wall, asked why the man would refuse water to a priest when he had the Pope's portrait in his house. "Pope?" repeated the farmer. "Wye, the peddler that sold me that picture said it was Harry Truman in his Masonic robes."

A legend goes that Truman was speaking at a Grange convention in Kansas City and Mrs. Truman was in the audience with a woman friend. Truman said to the Grangers: "I grew up on a farm and I think I know a little something about farming. One thing I'm sure about—farming means manure, manure, manure, and more manure." Down in the auditorium Mrs. Truman's friend whispered to her, "Bess, why on earth can't you get Harry to say *fertilizer?*" To which Mrs. Truman replied, "Good Lord, Helen, it's taken me thirty years to get him to say *manure.*"

In and out of the White House he was often given to pranks. When his daughter brought a school friend home, the President assigned them to sleep in the Lincoln Room and then told them it was haunted and if they heard anything or saw anything, it would likely be the ghost of Old Abe knocking about as usual. Later, sitting with Mrs. Truman, he decided he would put a sheet over his head and creep into the room and go "Wooooo!" Some-one vetoed the project.

He attended an important reception at the first United Nations conference in San Francisco. During the reception he spotted Merriman Smith and Tony Vaccaro, White House correspond-ents. He dragged them into the line just below his own position and they dutifully bowed and shook hands with the remaining guests. After which Mr. Truman wheeled around and shook hands and bowed to each of the correspondents.

Tony Vaccaro was the victim of another Truman joke. He was to accompany the President on a trip to South America and he was notified that he would have to take yellow fever shots. Mr. Vaccaro had a lively horror of the hypodermic needle and pro-tested, but he was escorted almost by force into the White House clinic. The doctor told him to lower his trousers and lie down on a couch facing the wall. He was lying thus, hull exposed, when he heard the door open. Footsteps across the room. Cold metal against his hide. Then a voice: "This won't hurt you a bit, Tony." He recognized the voice and whirled around and found the Presi-dent of the United States bending over him, holding a huge hy-podermic device ordinarily used by veterinarians. Mr. Vaccaro, when the shrieking of his nerves had subsided, said, "Mr. Presi-dent, I don't usually greet the President of the United States from this position."

Mr. Truman didn't care for fishing and said so, even when his advisers told him that the piscatorial bloc can make or break a politician. He didn't like to mow the lawn but his wife, whom he often called The Boss, felt he ought to cut the grass at their home in Independence after his retirement from the presidency. She bought a power mower and pestered him to use it and he grum-bled and made excuses. She kept after him and then one Sunday morning, at the precise hour when people were passing on their way to church, she heard the roar of the motor and there he was, vigorously mowing the front lawn in his shirtsleeves, desecrating the bejezus out of the Sabbath. Mrs. Truman rushed out and or-dered him to put the mower away and never again bothered him about it.

He was an original, whether in the White House, in Missouri, or traveling abroad. At the White House he had a horseshoe-pitching court installed on the south lawn, and he had a well-stocked icebox put in close by his bedroom so he could raid it at dawn. He usually got up at 5:30 A.M., leading his critics to remark that he'd thus have "more time to get both feet into his mouth." When he made his first television appearance from the White House, he was at his desk, the cameras were set, the script was at hand, the seconds ticked off, and then Bryson Rash of ABC noticed that the Presidential bow tie was askew. Mr. Rash leaped forward, sprawling himself across the desk, hastily trying to adjust the tie . . . and the show hit the air. "Ladies and gentlemen," intoned the announcer, "the President of the United States." And from coast-to-coast the nation's TV screens exhibited a startling butt view of Mr. Bryson Rash.

When he was Vice-President a chauffeur-driven limousine called for Mr. Truman each morning and took him to his office. At the same time a secret service man turned up and took the seat beside the driver. For a long time Mr. Truman thought the second man was a friend of the chauffeur, hitching a ride downtown. The Trumans at that time lived in a five-room, $100-a-month apartment and Mrs. Truman managed without a maid. When she got to the White House, where there were more than a hundred servants, she used to complain to her friends that there were so many people around she couldn't just throw on a kimono and go across the hall to visit with Margaret or Harry.

On his first return to Independence as President, the home folks gave him a parade. He was waving and grinning from the back of the car when a man's voice rang out, "Hi-ya Cap!" Mr. Truman turned, recognizing the voice, spotting its owner in the crowd, and then jabbing a forefinger at his own head. The man on the sidelines was Frank Spina, his old barber and war buddy, and the gesture meant that the President would be in for a haircut.

Some years after he retired from the Presidency he toured Europe with Mrs. Truman and he was a great favorite wherever he went. In Italy he told reporters that he had just enjoyed a dish of *fettucini* and when one unitalicized newsman asked what it was, he said, "It's like macaroni with no holes." Mrs. Truman was not amused when, studying the voluptuous figure of a dancer on an

ancient vase, the Missouri scholar said: "That girl's wearing fals-
ies."

Church groups often protested against some of his habits, such
as his use of profanity, his love of poker, his taste for bourbon, and
even the fact that he named the Presidential plane *The Sacred
Cow.* He apologized for none of these and remarked once that
he enjoys association with the kind of men who play poker. A
Washington correspondent told me once that he was present
when a delegation of Protestant laymen called on the President.
As they filed into the room Mr. Truman called out to them:
"Gentlemen, I want you to know that I belong to the best god-
damned church in the country!"

During his famous whistle-stop campaign tours, a semi-secret
encyclopedia known as The Book came into being. In this ledger
an attempt was made to size up each town in the country, with
notations about local industry, important citizens, agricultural
products . . . all manner of special information that might be
touched upon in an off-the-cuff speech. For example, arriving in
Grand Island, Nebraska, Mr. Truman called for The Book and
found that the town had given him a fancy pair of spurs on his
last visit. So he was ready—he gave them a speech on how he had
used those spurs on the no-good Eightieth Congress. Once the
campaign train was approaching a small town in Texas where the
President was to make a brief back-platform speech. He got out
The Book. The notation for this town was a cryptic: "wolf ex-
termination." He delivered a fiery speech denouncing wolves as
the orneriest critters inhabiting the earth and then worked things
around to the Republicans as being somewhat ornerier, and the
populace of the wolf-ridden town went wild

He seldom drew back from violating sacred tradition. In one
speech he said bluntly that George Washington never threw a dollar across the Potomac. It was a Spanish coin, thrown across the
Rappahannock at a point where a ten-year-old boy could have
done it with a dime. Further than that, said Mr. Truman, he had
strong doubts whether Washington, a notorious penny-pincher,
would ever have let go of even a Spanish coin.

At the same time he backed away from the ancient political custom of kissing or fondling babies, begging off by saying he had a
bad cold, or by protesting, "Afraid I might drop it."

The world knew that he had a deep and genuine love for his old mother, who was a Show-Me character in her own right. Whenever he left her after a visit, she usually said, "Now Harry, you be good." And sometimes she added, "But be game, too." When she was coming to Washington for the first time, her son told her that she would be sleeping in Abraham Lincoln's bed. An unreconstructed Confederate from who-laid-the-chunk, she sent word: "I'll sleep on the floor first." In her final illness he flew out to Missouri, established his office on her Mission oak table, and said he wouldn't leave her. "She's set up with me many times when I needed her," he said, "and I want to reciprocate when she needs me."

On his first full day in office President Truman, still aghast at what had happened in Warm Springs, encountered a group of newspapermen in a corridor of the Capitol. He paused long enough to utter one of his most famous remarks: "Did you ever have a bull or a load of hay fall on you? If you ever did, you know how I felt last night."

Eight years later, leaving the Presidency, he spoke of an epitaph in the graveyard at Tombstone, Arizona. He said that it described his feelings as of that moment, and then he quoted it:

"Here Lies Jack Williams. He Done His Damndest."

Indeed he did.

CHAPTER 32

AIG BREAD IN EGYPT

I'm growing so cantankerous that I even get into warm arguments about Egyptian bread. My father was of German descent (the part of him that wasn't Irish) and at our house in Southern Illinois (Little Egypt) the end piece of bread, known to some people as the heel, was called an opsott. There were entire hordes of children in the family and the cry would go round the table, "Ah want th' opsott!" or "Don't give me that ole opsott!" I have talked to German people by the dozen and I can't seem to find a single one who ever heard the word opsott applied to bread or to anything else. Even to an opsott.

Lately I was making some French toast for my breakfast and I fell to thinking how, when I was a kid in Illinois, we had it often, but we called it "aig bread." "Hey, Mom, cain't we have some aig bread for supper?" Just to make sure, I wrote to my kinfolks in Little Egypt and they all say that I'm out of my butter-churnin' mind. Aig bread, they say, is made out of corn meal and aig and cream and it's baked. I have one sister who admitted that aig bread is pretty much the same as French toast. "In restaurants," she says, "when I order it I always say French toast. 'Aig bread' sounds so country." I insist, however, that my relatives are wrong and I insist further that the Webster dictionary people are wrong. The Webster people define French toast as "bread dipped in a mixture of egg and milk and then sautéed." That, my friends, is aig bread, except that in Little Egypt we didn't know the word sauté. We said fry.

Now, what does Webster the Third say under egg bread? They say see spoon bread. They don't even know how to spell aig. How could they possibly come up with a sensible and acceptable definition? Spoon bread, which they in their Eastern Seaboard ignorance believe to be the same as aig bread, is "made of corn meal, with or without added rice and hominy, and mixed with milk, eggs, shortening, and leavening to a consistency that it must be served from the baking dish with a spoon." Not at *my* house. This country is so thoroughly shot to hell that a man can't even trust the dictionary any more.

Meanwhile, out of loyalty to my Egyptian homeland, I usually say to Room Service, whether at the Mills Hotel or the St. Regis, the Royal Hawaiian, or the Ponderosa Motor Inn, I say, "Send me up an order of aig bread." They always give me an argument and I end up saying, "Okay, damn it, one order of French toast." In the swank places, I've found, they sometimes put rum in their French toast. We never had any in our aig bread.

I've never even dared to ask Room Service for an opsott.

CHAPTER 33

JUST WHO *is* J. D. SALINGER?

A man named Visco, resident of Montclair, New Jersey, has written a letter to me advising me that recently he went into a New York City bookstore and bought a volume titled *How to Write Without Knowing Nothing*. The jacket bore my name as author.

When Mr. Visco got home to Montclair and took the wrapping off his package and opened the book, he found that its contents did not correspond with the description on the jacket and on the hard binding. In fact, the inside part of the book had nothing whatever to do with the art of writing, but was something titled *Franny and Zooey* and the author was identified on the title page as "J. D. Salinger." Mr. Visco said he was confused.

It came as no great surprise to me. Other copies of that book got into the stores—books described as H. Allen Smith's work on the outside and containing on the inside work by this J. D. Salinger. It happened once before to me when my publisher sent me a copy of another book of mine, *The Pig in the Barber Shop*, and on opening it I found that it contained a novel called *The Good Shepherd*, by C. S. Forester. I am in an idiot sort of business.

I could explain the more recent mix-up to Mr. Visco and to anyone else who happened to get a copy of Smith-Salinger by first stating that both *How to Write Without Knowing Nothing* and *Franny and Zooey* were issued by the same Boston publisher. So was *The Good Shepherd*.

The way it could happen is fairly simple. In the publisher's bindery, there on the banks of the Charles River, were large stacks of unbound, stitched sheets of my book and, alongside, much larger stacks of the book by "Salinger." Along comes a workman and his elbow brushes against the "Salinger" stack and a few dozen batches of unbound sheets topple to the floor. The workman hastily picks the things up and puts them onto the stack nearest him, which is the Smith stack. Those stitched sheets wind up, a few days later, neatly encased in hard bindings bearing the title, *How to Write Without Knowing Nothing.*

I *could* explain it that way, but I don't think I will. Sounds too much like the collapse of automation. Anyway, the time has come when I can no longer dissemble, when I can no longer keep a straight face in the presence of all this "Salinger" talk. I've got to tell the truth. Steel yourself. I *am* J. D. Salinger.

I am also Thomas Pynchon, author of the sensational novel V. That's what I said, V. That's the title of it. Almost nobody has ever seen Thomas Pynchon so it has been fairly easy for me to carry on this particular deception. His editor at the Lippincott company has never laid eyes on him; the press agent for Lippincott has never seen him; various other people who have had long-distance dealings with him wouldn't know him if they met him on the street. His own mother has seen him, but not lately, and when questioned about him all she is willing to say is that Thomas Pynchon is six feet four. A sort of warning, I suppose. It is all a lovely hoax and she is not really his mother, because she is not *my* mother; I am not nearly six feet four, but when I'm required to do it I can draw myself up. And if any among you smart-aleck litterateurs doubts my word in this Pynchon matter, please be advised that he, Pynchon, is said to do his principle hiding out in Mexico. Check my movements, please—I mean the movements of H. Allen Smith. I duck out for Mexico whenever I get the chance. Why? I have to pay Pynchon bills and clean up Pynchon correspondence that piles up week by week in Guadalajara. The correspondence, incidentally, consists mainly of letters asking, "Hey, Pynchon, just who are you?" or, in variation, "Listen, Pynchon, you crud, who the hell do you think you are?" As for my novel V, I wrote it with my left hand and can't remember what it's about, except that it's got a lot of alligators in it.

I may as well go the whole hog with this confession. I am also Xavier Rynne. I am he who wrote those marvelous "inside" accounts of Vatican Council II. In the book world there was great and feverish speculation about the true identity of Xavier Rynne because of his two works, *Letters from the Vatican* and *The Second Session*. Here is the story behind the story. I was down in Mexico, engaged in conspiracies aimed at deepening the mystery of Thomas Pynchon, and I got homesick, and in the middle of the night checked out of my hotel and climbed sleepily into a jet. Wrong plane. I ended up in Rome, and this Vatican Council II was in session and I stumbled into it while groping around for the Spanish Steps. I figured I might as well do something toward expenses, so I rapped out those two books about what I'd seen and heard. Imagine my surprise at the stir they created. Actually, this business of being Xavier Rynne is not very important to me, and I think I'll give it up. I've got other fish to fry. J. D. Salinger fish. The Salinger caper has brought in a lot of splendid money and it has been a most interesting game, cloak-and-daggerish in many of its aspects.

I started writing as "J. D. Salinger" back around 1940. I was just practicing. I had known a movie producer in Hollywood named George Glass, and so I started knocking out these trivialities about a family named Glass. All I was doing was searching for a Method, which I freely confess I never found. Those ragged-assed manuscripts got mailed out by mistake and before I knew what was going on, the stories began appearing in one of the *arrière-garde* magazines. I didn't show my face. I even hid the truth from my children.

So I lay low and turned out three or four perceptive and erudite books under the name of H. Allen Smith, and then, just for recreation, during two hot weeks in the summer of 1950, I did a little novel called *The Catcher in the Rye*. It had some dirty words in it, so I put the Salinger name on it. A publisher went out of his mind and issued it, and the nut kids in the colleges went ape for it when they should have been swallowing goldfish and swiping panties and riding to the moon in automatic clothes driers. That damn book sold like crazy and I, in the hidden role of Salinger, became a sort of public idol, a great literary hero to a generation of goofy kids. I want it clearly understood, however, that I had nothing to do with all that hair.

The money was nice so I just kept my mouth shut.

After a while the snoops from the newsmagazines began to close in on me. Rumors were kicking around. I had my reputation to consider, so I got nervous. My standing in the community was such that I simply couldn't afford to have it get out that I was J. D. Salinger. So it came about that I hired a young man named Jackson Daedalus Snug to impersonate me in the character of J. D. Salinger. I went up to New Hampshire and shopped around and finally bought a plain little old house with its own pump and cistern and an attic full of spinning wheels and a strong fence around the whole thing. Jackson Daedalus Snug moved in and put his initials on the mailbox and lived quietly there for a while.

Then, under my instructions, he began issuing forth, charging around the countryside in a jeep I got for him, holding his nose in the air and sometimes glowering at the rubes. When he had to go to town for groceries and erasers, I taught him to turn and run if any stranger came toward him. Soon enough the word began to get around that there was some kind of a filbert loose in the community, and Snug wrote me that he was afraid the townspeople might seize him and apply a priming coat of tar and feathers. So I sent him a homemade slingshot and told him to turn a withering fire upon any of the country jakes who tried to molest him. He still uses that slingshot, but mainly to sting the college kids who come to the fence and, between bottles of beer, howl through their hair: "Come outa there, J.D. We know who you are and we know you're in there. Come on out, you sweet son of a bitch. This here's ole Holden talkin'."

It has been a lot of fun, but I think the time has come to quit all this horseplay and devote myself to the philosophical pursuits which seem to be my lot in life. There will be some critics, of course, who will call me a liar and say that I, Smith, never had it in me to write as good as old J.D. They will say that the Jackson Daedalus Snug up there in New Hampshire is truthfully Jerome David Salinger and that I had ought to be ashamed of myself for claiming to be he. I say nuts to such people and advise them to hurry down to the doctor for an in-depth ECG.

To those who might entertain such doubts, I can also call attention to certain clues in the writings of "Salinger" which appear in the writings of H. Allen Smith. For example, consider the style used in Bessie Glass's inventory of all the items contained in a medicine cabinet, and in H. Allen Smith's inventory of all the items contained in the little black bag carried by doctors. These two passages *had* to be written by the same hand.

To me the most amusing outgrowth of my playful bit of deception has been the steady procession of scholarly disquisitions in which the work of "Salinger" is dissected and analyzed and praised beyond all reason. The professors and the critics have me dealing in symbolism and abstract notions that are as alien to me as so much Waldensian Trigonometry. It has been most revealing, for example, to find so many pundits saying that my Franny, when she was having all those fantods and collywobbles, was actually in the grip of a mysticism snit. Academic bullshit. She was *pregnant*.

It is time, then, that I say goodbye to my strange career as "Salinger" as well as my brief adventures as "Thomas Pynchon" and "Xavier Rynne." All of my serious, classical writing is done, of course, under the name of H. Allen Smith. I shall not suffer financially because of the foregoing revelations; in fact they will serve to focus attention on my true and basic self. Or maybe not. I'm actually not H. Allen Smith at all. I'm H. Traven, the natural son of B. Traven, who was called "The Mystery Man of American Letters" and who wrote *The Treasure of the Sierra Madre*. Pop never liked people. In the closing years of his life he hid out in the back room of a roadside taco joint near Acapulco. The last time I was down that way, playing my role of "Thomas Pynchon," I tried to see him. He snarled at me through the bead curtains and said he was not my father, B. Traven. He said he was Ambrose Bierce.

You know something? I believed him.

CHAPTER 34

THE NEW MATH

My neighbor Avery knows everything. I go to him consistently
with knotty problems and fatuous-sounding questions and he always has an answer—an answer with which I am contented and
which I respect as irrefrangible truth. Not long ago I asked him if
he knew about the New Math. Of course he did.

"There are two postulates which we——" he began.

"What is a postulate," I asked.

"We'll take that up next Wednesday," he responded, and then
continued, ". . . which we must take into account, two postulates, and each of these is best illustrated with a story. Both stories
are true and have to be true, else the whole edifice of applied
mathematics would crumble."

The first story was about Kopf, vice-president of a big insurance
company. Kopf, like many another businessman, was frightened
of flying but there were times when he had to do it. During the
period when the airliner bomb scares were at their peak, Kopf was
more distrait than usual. One day it became absolutely essential
that he fly from New York to San Francisco, so he called in his
company's top actuary.

"I have to catch the two-o'clock plane for San Francisco,"
Kopf said. "Can you figure the odds against a bomb being carried
onto that plane by some nut?"

The actuary said he could and went back to his big iron abacus.
A short while later the answer was on Kopf's desk; the odds were

twenty thousand to one that no bomb would be smuggled onto that plane.

Kopf thought about it a while and did a lot of frowning, and soon he began shaking his head in despair, and then he said to the actuary: "I don't like the looks of it. Not a bit. It's too damn close for comfort. Can't you work me out a better figure?"

At this point, my neighbor Avery told me, the New Math entered the picture. The actuary returned to his office and ciphered some more with his machinery and at length came up with the improved figure. He went back to Kopf and said: "The odds against a bomb being carried onto that particular plane on this particular day at that particular hour are still twenty thousand to one. But the odds against *two* bombs being carried onto the same plane at the same time by two different people . . . those odds are eighty thousand to one. So, Mr. Kopf, your worries are over."

"I don't follow you," said Kopf.

"It's simple enough. *You* carry on a bomb of your own."

Avery's second illustration is concerned with Virgil, the dumbest boy in a school noteworthy for its dumb boys. When Virgil was in the sixth grade his family moved to another town and nothing more was heard of him for years. Then one day he came back for a sentimental visit. He had grown dirty rich and was driving a Cadillac Eldorado and smoking cigars a foot long. His achievements in the world of commerce were a great perplexity to his former teacher, who held a peculiar belief that intelligence and personal merit have something to do with the acquisition of great wealth. So she asked Virgil to tell her the secret of his success.

"Nothin' to it, Miz Nicewonder," said Virgil. "I own a great big restrunt. I buy steaks for one dollar. I sell them for three dollars. That way I always make three per cent."

Thus did my neighbor Avery clarify the New Math. Just before leaving him I said, "One more question, friend Avery. Does dottle have to be knocked out of anything else besides pipes?"

"Gooseneck nozzles," he said. "Nothing else."

I went right home and knocked the dottle out of every gooseneck nozzle in the house. Got about a peck.

CHAPTER 35

THE MAKING OF A MUSICIAN

I spent about forty years wanting desperately to be a musician and telling myself that it could never happen. Then along came television with its insidious practice of showing expert musicians performing almost in my lap. They always made it look so damn easy.

The first instrument that got me was the piano (we had a baby grand in the living room for décor). One evening I was sitting before the TV screen when the camera moved in tight to a piano keyboard and I watched a man's fingers gently playing *Star Dust*. I leaned forward in my chair and stared at the simplicity of it, the ease, the slow graceful gait of those fingers. For a moment I was tempted to shut off the barrage of electrons and go to the piano and play *Star Dust* the way I had just observed it being played. Then I remembered that I had tried the piano before with no success. I have no musical education at all and my virtuosity reached its peak many years ago when, for portions of one entire afternoon, I played a kazoo.

In common with many of my fellow men I yearned to play the piano, and now the temptation was strong within me—I might even summon a music teacher and go for broke; but I fought it off for a few days. Then this kid appeared on the television screen, a tiny child, five years old, sitting there whamming away at the keyboard, playing something quite beautiful by Chopin or Buddy DeSylva. That little bastard flat-out infuriated me. Here was a mere infant playing piano expertly at an age when I had been unable to place one wooden block on top of another wooden block. I cursed him to hell. This time I did sit down at the piano and worked diligently for perhaps fifteen minutes, and then I abandoned that instrument forever.

Now, on television, I began watching other musicians and finally I got the accordion fever. After looking at two or three accordion players close up, I concluded that here was a thing I should be able to do, and I was about to open negotiations for the purchase of an instrument (they cost almost as much as a hysterectomy) when someone mentioned an important fact that I had overlooked.

"He's doing things with that other hand," I was informed. "Lots of little buttons over on the left there, and he has to play those buttons as well as the keyboard on the other end, and in addition to that, he has to keep squeezing the thing back and forth."

Specimen on that. I was cured of the accordion before I had ever taken sick. I began watching for some kind of music in which the fingers don't figure too much, such as the triangle. I soon found out that fingers are more important in music than they are in picking cherries or hanging up the wash or scratching. Then I arrived at the guitar, light-years before every hairy hoodlum in the land had taken it up.

I watched closely whenever a guitarist came on the screen and studied his operations carefully, and then just to be on the safe side I inquired around and everyone said: "Oh, anybody can play a guitar." Everyone knew somebody who played the guitar and in each case it was the same story: "He just picked it up, fooling around with an old guitar he found in the attic."

So, I got out the mail order catalogue and sent away for a Spanish guitar "with highest quality pick" and a book of instructions. While I was waiting for my instrument a scene came up on television in which a couple of lovers were sitting on a bench in a patio. Back in the shadows, on another bench, was a Mexican with a guitar and he was playing *Solamente una vez* and it was the prettiest god-damn thing I had ever heard, and an intense eagerness came over me, an eagerness to get my hands on that guitar.

When it came I began with the instruction book but almost immediately I found that if I used the book I would have to learn to read music, and this I was determined not to do—I was going to learn to play the guitar by ear, by just fooling around with it as if I had stumbled across it in the attic.

From the book I did learn how to tune the instrument and then I fooled around for about two weeks, picking out melodies. This, I now know, was a mistake—I should have been learning chords—but I went ahead and through hard work and perseverance reached the point where I could pick out the melody of *Red River Valley*. I couldn't sing along with it because it required every ounce of concentration to remember where to put my fingers and, even then, I played the slowest *Red River Valley* in musical history. After that I learned to pick out *September Song*, and then *My Blue Heaven*, and now I had a repertoire of three numbers. I played them over and over until the tips of my fingers were so sore I couldn't run my typewriter.

I was now ready for a brief performance in front of someone outside the family circle. One evening a friend came to the house for dinner and for a while I didn't say a thing about my achievement in music. After dinner, in the living room, I let him discover the guitar standing in the corner.

"Well!" he exclaimed. "What do we have here? A guitar! Who plays the guitar around here?"

"Oh," I said casually, "I fool around with it, a little."

By this time he had the instrument in his lap and was flicking his fingers across the strings.

"My god!" he said, "it's out of tune."

And so he tuned it. He tuned it and destroyed a month's hard work. I had learned to play my three songs with the guitar tuned a certain way, and now he had changed the tuning, and my repertoire was reduced to absolutely nothing. After this wretched Samaritan had gone I sat down and started all over again. I had no inkling of how the guitar had been tuned before. *Red River Valley* and *September Song* and *My Blue Heaven* had to be fingered in an altogether different way, of course, with the instrument retuned, but I kept at it and in about two or three more weeks I could play those melodies again, in a new way.

Came a day when I was away from the house for a few hours, and when I got home my wife had news for me.

"Maxine stopped by," she said, "and had your guitar out. She said somebody had tuned it wrong, that it was tuned for a Hawaiian steel guitar, and that was all wrong."

"So?" I said.

"She tuned it."

I snatched up the instrument and tried the opening of *Red River Valley*. It was gone. Gone again. I cussed feelingly and decided that if I ever learned those songs again, I'd keep that instrument locked away from itinerant guitar tuners. And so I went at it again and it took a long time, but finally I had my three songs once more.

I realized more and more that my whole approach to the guitar had been wrong because of that Mexican on the bench. Learning to play melody, plucking one string at a time, was no good. I wanted to be able to play and sing simultaneously, and the kind of playing I had learned was not suited to singing. I still needed to learn chords. But, try as I did, I simply couldn't do it. What I needed was the advice of some practical down-to-earth guitar players.

I remembered the two professors. During the previous year I had been visiting friends in Chapel Hill and there had been a party and among the guests were two professors from the University of North Carolina. One was a professor of law and the other was a professor of Romance languages and between them they had a guitar. During the party they played that guitar, using chords, and did considerable singing along with it. The professor of law would play and sing for a while and then he'd pass the guitar over to the professor of Romance languages and he would sing and play for a while. I remembered that the professor of law had told me that the guitar was very simple—nothing to it at all —and that he had just picked it up, fooling around with an old guitar he found in the attic.

I figured that if those friendly professors could show me just five or six basic chords—show me where to hold my fingers for those chords—then I might get somewhere. I wrote to my friend Jim Street in Chapel Hill and got this response:

"Professor F. B. McCall of the University of North Carolina College of Law is a steel-string man. I am referring your query to Professor N. B. Adams of the Department of Romance Languages of the University of North Carolina. Professor Adams is a gut-string man."

This confused me a little since, by merest chance, I appeared to be a steel-string man, but I let it slide and before long Professor Adams came through with a fat letter, most of which consisted of an impassioned defense of gut strings as opposed to steel strings, and enclosing a gut-string price list put out by a dealer in Nazareth, Pennsylvania. Professor Adams then urged that I "learn to make the *grand barre*" at once and he sketched a diagram of this *grand barre*, as follows:

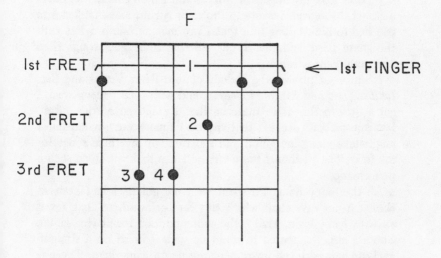

THE GRAND BARRE

If you have ever fooled around with a guitar, or if you have a guitar stuck away in the attic that you can fool around with, please get it out and try the *grand barre*. You won't be able to hold a fork in your left hand for a week. I tried it and kept trying it and before long the muscles were aching clear up to my elbow and beyond and, on top of that, I couldn't get anything remotely musical out of the *grand barre*. It is my firm conviction that Professor Adams misplaced some fingers and left out some frets when he made his sketch.

About this time Sybil Bock from Hollywood came to spend a

few days with us and, being a musician herself, thought it was wonderful that I had taken up the guitar and she wanted to play a simple piano accompaniment while I, with highest quality pick, rendered the melody of *Red River Valley*. She played very slowly, but I still couldn't keep pace with her because of the lameness in my arms and fingers, chargeable to that Tar Heel *grand barre*.

"You've got to expect," said Sybil, "that your fingers will get real sore. I've been working around radio musicians for years and I know what you ought to do. Soak your fingers in vinegar and then hold them over a gas jet. That'll toughen them up."

"Thanks," I said. "You're very kind."

I didn't soak my fingers in vinegar and I didn't hold them over a gas jet. Moreover, I wrote to Professor Adams and thanked him and lied to him, telling him that I was making fine progress with the *grand barre* and that I was ordering some gut strings from Nazareth, Pennsylvania.

I continued playing the melody of *Red River Valley* and *September Song* and *My Blue Heaven*, and with each passing week I got a little better at it, meaning that I could go a trifle faster. I had just about decided that the next time I was invited out I might take along my guitar and run through my three songs for the folks. Then I thought of a circumstance that precluded such a performance.

All the many hours I'd spent with my guitar, I had been reclining in an easy chair which tilts far backward, so that I was virtually lying down. That is the wrong position for playing guitar. You are either supposed to stand up with it or sit on a straight-backed chair with the instrument resting on your thigh. The way I had learned to play it, I was supine if not prostrate, with the guitar lying flat across my stomach. It occurred to me that if I took my guitar to someone's house and if they urged me to play it, I'd be compelled to say:

"Okay. Be glad to. Where's the bed?"

Somehow after that the whole thing turned into a bore and I took the guitar and stored it in the attic, where it could await the coming of some person with more patience than I.

After that unhappy experience it is still an astonishing thing to me how quickly I learned to produce recognizable music out of the Hammond organ. I had a friend named Bob Smith who was a musical moke (played fourteen or fifteen different instruments) and one evening at his house I sat enthralled while he played the organ. Subsequently he said to me: "I never took a lesson in my life." Soon after that I sat in the home of a new acquaintance, Campbell Lorini, and listened while he played his Hammond for two hours. He finished off with the declaration: "Never took a lesson in my life."

The next morning at store-opening time I phoned Steinway in Manhattan and said send me one of them things.

I had an office separate from the main house and I ordered the organ put out there so I could fool around with it privately. I figured it would take at least a year before I'd be able to play a single number that would be recognizable for what it was. When I reached that point I'd move the instrument over to the house.

I moved it one week from date of delivery, at which time I was playing *Girl of My Dreams, September Song, If I Had My Way,* and *Song of the Islands.*

It appears that like the late Robert Sherwood I have an enormous amount of popular music stored up in my head. Once I fooled around with a tune, worked it out, then played it for a neighbor and asked him if he knew what it was. He couldn't think of the name of it, so he telephoned a relative who was a musician, hummed it, then came away from the phone and said, "Good god, you're playin' grand opera!" It was *My Heart at Thy Sweet Something.*

As of this writing I have been fooling around with the organ for almost twenty years. If, some day, you come to visit me and you are a blood relative and hold two mortgages on my house and you demand that I play for you, I'll probably do it. I am an amateur, however, and I take pride in the fact that Edward R. Murrow brought his television cameras into my house one evening and while we were on the air, coast to coast, asked me to play. I said no. He said why not. And I said because I don't want to. I shall now attempt to explain myself.

One of the great evils of present-day social intercourse is the doggedness with which certain people beg amateur musicians to perform. Their constant cry is: "Oh, come on now and play!" They are responsible for some of the most horrible hours I have had to spend on this earth.

There is at least one at every gathering, usually more. They find out that Junior is studying the clarinet or Sweet Sue is learning the banjo. "Oh, come on now and play!" they say to the youngsters. Junior bridles, and paws the carpet, and wishes he was out somewhere sucking eggs. Sweet Sue blushes down past her kneecaps and then vanishes in the direction of her room. "For heaven's sake," the company cries, "don't be bashful! Come on now and play!" And they keep at it and keep at it, and then Junior's Mama gets into the act—she orders Junior to get his clarinet and play. A command performance. So Junior plays. Not once. He goes through his first selection, producing noises that would curdle blood and send wild animals and gaily plumaged birds shrieking for sanctuary in the deep forests. Now there is tumultuous applause and Mama, glowing with pride, commands: "Play *Glow-Worm*, Junior." It may go on for an hour or more after that.

Some people will argue that a juvenile musician needs precisely this sort of encouragement. He needs to have grown people urge him into impromptu concerts and applaud him afterward, if he is to go on to greater things. If that is a requirement of learning to be a musician—if it is necessary that a roomful of mature people sit around and have their nervous systems shattered—then I contend it is time we learn to get along *without* music. We can substitute some other art form that is quieter in the learning, and more soothing, such as hooking rugs, or decalcomania, or whittling. I for one hope to see the day come when a person who urges a young musician to "Come on now and play" will be regarded in popular disesteem as a social leper, ranking below the person who, after three cocktails, takes out his false teeth and gnashes them at arm's length.

These observations have nothing whatever to do with the garbage that passes for music nowadays amongst the teen-agers. I have spoken my piece at length, and in print, at least a dozen times with reference to rock plus country plus western. If you do come to my house and I play the organ for you, I promise that you will get none of that hideous crap. And don't ask me to favor you with a little Johann Sebastian Bach. That's what the people of quality always ask an organist to play. I do not know how to play a shred of Bach, but I don't like to show my boorishness, my lack of culture, so I hit them with a set speech that goes:

"Please! Don't ever ask me to play Bach. He's not my style. Considered contrapuntally, he had a tin ear. He was a substantial and solid family man. He didn't smoke opium and he didn't cheat people and he didn't go around knocking up serving girls and duchesses. He had no impermeable strictures to take to his doctor, and he harbored no crotch-crickets and he usually told the truth. What kind of a man is THAT to be writing music?"

Just one more instance of my artistic sensitivity.

CHAPTER 36

FURNITURE TALK

The first caster for furniture was invented by Philos Blake, Eli Whitney Blake, and John A. Blake of New Haven, Connecticut. On June 30, 1838, they were awarded a patent on "a mode of constructing casters and applying them to bedsteads."

The achievement of these Blake boys is saluted in the books, but it doesn't throw me into a swoon. It took three of them to devise a plain little old thing like a caster, whereas I played a lone hand in my reformation of the furniture industry.

I am related by marriage to some people who are prominent in the furniture dodge in North Carolina. Because of this relationship I have been in a position to effect some significant changes in English as she is spoke among furniture builders and furniture salesmen. It saddens me that Mr. Mencken is not here to record my triumphs in his great work on The American Language.

After my daughter married into furniture she began speaking in tongues, employing the jargon she heard all around her. Some of her locutions were jarring to my sensitive soul, and I quietly resolved that I would set matters straight.

Being thrown into the company of furniture people from time to time, I found that they committed various conversational sins that fell harshly upon my ear. I'll give you just two instances in which, by persistent nagging, I persuaded my branch of the furniture fancy to change their manner of talk.

Almost to a man they spoke of a bedroom soot, or a living

room soot. An atrocity! Real country! I challenged them about it, told them they should say bedroom sweet, urged them toward the paths of cultural living. They countered my challenge by leading me to the dictionaries and showing me that soot is an acceptable pronunciation, second choice.

I told my daughter sternly: "Always go first class. Don't settle for second choice. It's sweet. Living room sweet. Soot is all right in one minuscule contingency. When Jimmy——"

She interrupted me. "What's a minuscule?"

"Never mind. When Jimmy Durante used to speak of his corner soot in the Hotel Astor, that was proper usage, eminently correct."

Mr. Durante would sometimes start off a story by saying, "I was a settin' up there in muh soot at the Astor, when . . ." In his own way he is a classicist and a strict constructionist. Soot comes trippingly on the tongue for Durante. Everybody else should say sweet. And as for the dictionaries, there were moments when Noah Webster couldn't locate his butt with both hands.

Another grating word employed for many years in the furniture trade is commode. As meaning a toilet. The can. Back where I come from, and elsewhere, a commode in the home is one of three items: a low chest of drawers; a movable sink or washstand; or (Webster's third choice) a chair or similar framework holding a toilet utensil under an open seat. Now, I ask you! Do you have such a contrivance as that last-named one in your house (or in your sweet)? I need to add that Webster Three suggests turning to *chamber pot* for further information on that unflushable "toilet utensil" that is rattling around under that open seat.

Well, as in the case of soot I went to work on commode. And it pleasures me to report that people I know in the furniture line are mending their ways. They speak nowadays of a bedroom sweet or, in a spirit of compromise, of a dining room set. When discussing fixtures for the bathroom they refer openly and unblushingly to the toilet, not the commode. I am told that this intelligent usage is spreading across the country and I feel that I am largely responsible for the extirpation of both soot and commode from furniture talk. One way or another, I intend to rank as a man who had an impact on his times. Despite the fact that . . .

I have just shown the foregoing paragraphs to a professor of

English of my acquaintance, a man I frequently consult in order to get academic support for my opinions. He quickly obliged.

"You," he said, "are wrong on both counts."

English professor indeed! The man's more inept than Noah Webster!

CHAPTER 37

HOW TO TIE A MATTHEW WALKER

The Bar Pit Drug Store is a plain dusty structure with clapboard front, facing one of the principal east-west highways in West Texas. It is distinctive for several reasons, notable among them being the fact that it handles no drugs except aspirin and styptic pencils and cough drops.

Beyond the soda fountain in the rear of the store are two wooden tables, and here the ranchers and their hired hands from the surrounding countryside gather to swill coffee and narrate rat-killin' tales of The Last Frontier. The congregation is usually joined by Chad Bentley, proprietor of the Bar Pit.

To this drug store I was drawn one day by an urge to find out if, after forty years of profitable writing, I really knew how to write. In my files I had come across a clipping I had squirreled away years back, a quotation from Hilaire Belloc, an English writer of some renown. Quoth Hilaire:

"Ropes more than any other subject are a test of a man's power of exposition in prose. If you can describe clearly without a diagram the proper way of making this or that knot, then you are a master of the English tongue."

I resolved at once to give myself the knot test. The first requirement was that I settle on a knot, the kind of knot I wanted to describe. Then I'd have to get somebody to sit in front of me and tie it; I felt that tying the knot myself, without witnesses, might somehow smack of duplicity, if not knot-barratry. I am not personally adept with knots and, in fact, my shoelaces come undone every day of my life.

One afternoon I was buying some styptic pencils in the Bar Pit Drug Store and Hilaire Belloc's challenge popped into my mind and I spoke to Chad Bentley, Prop., about it. Did he know any cow persons in the neighborhood who might be expert at knots? Of course he did. Oash Gowdy. Oash is pronounced the same as the first syllable in *Ocean*. Oash Gowdy used to make the rodeos with a trick-roping act and in those times he became known as Ocean Wave Gowdy; he was expert at a roping maneuver called the Ocean Wave. And he knew knots.

I tried to explain to Chad Bentley what was on my mind, what I would like to have Oash Gowdy do for me, but the technicalities involved were so complex that even Hilaire Belloc would have balked at them. I finally suggested that if Mr. Bentley could get Oash Gowdy in the store the following afternoon, with a piece of rope, I would be present and issue instructions and ultimately I would buy Mr. Gowdy a bottle of tonsil varnish and maybe a box of cough drops.

Thus it came to pass that on the following day we assembled at the back tables: Oash Gowdy with a length of half-inch rope; Mr. Bentley with his coffee urn fired up; myself; and Mr. Muley Holland, a rancher with a pound and a half of Days Work plug in his cheek. Muley Holland was a wealthy man, working one of the biggest ranches in the area, but he would have been blackballed out of a hobo jungle for untidiness beyond the call of duty.

After he got it reasonably clear in his head what I wanted him to do, Oash Gowdy tilted his greasy Stetson onto the back of his head and said: "I could do you a rosebud. That's the name of a knot we use when we want to——" I said no. A cowboy tying a knot called a rosebud would somehow detract from the main purpose of the experiment.

Mr. Muley Holland wiped off his mouth with the back of his hand and spoke: "How 'bout doin' him a Mormon tangle, Oash? He wants a kinda complicated one, so give him a Mormon tangle."

"What's it used for?" I wanted to know.

"It's sometimes called a squaw's hitch," said Oash. "It's to hold a load onto the back of a burro."

"Do him a Mormon tangle," urged Muley Holland.

"Look, Muley," said Oash irritably. "I'm the knot man in this crowd and I ain't tyin' any Mormon tangles because in the first place you got to have a burro with a panner and a longer rope than I got and——"

"Oash," put in Chad Bentley, "you know how to tie a Matthew Walker?"

"There ain't a knot on or off the ocean," said Ocean Wave, "that I don't know how to tie."

"What's a Matthew Walker knot for?" I asked.

"It's a stopper knot," said Oash. "Keeps a rope from slippin' through a hole. Here, I'll show ya."

He picked up his length of rope. "Now," he said, "the first thing you do is unlay the ends of your rope like——"

"Unlay," I repeated. "That's a strange sorta word. How do you unlay anything?"

"It means in rope-talk," said Oash, "to unravel the ends. Like this." He began unlaying, and then resumed, "Watch me now. I'm passin' the first strand around the rope and then through its own bight. Damnation! If I look clumsy today it's my arthritis."

"Oash," put in Muley Holland, "I tole you oncet I tole you a thousand times, but you had to quit wearin' that copper bracelet."

"And I tole *you*," said Oash, "that it's pure superstition. The things you people will believe!" He turned to me. "I ran into a fella once, from Odessa, a lawyer, says a rabbit's foot is a certain cure for arthritis if you carry it with you all the time and put it under your pilla at night. I give it a try. Pure warp and woof! The next time I saw that lawyer I bawled the oatmeal outa him. But he said I didn't do it right—the rabbit's foot has to come offa the left hind leg, and the rabbit has to be shot when the moon is full. Lor-dee! The things some people will fall for!"

Oash Gowdy had forgotten all about his Matthew Walker knot, but now he looked down at the rope and remembered and was about to start anew when Chad Bentley spoke up.

"Strange thing to me is," said Chad, "how ever' dern town in West Texas has its own cure for arthritis. I got a sister-and-law over at Botts, claims that eatin' alfalfa clears up her arthritis like magic. There may be something in it . . . most of the folks in Botts believe in it, but I be god dern if I'm gonna sit around like a fool eatin' alfalfa. This sister-and-law of mine averages a bale of alfalfa a month."

"Superstition," said Oash. "Flat out superstition."

"No it's not," snapped Chad. "She says the San Antonio doctor who give her the alfalfa prescription uses it for *his* arthritis. This is a funny thing. Ever'body who's got a cure for arthritis always says their doctor uses it for *his* arthritis. Some people claim that if you eat a tablespoon of powdered alfalfa everyday of your life, you'll never get cancer. So there must be——"

Muley Holland interrupted him. "That," he said, "is almost as ridiculous as the Mescans and their tomato cures. A Mescan gets a sore throat or a bad cold or a earache, he'll pour canned tomatoes in his shoes and then put the shoes on and walk two mile in them, and then he'll claim the tomatoes draws the sickness away from his head and down through his feet and into the tomatoes. Mescans are the most superstitious people on the face of the earth."

Ocean Wave Gowdy was getting sore. This was supposed to be *his* party.

"Now you birds listen," he said. "I'm here to show the gentleman how to tie certain knots and not to listen to all this bullroar about shoes fulla tomatoes and dumb females that eat a bale of alfalfa a month. I happen to know a rancher lives near Kermit who scrapes the frost outa his deep-freeze and eats it and it relieves his pain. He eats that freezer frost all day long and the machine never stops runnin'. Makes more sense than eatin' alfalfa. Now, let me see, where was I?"

He began a fresh maneuver with the rope, explaining that he now had to pass the second strand around the rope, then through the bight of the first, and after that through its own bight. I was losing him. I somehow had the notion set firmly in my mind that the bight is the end of the rope, which it is not. I bombed out of the Boy Scouts before I ever made Tenderfoot . . . cashiered out for playing with matches.

Once again Oash paused in his knot tying, elevated his chin, and gazed at a shelf of assorted hair ointment. It must be remarked that, in this part of the country, ball bats could not keep an adult citizen from talking about arthritis cures once such talk got started. Oash said that over to the east, around Menard, people with arthritis in their feet would drill a hole in a dime and run a string through it and wear it around their ankle. He said he had heard of folks who cured arthritis of the feet and toes by propping their shoes against the wall at night, toes pointed upward. He thought there might be some merit in this procedure, although the best way of curing foot pains was to have a bee sting you on the big toe. He told about the vengeful war between the Buckeye and the Horse Chestnut adherents. Chad Bentley now barged in with the details.

"Over to Chaney," he said, "Volney the banker started givin' out buckeyes to his customers that had arthritis. Great lord, the people were lined up outside his office! Then Banker Ketcham at Botts, he heard about it and he let the word out that he was given' away buckeyes. So Banker Volney he put an ad in the paper that the buckeyes that Ketcham was givin' out was really horse chestnuts. He said in his ad that horse chestnuts come originally from Europe while buckeyes was one hundred per cent native American and anyway, the only buckeyes that would cure arthritis was buckeyes from Ohio, and he said he had a dealer in Bucyrus, Ohio, who was sendin' him buckeyes in gunny sacks, a hundret pounds at a clip. And Volney then said in his ad that horse chestnuts was poison to little childern and if they et any it would kill them."

The little snaky pile of rope lay at Oash Gowdy's feet, representing a fragmentary part of a Matthew Walker knot. Oash had been looking for a spot to break in, and he found it now.

"That buckeye business," he said, "is an old wife's tale. Maybe I could go for the Irish potato deal, but not the buckeyes. Homer Kane carries an Irish potato in his pocket till it turns black and shrivels up to the size of a walnut. Long as he has that potato on him, he never has any pain. But you have to carry it in your hippocket—nowheres else."

"I've heard it said," put in Muley Holland, "that you can get rid of arthritis forever by eatin' nothin' but poke salad for ten days hand-runnin'. Not even coffee with it—just poke salad. And all durn that ten days you make up a salve by mixin' rattlesnake fat and coal oil and rub it on the places that hurts."

Oash Gowdy dropped his chin and his eyes fell on the little snarl of rope that was his Matthew Walker knot, waiting to be tied. He didn't seem to recognize it.

"Poke salad!" he snorted. "Ten days straight! Witch-talk! Lot of foolishness! I've tried nearly ever'thing I ever heard of and I tell you, there's only one real cure, and I got it and I use it and it works. It was told to me by a minin' man from Arizona. You fill a quart jar half full of raisins and then you fill it up with Bourbon whiskey. Let it set two weeks. Then you take two raisins a day, same as if you was takin' pills, or you can take a tablespoon of the juice three times a day with meals."

"I'd take the juice," said Chad. "Takin' the raisins would be too slow."

Oash said: "I'd a heap rather take the raisins than eat nothin' but poke salad ten days in a row." He looked up at the clock on the wall and then turned to me.

"We'll have to do the rest of this knot some other time," he said. "I got diss-tracted offa knots by these knotheads here, and their superstitions about arthritis. Leave Chad know when you can come by again. Right now I'm overdue at home."

I had a suspicion that Oash was in need of his raisins. And I knew no more about how to describe the tying of a knot than I knew when I walked into the Bar Pit Drug Store. I could not, in fact, describe the beginning stages in the fashioning of a Matthew Walker. I had learned precisely two things . . .

Don't eat horse chestnuts.

I can't write.

CHAPTER 38

MY VERY OWN CONGLOMERATE

In common with many other professional writers I have periods
when I entertain a condition of daydreaming in which, walter-
mittywise, I become a large wheel in the business world. It used
to be that these pleasant hallucinations were located in the area of
athletics where I was wont to perform superhuman feats of
strength and skill and cunning. But I've been getting a trifle
older. The slow but steady disintegration of the meat will no
longer permit of my riding the winner in the Kentucky Derby or
of my ending the World Series with a tremendous blast over the
wall at Yankee Stadium.

Today I sit at the head end of long glistening tables in corporation board rooms and make decisions affecting empires on the
one hand and widows and orphans on the other. I am good to
widows and orphans. When I first started out dreaming com-
mercially, I was a captain of industry in the classic mold, although
altruistic and noble. A kindly robber baron.

Sometimes I fancied myself as a banker. Not the sleek and
streamlined variety of today, whose desk has no drawers in it. I
was the stern and granitic character of yesteryear described by the
late Lucius Beebe in the course of his endless yearnings for a return to the olden time. Mr. Beebe said that if he could find a
banker in a square hat with a square face framed in muttonchop
whiskers, stepping out of his Stanley Steamer and brandishing
his cane angrily at a street urchin . . . that man, said Mr. Beebe,
would get the Beebe account.

I came to realize in my dreamland role as a top financier that the operational procedures, the over-all milieu, of big business have changed, and so have the men who run things. Achievement of the highest order lies today in the adroit manipulation of big corporations. I quit banking.

I have daydreamed myself into the top spot in several large corporations. One reason I am good in this field is that I keep in tune with the times. I can roll with the punch. This being the era of the merger, I merge. I can't play my little game of tycoon for three minutes before I begin organizing unbustable trusts. I'm the kind of operator who might cook up a sensational merger between putts on the golf course.

My corporate absorptions are not undertaken on as great a scale as those of, say, a Henry Kaiser, a Howard Hughes, or a Consolidated Food. I am not vain. I'd gladly tackle a project as intricate as swallowing IT&T into one of my conglomerates, except that the arithmetic is a little too tough for me. I keep my mergers down to reasonable proportions where I can at least *try* to understand what's going on. To be perfectly candid about it, there are many aspects of conglomeration that confuse and baffle me. If someone asked me point-blank to explain the *modus operandi* of a stock swap, I'd plead urgent business elsewhere and depart hurriedly for another office. No, I like it small and neat. Let me outline my latest coup, so that you may understand my methods and learn from them. Pay close attention—it takes an alert mind to follow this sort of maneuvering.

About a year ago I found myself adrift in a fantasyland where I was Mr. Big at Smucker's, the people who make those good jellies and jams in spite of their name. I moved into the top executive post at Smucker's, had a cursory but keen look at the general picture, sacked some administrative deadwood, put a little more zing into our TV commercials, and then . . .

Well, I knew that if I were to continue on this dynamic course I'd better get busy with some amalgamating. Smucker's, under Smith, cried out for a merger. I spent a few weeks surveying the food industry and then I got the answer. I was rummaging through an old collection of travel pamphlets when I came upon a folder I picked up a dozen years ago in Smithfield, Virginia, where those famous hams originate. The pamphlet had been issued by a celebrated packer down there, a company whose name alone would do much toward enhancing the image of our corporation, to wit: Gwaltney. An ancient and honorable cognomen in the ham game.

Smucker's & Gwaltney's. A fine, rich-sounding corporate title, a name that would glow and sparkle on the financial pages of the nation. It would command confidence and trust. It would make mouths water. Without hesitation we at Smucker's gobbled down Gwaltney's and the moment the deed was done, our board of directors gave me a standing ovation. When the cheers died away our beloved chairman emeritus, Smeed Smucker, cried out: "Ole H.A. has done gone and wrought another shining page in the economic history of our glorious country!" I felt good. Real good. But my euphoria was not to last for long, as I shall quickly show. The historic meeting culminated with a buffet—Gwaltney's ham on rye smothered in a drench of Smucker's jams and jellies. Whew.

Within a very few months of this coup I began to have misgivings. It wasn't a decline in quarterly earnings. It was not the crisis we experienced during the 1966 barrel-stave shortage. It was a simple matter of euphony. I began taking long and lonely walks, during which I would mumble over and over, "Smucker's & Gwaltneys. Smucker's & Gwaltney's, Smucker's & Gwaltney's." There was a flaw in it. I tried it as "Smucker & Gwaltney" without the possessive, and I tried it other ways, but the beat was still just a trifle off. The music wasn't quite true. There was something lacking, and I knew that the missing ingredient was important and that the lack of it might in the end destroy our company altogether or get it gobbled up by IT&T or somebody.

The thing became an obsession with me and for a time I was the unhappiest of mortals, though real rich. My doctor said that I ought to get away for a while and try to forget Smucker's and jams and Gwaltney's and hams. I was not even to let my mind dwell on the goodness of good old Smeed Smucker.

I got into my car and drove cross-country, aimlessly wandering from state to state, but there was no escape—down the long smooth highways I traveled and the pulsing of the motor was a dissonant threnody: "Smucker's & Gwaltney's. Smucker's & Gwaltney's. Smucker's and . . ."

At length I found myself in a small city in West Texas. I was exhausted. Hadn't had a good night's sleep in weeks. Nerves all shot. I checked in at a motel and bought a local paper and climbed into bed, determined to get some rest. I was glancing through the newspaper when my eye fell on one of those full-page supermarket ads.

They were featuring packaged meats, processed by a company named . . . glory be! I leaped up in bed as if someone had thrown a prairie rattler into the blankets. I rushed to the phone.

It was a Texas company, headquartered in Abilene.

Gooch.

GOOCH!

The Gooch people were flourishing and expanding in the West, the very locality where Gwaltney was weak. But that was not the real important thing. It was the *music*. I drove excitedly to the airport, silently calling down blessings on the head of my doctor who had sent me into this far-off part of the country, and I caught the next plane for New York.

In twenty-four hours we had ingested Gooch.

And after that . . . I stepped down, relinquished my corporate command. The time had come for younger hands to take over. I had furnished them with a foundation to build upon and now I could rest and relax a while and murmur the melodious words: "Smucker's, Gwaltney's & Gooch."

That's about the way I operate in my autistic handling of the merger game. I'd devote all of my time to it if circumstances would permit . . . but I just can't seem to kick this writing habit.

CHAPTER 39

A SESSION WITH MCCAREY

On a Sunday morning in the summer of 1969 I was working on a collection of stories and anecdotes and it happened that the tale at hand concerned Leo McCarey and the filming of *The Bells of St. Mary's*. I had just finished typing the anecdote and had gone on to some others when my wife came in and said that the radio had just reported Leo's death.

I left my desk and went outdoors and walked around a while, thinking back twenty years to a session I had with Leo in New York, and to the rather unusual circumstances attending that reunion.

Leo was a man who liked to drink. So was I. He entertained a contemptuous attitude toward New York City and he had a McCareyesque method of demonstrating that contempt. Every year or so he'd get on a train in Los Angeles. When his Pullman reached Grand Central he'd get off, take a cab at an underground taxi stand, go straight to the Waldorf-Astoria's underground entrance, step out of the cab and into an elevator, and ascend to his suite in the Towers. He'd stay perhaps a week and never once set foot outside his quarters. If anyone wanted to talk to him, he could damn well come to the Waldorf. In a sense McCarey was never outdoors from the time he left Los Angeles until he got back.

He phoned me one day in the autumn of 1945 and asked me to come and see him at the hotel. It happened that on that day I was introducing my home-from-college son to the poisonous wonders of Belmont Park. As I remember we watched seven races, got cleaned, then found a cab and headed for the Waldorf. McCarey was expecting us and he was in good fettle. We sat and talked a while and had a couple of drinks and then the phone rang.

"Come on down," Leo said into the phone. "Got somebody here I want you to meet." He didn't say who the caller was.

In about five minutes a woman arrived. I didn't pay much attention to her—she seemed to be rather plain-looking. Leo introduced her but my mind was on something else and I didn't catch the name. She sat down on a couch next to my son and they began talking, mainly about the boy's studies in chemical engineering at Cornell. Leo and I continued with our own colloquy—consisting mainly of stories about such sterling characters as Gene Fowler and Barney Dean and Bing Crosby.

At length the plain lady got up and excused herself and left, and an hour later my son and I were on the train headed into Westchester.

"How'd you like her?" my son said to me.

"Who?"

"Ingrid."

"Who?"

"Ingrid Bergman. That was Ingrid Bergman. You mean you didn't recognize her?"

"My god," I said, "I had no idea!"

I really didn't.

I think I must have been very fond of Leo McCarey.

CHAPTER 40

EXERCISE IN LITERARY TECHNOLOGY

As most people with adequate eyes and ears surely know, an author with a new book is apt to be asked to appear on radio and television shows, the theory being that such appearances will stimulate the sales of his masterpiece and, at the same time, entertain and instruct the public. A highly questionable supposition.

I have been indulging in this sort of thing as long as I have been writing books, something over thirty years. I can't remember which of the book shows was the first on radio, but I think it was *The Author Meets the Critics*. I performed on that one many times, both as author and as critic. In passing I would like to say that out of all such programs, radio and TV, that I have done business with, the best by far is the current *Book Beat* television show which comes out of Chicago and is masterminded by the serenely erudite Robert Cromie.

In the last few years I have several times taken part in a new form of radio interview. The gimmick was for me to sit in my home in New York (and later in Texas), connected by telephone with a radio station in Ohio or Iowa or Utah. Let's say it's Dayton, Ohio, as it actually was on one occasion. The guy who runs the program talks to me briefly and then he asks his Ohio listeners to phone the station, and he'll hook them in with me, somehow, and they are free to ask me any questions that come into their minds. The technology involved here is a little mystifying to me. I'm inclined to think back to the Paleolithic time of the popular radio show "Information Please" when Clifton Fadiman asked Franklin P. Adams, "Do you understand, Mr. Adams, how radio works?" Mr. Adams replied, "I don't even understand how the telephone works."

All this effort in Dayton, and elsewhere, getting the guest arrangements made, the time set, and the telephone hookups welded solidly into position, and what do we have? Intelligent cultural exchange, that's what, as I intend to demonstrate.

One afternoon I was sitting in the living room of my home in New York, and I was hooked up with radio stations in three different towns in one of the Corn Belt states. After the show got to rolling a man telephoned one of the stations and the interlocutor asked him if he wanted to speak with Mr. Smith.

"No," said the caller. "You'll do."

I could, of course, hear every word that was said by everyone. I was not overly enchanted.

"I want to find out," said the man who was phoning from the middle of a cornfield, "if Mr. Smith is the same fella that wrote an article in the *Reader's Digest* a few years ago."

Whether he wanted to talk to me or not, I now broke in. "I write occasional articles for the *Digest*," I said. "Tell me what the article was about."

"Well, sir, it was the funniest one thing I ever read in all my born days. It was about this cat. Funny? I never laughed so hard at one single thing in my whole life. Laugh? I *thought* maybe you were the one who wrote it. You did, didn't you?"

"I can't remember writing anything about a cat in the *Digest*," I said. "Maybe I did. I've written a couple of novels about a cat. Tell me, what did this particular cat do?"

"He walked along on top of a fence. Comical? I tell you, I thought I'd die! I've ram-sacked this house, top to bottom, can't find head-ner-hair of that copy of the *Reader's*. This cat was walkin' along the top of this fence. I remember that."

"Yes," I said, "but what did the cat do? I mean what did he do that was so funny? It's not all *that* funny, just for a cat to walk along the top of a fence. What was it he did that doubled you up?"

"That," he said, "is the part I can't remember. All I know is it was the funniest thing I ever . . ."

"It doesn't sound like anything I ever wrote," I interrupted.

And so he grumped and growled a little, saying a man oughta *know* if he writes something that is that comical, and then he hung up. There were a couple of other calls, including one from a woman who wanted to know if it were true that I was "a gourmet eater." I was in an unpleasant mood after that bout with the cat-on-the-fence character and so I told her it was true, that I have a gourmet for breakfast every morning. This was a form of New York style comedy and I don't think it registered with her, or perhaps she didn't even hear my response, for she said, "That is *real* innaresting."

Then another man phoned in from the prairie. "That gentleman that called in about the cat on the fence," he said. "It was sure enough in the *Reader's Digest*. I remember it real well. I agree with him. It was the funniest thing *I* ever read in *my* life. I laughed till the tears run down my face. I just howled."

"What was so funny about it?" I broke in.

"Well, the other gentleman had it all wrong. It wasn't a cat. It was a dog. This dog was walkin' along the top of this fence. That's the way it started off."

"That," I said, "is a little funnier than the cat walking along the fence. But I don't think it would bring tears to my eyes. What *else* did the dog do?"

"Well," he said, "as I recollect, he was a-scared of something. My wife says to this day that when I read that thing I laughed so hard I almost split my gizzard."

"What was the dog a-scared of?" I persisted.

"Darned if I can remember. I called in because I know it was a dog instead of a cat, and I can help the other gentleman out with that much, and maybe if him and me could get together and compare notes, we could get it straightened out and remember the whole thing."

The cat-dog-fence matter was now concluded. There was one additional call of interest. A man with a telephone in his automobile called one of the radio stations, from the-hell-and-gone out in the country, and he was relayed on to me.

"Yes," I said, "what can I do for you?"

"Not a thing," he answered. "I was just listening to this program and decided it would be fun for me to call you from my car out here on this country road all the way to New York."

The man at the radio station spoke up. "Don't you have anything to ask Mr. Smith?"

"Not a thing," said the man in the automobile.

And so, on that strong cultural note, the program petered out.

The radio stations unhooked themselves and launched into other less intellectual programs, but the emcee stayed on the phone with me for a minute or so longer, wanting to thank me for my participation.

"That first guy," he said, "that called in about the cat on the fence, he heard the second guy say it was a dog instead of a cat, and he got furious about it. He said he wasn't going to sit there and have his word questioned. He got to yelling over the phone and calling the dog-guy a liar, and then he began cussing the dog-guy and cussing you and the station. We couldn't put him on the air again, the kinda language he was using. He was really bugged."

So we said our farewells, with thanks all around, and of course the sales figures on my then current book surged. In what direction I am not prepared to say.

CHAPTER 41

WHY WHY? WHY NOT WYE?

During the last year I have been engaging in a spirited campaign aimed at spelling reform. Almost every professional writer goes through this phase at one time or another and usually, in the end, regains his health.

My efforts have not been as extensive as those of such dedicated revolutionists as George Bernard Shaw and Theodore Roosevelt. Shaw was fond of pointing out that if we clung to the old-fashioned orthography, the proper way to spell *fish* would be *ghoti*. The *f* sound is spelled as in *rough*. The *i* sound as in *women*, and the *sh* as in *nation*.

Ghoti er cut bait.

Teddy Roosevelt bellowed wantonly for simplified spelling. When Taft succeeded him in the White House, the New York *Sun* commented on the departure of T.R. with a one-word editorial: THRU.

H. L. Mencken never espoused spelling reform, but he had a great relish for bizarre usages. In one of his books on the American language he called attention to a sentence spoken by a woman in the Ozarks, a sentence Mencken himself sometimes quoted in his casual conversation. This Missouri woman, wife of a hillbilly investment banker and a very proper lady in her community, once addressed her teen-age daughter in public: "Git a rag an' snot that young-un." Don't look at *me*. It's part of authentic American folklore and may one day be set to guitar music.

My own campaign is directed against a single word: *why*. Why should *why* be spelled *w-h-y* when it is used to indicate a sort of pause, or a moment taken for thought; when its definition is, in fact: er, uh, ah, weh-ull? As in such a sentence as, "Why, I wouldn't really know about that." Or, "Why, of course I'll do it."

Whywise, why should *why* be spelled *w-h-y* when it is used as an interjection at the beginning of a sentence, as meaning *lawsy, gosh, zounds, egad?* As in, "Why, bless my soul, here he comes now!" Or, "Why, I'll thrash the son of a bitch within an inch of his miserable life!"

Every time I write the word *why* in either of these contexts, I die a little. It goes against the grain. I see one thing from the viewpoint of the reader, of whom I am one of which. To me, when a sentence begins with the word *why*, my razor-sharp mind usually advises me that a question is coming up.

It is my recommendation, then, that the word be spelled *wy*, or *w'y*, or, best of all, *wye*. It would read better. In one or two places earlier in this book I've tried it as *wye* just to see how it looks. It looks pretty sensible to me.

I hope to win this campaign and have my reform accepted by the end of the present year. Next year I'm going after that bugger *mulct*. Just look at it! *Mulk-tuh!* Ought to be forbidden by law.

CHAPTER 42

HILDY JOHNSON SCOOPS THE TOWN

It was a warm and humid day that twenty-sixth of July in 1938 and I was on rewrite in the city room of the New York *World-Telegram*. The summer heat had mesmerized the city into a state of sweaty lethargy, and there were even people on the streets walking at a slow and unfrenzied gait. The town being sluggish, there was little in the way of news breaking, and I had my feet up on the draw lid of my desk, indulging in vulgar badinage with a couple of hard-bitten copy boys out of the Flatbush section of Brooklyn. In ten minutes it would be noon and I would head out for Nick's for cold beer and maybe a nibble of lunch.

Elmer Roessner, who was running the city desk, yelled over to me: "Off two, Slanthead!" I swung my feet to the floor, picked up the headphones, lifted the receiver off the hook, and while whirling a sheet of copy paper into my typewriter, told Ella on the switchboard: "Gimme the call off two."

Click.

"Smith, rewrite," I said.

"This is Lee Tracy," he said. "Listen, I got what might be a hell of a story——"

"Did you say Lee Tracy?" I broke in.

"Yeh."

"You mean Lee Tracy the actor?"

"None other."

I read his voice loud and clear and knew that it *was* Lee Tracy and not some joker. Jokers are always in abundant supply around newspaper shops.

"And," I went on, "did I hear you say you had a hell of a story?"

"Come on," he almost snapped at me, "let's get moving. Ten, fifteen minutes ago I stepped out of the Hotel St. Regis and . . ."

But let's interrupt that telephone talk and move uptown about four miles to the intersection of Fifth Avenue and Fifty-fifth Street. On one corner is the venerable St. Regis and directly across Fifth Avenue, the Gotham Hotel. At about 11:30 A.M. that July morning a pedestrian chanced to glance at the upper façade of the twenty-one-story Gotham just at the moment a man climbed out a window on the seventeenth floor. The stone ledge at this level was about two feet wide and the man walked along it until he was midway between two windows, both of which were open. Then he moved casually out to the very lip of the ledge and stood there, teetering slightly.

Thus began one of the most dramatic and suspenseful news stories of our time. It was literally a cliffhanger and in my own experience ranked second in prolonged suspense to only one other—the Lindbergh flight from New York to Paris.

The Man on the Ledge, as he was called in books and in a motion picture, was John Warde, a dark and handsome boy of twenty-six, a manic-depressive with a history of two suicide attempts.

Nobody knows the name of the pedestrian who looked up and saw John Warde come onto the ledge. But within ten minutes the intersection was aswarm with people, vehicular traffic was snarled, and police and fire department rescue squads were screaming in, along with hook-and-ladder trucks.

Minute by minute the crowd grew larger on the sidewalks and the pavement, and other people were hanging out windows of nearby office buildings and hotels. Heads were tilted back as the spectators kept their eyes fastened on the young man, not wanting to miss his wild leap when it came . . . and it was expected at any moment.

The nearby radio networks soon had men and equipment on

the scene, setting up mikes in the street and putting their best newscasters to work. The running description was broadcast from coast to coast and across both Canada and Mexico. As the hours wore on, it almost seemed that every human being in North America was following the story, tensed and eager, waiting for the jump.

In the hotel rooms behind the two open windows were policemen and firemen and a crazy assortment of preachers and priests and faith healers and yogis and people who make a profession out of soft-talking would-be suicides out of jumping off of high buildings, or bridges, or water towers. A policeman with a reputation as an actor put on a bellhop's uniform and spent hours leaning out a window and talking to John Warde, promising him fun and frolic with girls and booze if he'd only come off the ledge.

Long periods of scheming were devoted to possible methods of grabbing him by an arm or a leg and dragging him in. But he played it cagey. He was friendly and receptive toward the cop-bellhop, but he was also suspicious. They handed water out to him, setting glass after glass on the ledge and then withdrawing, on the theory that if he drank enough he'd have to come in for a visit to the bathroom. He drank the water and stayed on the ledge. His sister arrived and pleaded with him but to no avail. After a while she collapsed and had to be put under sedation. Psychiatrists came, offering their know-how, and a hypnotist, and a policeman skilled in the use of the lariat. Finally a cargo net was brought to the scene and ropes were lowered from the hotel roof and a crew of workmen began trying to rig a large net beyond which John Warde would be unable to jump. (One thing I learned that day: the circular canvas life net which firemen hold for people jumping out of burning buildings is no good when the jumpers are more than six or seven stories above the ground.)

The afternoon wore on, and John Warde stuck to his ledge, sometimes sidling up to the edge and setting the women in the crowd to screeching. All kinds of ruses and tricks were attempted but Warde played it his own way; he played it shrewd.

Down in the street newspaper photographers lay on their backs, aiming their cameras upward, yelling curses at spectators who walked on them. There were no television cameras, no Cronkites or Brinkleys or Howard K. Smiths, but all the newsreel people were present. By midafternoon hucksters from nearby Times Square were on the scene selling cheap opera glasses and assorted novelties. Also dancing attendance were members of the gambling fraternity, calling out such proposals as, "Five'll gitcha eight he don't jump."

Dusk came on, and then darkness, and John Warde stood firm. The cargo net had gotten fouled up and was hanging flat against the façade of the building. Now and then John Warde sat down to rest his feet, and occasionally he'd smoke a cigarette. The mob in the street below hung on. Nobody wanted to go home. Night came and floodlights illuminated the whole front of the hotel.

About 10:30 that night they got the cargo net untangled and they had devised a new method for rigging it in place. Bosun's chairs were ready to be lowered from the roof. They were getting John Warde boxed in. But somehow he sensed what was going on and after eleven hours on the ledge, he jumped.

He struck a cornice and his body whirled downward, hitting the hotel marquee and landing at the curb. The screaming of the women was frightening, even to the cops and firemen; scores fainted as John Warde died. It required the efforts of three hundred policemen to keep the surging mob away from the body. They wanted to rip off strips of his clothing to take home as souvenirs.

And so we return to the beginning of this story, and the telephone call from Lee Tracy.

". . . I stepped out of the Hotel St. Regis," the actor told me, "and turned toward Fifth, and immediately I saw that crowd gathering. I looked up and saw this guy. My god, he looked like he was a mile up the front of that building. I counted the floors and stood around a few minutes and the fire trucks were tearing in and the crowd was getting bigger and it was pretty clear this guy was ready to jump. Know what I said? I spoke right out loud, 'Jesus! This could be a big one! I've got to call the paper.' I turned around and was hurrying back to the St. Regis entrance before I realized I *didn't have a paper to call!*

"You probably know that just about ten years ago I played the part of Hildy Johnson in the Hecht-MacArthur play, *The Front Page.* That did it. Ever since then I've been playing newspaper reporters, with my hat turned up in front and a pint of red-eye on my hip. I've not only been typed by Broadway and Hollywood, I've been typed by myself. The minute I saw all those people and the guy they were looking at, I went straight into character. I had to call my paper. For some reason the *Telly* popped into my head, and here we are."

"Do me a favor," I said to Tracy. "Run out there and have another look and call me back in about three minutes with any new developments." He did. He reported that the crowd was still swelling. Whole brigades of police and firemen were swarming in. Traffic seemed hopelessly snarled. The guy was still on the ledge.

I thanked Tracy and then wrote it in takes (one quick paragraph at a time, each sheet being snatched out of my typewriter by Elmer Roessner) and I dressed it up a bit, placing emphasis on the colorful crowd and the traffic tie-up and the stalled buses and the whooping and yelling and the heads poking out of windows and so on. You might be surprised how much copy an imaginative rewrite man can get out of a few sentences spoken to him by a reporter on the phone.

The *World-Telegram* hit the street soon afterward with a scarehead over the story on Page One. We scooped the rest of the town by a good forty-five minutes. We walloped the opposition good on the biggest local story in years. And all because a li'l ole Georgia boy had been typed as a demon newspaper reporter.

I think perhaps that I sometimes miss those years I spent as a newspaperman. Everything happened. And that play, *The Front Page*, was not altogether fiction.

CHAPTER 43

FOUR BOOK REVIEWS

THE HOME BOOK OF HUMOROUS QUOTATIONS, Edited by A. K. Adams (Dodd, Mead, $10).

This reviewer wishes to put forward a theory that A. K. Adams does not exist. It may sound a trifle wild, but I have a hunch that the girls in the stenographic pool at Dodd, Mead decided to put together some kind of a book as a Christmas surprise for Mr. Dodd and Mr. Mead, and this ten-buck thing was the result. If it happened that way, then I have a further theory: those clever little girls, in the course of assembling their gift book, somehow got themselves good and zonked.

Someone committed the deed, and for convenience let's just call him (it) A. K. Adams. He must have had some reason for putting the word "humorous" in the title. You might hazard a guess and say maybe he had a lot of hilarious jokes and funny sayings in the collection. Not so. The title is pretty long as it stands, but it should have been sprangled out to: *The Home Book of Quotations of Which Maybe a Dozen out of the Nine Thousand Selections Are Vaguely Humorous in Character*.

I keep going back to the original thought: there simply couldn't be an A. K. Adams. No one man could stand up under the awful responsibility of committing such a book as this. Page after page after page without even a hint of anything humorous. Just straight quotations, such as you might find in Bartlett or Seldes or Mencken or Bergen Evans.

Originally appeared in the El Paso *Times*.

It might help you to know that A. K. Adams desecrates the memory of Fred Allen with a long series of vapid, senseless, and unfunny gags largely out of Mr. Allen's beginning days in vaudeville. Or that A. K. Adams (it *must* be those dizzy girls) regards a Broadway mushhead named Joey Adams as one of the funniest men who ever slapped shoe leather. Or that old A.K. even quotes the Mad Gaekwar of Alpine from time to time, inconsequentially. Gaekwar in Sanskrit means Protector of Cows.

Considering my irresolute and vacillating uncertainty about this volume, the best way to summarize it might be with a few apt aphorisms which A. K. Adams overlooked. O.K., A.K.? Here we go:

"The covers of this book are too far apart."—Ambrose Bierce.

"He has a real elementary sense of humor, and by elementary I mean grade school."—Sayings of Avery.

"I may be wrong, but I'm not far from it."—Dave Clark. (The Lake Hopatcong Dave Clark.)

"Who steals this book steals trash."—Shakespeare. (Claude Shakespeare.)

And one other: "Comparisons are odious, and so is this book." Which is a true quotation from the author of this review.

MENCKEN, by Carl Bode (Southern Illinois University Press, $10).

No person who admires H. L. Mencken, or has ever admired him, or has read anything he ever wrote, or who despises his memory, should miss this book. People who have never read him, or who belong to that vast majority who have never even heard of him, should pass up this ten-dollar beauty and proceed with their Jacqueline Susann homework and their scholarly probings into the motivations of Harold Robbins and Rod McKuen.

Several biographies have been written about Mencken. As far back as 1925, when he was a sensation in the land, Isaac Goldberg did a full-length treatment of his life, and books have been appearing since his death in 1956. Up to the present year the best of the lot has been *Disturber of the Peace*, by William Manchester, the guy who kicked up such a fuss with his book about the assas-

Originally appeared in the El Paso *Times*.

sination of President Kennedy. It is now my firm opinion that Mr. Bode's book is the best.

One of the major elements in my own dissolute life was an acquaintance with H. L. Mencken extending over a period of thirty years. And a major flaw in his own character was the fact that he approved of me. He became a hero to me before I ever set eyes on him, and he remains a hero to this day. This friendship with HLM has caused me to take down with Critic's Disease—a meticulous and finical searching for blunders and bad writing by people who deal with a subject I know something about. Sometimes called nit picking.

Carl Bode is a professor of English at the University of Maryland and his book, to me, is the best of the biographies because it is the most complete. The essential facts are here, in volume, and the book is quite readable. Some early reviewers have criticized the writing as pedestrian. To me it doesn't seem necessary that a man composing a biography needs to write like an angel. (Come to think of it angels, while pretty good fliers, are notoriously inept at the typewriter.) The Bode prose is adequate. He has a slight tendency toward clichés, but so have I, so it's all right.

One very pleasant thing about his book is the chance the reader has of meeting up with most of the literary whales of the period. Theodore Dreiser, Sinclair Lewis, Sherwood Anderson, Edgar Lee Masters, Willa Cather, F. Scott Fitzgerald, Anita Loos, Upton Sinclair, and, of course, George Jean Nathan—these and a host of others appear on the stage wearing their warts.

There is one memorable document Mr. Bode didn't consult, possibly because he didn't know about it. I have reference to the shortest thing Mencken ever wrote. It is in my possession. I was a reporter in New York in the early 1930s and one day I learned that HLM was on a transatlantic liner returning from a vacation in Europe.

I sent a radiogram to the ship in mid-ocean asking if I might meet him for lunch at the Algonquin Hotel on the day after his arrival.

Back came his response by radio:

"OKE."

That's what I call writin'.

MARK TWAIN, by Charles Neider (Horizon, $6.50).

Now in the early part of 1967 comes Brother Neider with a book about The Master. Books by Mark Twain and books about him are always welcome at my house, though they have been coming so fast recently that soon I'll be forced to pitch a tent in my back yard and live out there.

Unhappily for Mr. Neider, his book will have to stand comparison with Justin Kaplan's *Mr. Clemens and Mark Twain*, which made the joyous scene six or eight months ago. In my own opinion and in the opinion of professional critics, Mr. Kaplan's book is probably the best book ever written about the man from Hannibal. Yet it would not be fair if Mr. Neider's work were to suffer under such a comparison.

He has involved himself with the writings of Twain for at least half a dozen years, principally as an editor dedicated to bringing order out of the vast disorder his subject bequeathed to the world. He is the man who fetched *The Autobiography of Mark Twain* out of chaos and confusion, throwing out the dross and dribble of a faltering and querulous old man and adding about forty thousand words that had never seen print before. In that instance, he took aholt of a massive jumble and made a legitimately splendid book out of it.

His present work is a collection of eleven pieces, most of them written as introductions to anthologies which Mr. Neider has been putting together in recent years. Two of the pieces are fresh work and of these, the one on "Mark Twain Censorship" strikes me as the best thing in the collection.

The book presupposes that the reader enjoys a basic acquaintance with Mark Twain's life and works. It is, in large part, a critical discussion of the novels, travel books, essays, notebooks, sketches, and short stories. There is a fine chapter on Mr. Neider's dispute with the Moscow *Literary Gazette*, which hit the front pages in 1959. And another chapter describing how *The Gilded Age* by Twain and Charles Dudley Warner was ripped up and made into *The Adventures of Colonel Sellers*, in which all of

Warner's chapters were thrown the hell out, as they should have been in 1874.

There is fine informative stuff in Mr. Neider's *omnium-gatherum* (Great god, look at me talk Latin!). I do wish he had forborne saying that in his view Mark Twain was "a profoundly religious man." So many people chicken out and make the same ridiculous kind of statement. Clara Clemens, up to the time of her recent death, said it over and over when she wasn't looking under the bed for Communists. A woman named Harnsberger turned out a sinful forty-seven-page book a few years ago seeking to prove that Mark Twain was as religious as Billy Graham, if not more so. Her argument was based on her evaluation of Twain as a *good* man, a man who was *nice* to people. A clean flub. Most of the time he was as mad as a soppin'-wet hen and as mean as a tromped-on snake.

How can these people support such an argument, knowing that Mark Twain almost outdid Robert Ingersoll in attacking religion? Twain did it in a cold fury, ridiculing the Deity, blistering the clergy, challenging the Bible, denouncing any and all churches, from the youthful days of *The Innocents Abroad* right down to his final months at Stormfield in Connecticut. How, I repeat, can they call him a profoundly and innately religious man in the face of all his bitter and acrimonious assaults against religion? Of course he faltered, ever so slightly, on a few occasions, but he always shook off the moment of weakness and returned to the attack. Mark Twain was Satan's Angry Man.

He spent a good part of his writing life berating "the damned human race" and the famous phrase popped into my head several times while I was reading this book. The cross section of humanity involved, one way or another, in the editing and publishing and criticizing of Twain's works, and in the management of his estate, is as grubby and unattractive a group as might be imagined. Even Clara Clemens seems to have been something of a termagant. I once made arrangements to visit her in California with the intention of writing a magazine article about her, but something came up and I couldn't make the trip. I'm glad. Among them all, never such petty behavior, never such underhanded, cheap, and sleazy backbiting. And every one of them a card-carrying member of the damned human race. I wish The Old Man could have been turned loose amongst them—he'd have blasted the britches off of them all—male and female alike.

MOVING ON, by Larry McMurtry (Simon and Schuster, $7.95).

The publisher's man describes this book, on the jacket, as "the most powerful and gifted novel to come out of America in many years . . ." Publishers never exaggerate, no more than used-car dealers would exaggerate, so let us accept that verdict.

It needs to be accepted for moral reasons. This novel, so powerful and gifted, is intended as a reflection of life as it exists today among the people who are under thirty and over twenty. The book stands, then, as a revelation and a confirmation. It confirms this reviewer's judgment that the young people of our time are, by and large, a sad lot of slobs. Through 794 pages these poor creatures, who imagine all along that they are leading standardized and normal lives, exist in a dreary world of hang-ups and cop-outs.

Brother McMurtry shows, whether he meant to or not, that the New People are dull and dissolute, and his book points up the incredible sterility of their lives. They get their kicks from the kind of sex known in Arkansas as "slippin' around." And from smoking pot, from driving a hundred miles an hour in traffic, from questionable intellectual pursuits. They do a lot of reading, but their books don't sound like fun and they don't discuss them afterward. There must be thirty or forty contemporary books mentioned in the novel, and I can't remember a single one of them that I've read or would want to read. The same for the music they favor; in fairness to cows everywhere, I refrain from calling it tripe.

They appear to enjoy their nagging hopelessness. There is no ambition among them. The women weep great hogsheads of brine, and the men cry like babies from time to time. Never in literature has any character bawled the way the book's principal character bawls. Her name is Patsy and she can look at a burned-out light bulb and burst into tears; she can dwell upon her tendency to cry and then start crying about *that*.

The one occasion when, strangely, she doesn't shed a tear is

Originally appeared in the El Paso *Times*.

the funeral of a good-natured and kindly old man who has willed his ranch to Patsy and her husband. And among all the people in the story, this old rancher is the only one who seems to be satisfied and serene.

This book is a must for people of the Decrepit Generation. It will make them feel less villainous than they have been painted by their get. Most of them, if you spoke of a hang-up, would think you meant putting the phone back in its cradle.

It all brings tears to my aging eyes, and makes me despair, but then I think some more about these slow-headed waifs and their day-by-day pursuits and I feel real good about belonging to my own generation. And I'm able to say: if *Moving On* is an accurate reflection of life in 1970, then the race is in a very bad way.

CHAPTER 44

THE TROUBLE WITH THEM IS US

A man named Walter B. Pitkin once set down a small parable to illustrate the somewhat extensive differences that exist between people in the United States and people in distant lands. A sweet old lady in Boston, member of a missionary society, is knitting a pair of socks destined for the feet of a savage chieftain in the South Pacific. On his faraway island this same savage chieftain, turning his mind to the little old lady in Boston, smacks his lips at the thought of how good she would be . . . barbecued. It is a nice little parable, though not to my liking; if I had to eat barbecued lady I'd prefer a springer—something about high school age.

It takes no great research to turn up foreigners who are as different from us as the Bronx is different from Bronxville. Take Egyptians. They grow a lot of henna, needing it for a red dye used by their women to stain the palms of their hands and the soles of their feet, and used also to henna the tails of their horses. In this country we prefer the extremities of our women and the tails of our horses unreddened.

Or the Swiss. They invented the bouillon cube and perfected the yodel and thus stand condemned before all humanity. All we did was invent the electric back-scratcher and a sundial that is set ten minutes ahead for people who are commonly late for appointments.

In Japanese restaurants, where the menu may include frizzled octopus and broiled ape shank, it is considered good luck for a customer to see a rat scamper across the floor. This is never true in American restaurants. Almost never.

Every male Italian past the age of eleven, up to and including the age of one hundred and three, spends a good portion of his time pinching the *gluteus maximus* portions of lady tourists, right on the main thoroughfares. In South America there is a game called *piropo*, a degeneration of or improvement on the Italian sport; *piropo* players come up behind a lady tourist on the main thoroughfares, pinch her on the bottom, and, at the same time, make pointed remarks about the beauty of her chest. In the United States we never do such depraved things—on the main thoroughfares. Only on the side streets.

No matter where you go in foreign lands, you will probably run into a cathedral built with cement that was slaked with vintage wine. Barrels and barrels of it. Each of these wine-impregnated cathedrals is certified as the only one of its kind in the world. There are none that I know of in the United States, although I have heard it said that the mortar used in Milwaukee's County Stadium was laced with lager beer.

In the Netherlands they put nutmeg in everything. This is quite disturbing to most American visitors. In Greece, on the other hand, they stir rosin into their wines. Over here we wouldn't think of doing that; we put rosin on our fiddle bows and enclose it in a small white bag so that Dizzy Dean can speak of it as "rozzum."

All these fascinating things—the business of the horses' tails and the broiled ape shanks and *piropo* and the yodel and the wine-soaked cathedrals and the rozzum bags—all these are true international differences. There are also widely held misconceptions concerning the manners and morals and customs of foreign peoples. And it remains a sad truth that many of us who travel abroad harbor an intense dislike for the differences we encounter when we stand amid the alien corn. The American tourist who howls for ham-and-eggs-country-style in the Tour d'Argent and asks sarcastically, "How much is it in *money?*" was not invented by the travel writers, though he may have been drawn large at times. Our top business leaders are customarily cautious, meaning tactful, meaning chicken, when it comes to making critical remarks about the consumer. Yet in 1963 Conrad Hilton, who should know, said: "I do not think American tourists behave themselves as well as they should when they are overseas. They create the wrong impression of America. There is too much cockiness."

My neighbor Avery, when it comes to foreigners, is a man with strong opinions, most of them wrong. He has congenital attitudes that are mainly emotional and grounded in both misinformation and pure human orneriness.

Avery has traveled abroad. Years ago he spent a sweaty afternoon in Juárez, then a malodorous hellhole across the border from El Paso, and came away with the conviction (often given tongue to) that "Mexico is a god-damn mess." And he once drove two hundred miserable miles in a foreign land (Canada), between Niagara Falls and the Blue Water Bridge at Sarnia.

"Dullest, dumbest damn country I ever been in," Avery, now the world traveler, said afterward. "Flat and dreary and dry, and the people all got that gray look. But . . ."

That "But . . ." proved to be important. Avery *had* seen something that piqued his interest. "All through Canada," he said, with reference to those two hundred miles, "I noticed that they got the best-dressed scarecrows on earth. The farmers up there seem to compete with one another to dress up their scarecrows in fancy duds. Garage fella told me the styles change every year or two, same as with people. This year the scarecrows have all got on sports jackets. I saw one, gray check, modified drape, two-button job, my god I'd like to have had it myself. This garage fella said a few years ago all the scarecrows in his neighborhood wore hunting jackets and red-flannel caps. How about *that?*"

Avery appears to be coming along. He will yet discover that there are other beguiling deviations and divergencies in the world, beyond the stylish costuming of Canadian scarecrows. But first he must divest himself of sixteen tons of misinformation he has accumulated over the years. He stands today as a depository for every cliché ever uttered by his fellow citizens regarding the people of other lands.

In the realm of ethnology Avery believes that:

French women of the *haut monde* slosh themselves with perfume to avoid the nuisance of taking a bath.

All Swedes, male and female, are sex mad.

In Wales, after you've seen a gang of coal miners yelping away in an eisteddfod, you might as well move along to greener and quieter pastures.

Italy never pays her debts.

Everybody in Ireland is dirt poor but deliriously happy.

Mexico has the wildest, most reckless automobile drivers in the world.

All Englishmen have extremely long upper teeth, which they bare at one another whilst ejaculating, "Pip, pip!"

In Madrid the guides enter into a conspiracy with the merchants to whipsaw the American tourist.

The water that comes out of every foreign faucet is as unsettling to the stomach as a cup of fer-de-lance venom with a dozen mole-nots stirred in.

England never pays her debts.

All Frenchmen have liver trouble, usually cirrhosis of the.

The guides in Rio de Janeiro conspire with the merchants to swindle American tourists.

In Japan they do everything in bathtubs except shoot pool.

Spanish señoritas fall over backward if you twang a guitar at them and crack your heels on the floor.

Waltz music never sounds right unless you listen to it in Vienna.

Driving on the left-hand side of the road is about the stupidest idea ever to emerge from the mind of man.

In order to speak French properly it is necessary to have a certain flexibility in the roof of the mouth, whereas most Americans have roofs of the mouth that are somewhat stiffer than automobile fenders.

Tour escorts in London conspire with shopkeepers to strip Yank visitors of every bob and farden they possess.

A citizen of Holland would not know what to do with footwear made of leather, being obliged by tradition to go through life wearing either wooden shoes or silver skates.

Andorra never pays her debts.

No Frenchman should ever be permitted behind the wheel of an automobile; no Frenchman should ever be allowed to occupy the saddle of a bicycle, and no Frenchman should ever be permitted to pedester.

The Irish grow so many potatoes that they don't know what to do with the surplus so they churn them up and make Irish whiskey and come home late at night and flog the bejabers out of their wives.

If you keep yourself on the kwee vivvy when you are in Australia you might chance to see an ostrich and a kangaroo engaged in kicking each other to shreds.

Taxi drivers in Tahiti conspire with the Chinese merchants to horn the tourist when they are not swoggling him.

English women don't know how to fix their hair.

Pago Pago has the wildest, most reckless automobile drivers in the world.

A Frenchman can't get within half a mile of a piece of fruit without trying to candy it.

The dancing girls of Bali (in addition to everything else) have developed specialized neck-knuckles which make it possible for them to move their heads from side to side without moving their shoulders.

All the people in Puerto Rico are like the Puerto Ricans who clobber and mug folks in Central Park, and it must be awful down there.

To get a French actress—any French actress—to appear on stage without a stitch of clothing on, it is necessary to ask her to do it.

If you speak in a loud firm voice, pronouncing each word carefully, even shouting out the syllables, you can make any Norwegian lemming-herder understand English.

The tailors of Hong Kong conspire with the rickshaw jockeys to con the American tourist out of everything he has in his pocket, including his vaccination certificate.

As soon as the sun gets high in Mexico all male citizens wrap themselves in serapes, put on hats the size of wagon wheels, and go out and sit with their backs against adobe walls to sleep and dream about banging Dolores Del Rio.

Cat Cay never pays her debts.

The foregoing is but a sampling of the beliefs cherished by my neighbor Avery. It is my hope that before he gets too old to navigate, he'll make it to Europe and even to those remote places where wyverns and griffins and hippogriffs and cocodrills stalk the land. He insists he doesn't want to see Europe. "They've had it," he argues. "All worn out. No future."

I've tried to convince him that an American can learn an enormous lot about the art of living by visiting Europe and observing the European way of doing things. I've tried to show him how the French have no peers in the culinary arts and the bibbing of wine; I've spoken earnestly of the Italian's way with a guitar and his all-around oleaginous euphoria; I've told him of Switzerland's example of shining cleanliness and respect for other people's property and of Germany's endless scientific achievements, especially in chemistry, with special reference to the mixing of malt and hops and mountain water. I almost had him convinced that the British could teach us plenty about integrity in government and then along came that damn Christine Keeler, I mean that damn Profumo. Again I almost scored when I told him how the Romanians hate spinach so much that their word for it is the same as their word for garbage. (Avery roused himself enough to say, "Hoo-ray for the Roo-manes!" but he expressed no desire to go and watch them spurn spinach.)

Occasionally I've tried to humanize international relations, telling him how in Germany the Bronx Cheer is known as the Bavarian Salute; that the people of the Netherlands never heard the story of the little boy with his finger in the dike until the American tourists brought it in; that there is a tribe of salt-water gypsies who live on ragged sailing vessels in the Sulu Sea and who get violently sick to the point of throwing up if they have to spend more than five minutes on steady land; and that when an Argentine widow goes into mourning she wears black underthings.

None of these fascinating matters has, thus far, impressed him much. The thing that Avery and others of his intellectual bracket fail to see is that in international judgments, much depends on the judge's point of view. One man's meat.

It was Ruggles of Red Gap, an English butler suddenly transported to a western cow town, who was startled when certain cattle persons referred to him as a foreigner. Most peculiar, he observed, that they should call him such a thing when, in truth, *they* were the foreigners. A kind of reverse English can be applied to this mode of thinking. Twenty-odd years ago I happened to find myself standing beside the playing fields of Eton. I felt the stirrings of history, and gusts of emotion swept over me, and I murmured: "Just to think! Here is where the Battle of Yorktown was lost!"

A city such as Venice can stir widely divergent emotional response, depending on the point of view. Ulysses S. Grant, after a visit there in 1879, said that it would be a splendid community if they ever got it drained. My father always said that Venice was the place where he'd like to spend his declining years—he had heard that it was the only city in the world where you could sit in a saloon and fish out the window. When Robert Benchley arrived for his first visit in Venice he quickly cabled a friend in New York: STREETS ALL FULL OF WATER. ADVISE.

It would be difficult for my neighbor Avery to travel among the Chinese and contemplate their conduct with aplomb and understanding. Lin Yutang himself has observed that a Chinese whiles away the hours tasting spring water, flying kites, whining operatic music through his nostrils, playing shuttlecock, matching blades of grass, working wire puzzles, pawning his clothes to pay off his gambling debts, stewing up a mess of ginseng, watching cock fights, taking naps, observing the twitter of cage birds, playing finger games (like *piropo* maybe?), gossiping about the fox spirits, beating on drums and gongs, blowing into flutes, munching duck gizzards, fondling walnuts and bits of jade to settle his screeching nerves, training eagles, gulping down aphrodisiacs, begetting children, smoking opium, standing on street corners with his hands in his sleeves, shouting insults at airplanes, practicing deep breathing, catching crickets, gambling for moon cakes, lighting colored lanterns, burning incense, eating noodles until they are drooling out of his ears, training pot-flowers and, except for these things, generally carrying on like some kind of a nut.

Avery would snort and snigger at such behavior. Yet I'd hesitate to set down in cold print all the things that he, being now retired from business, does in the course of a single day. It is entirely possible that there are a few minor flaws in the near-perfect civilization we have wrought in this country, and so it might be a good thing if we kept our big carping yaps shut when traveling abroad. A long time ago Samuel Johnson said: "I am willing to love all mankind, except an American." Strange to relate a few other foreigners, down through the years, have had harsh things to say about us.

I think there is a solution to the problem of what to do when we witness seemingly perverse or idiotic behavior in a foreigner—and it does not involve creating an unpleasant scene or being humble and losing face. Whenever I meet with such a situation abroad and feel the urge to wax nasty, I grit my teeth and say to myself:

"Hold it, boy. Go easy on them. How could they possibly be anywhere near as smart as *you* are?"

Meaning me.

CHAPTER 45

THE LUSH ON THE SUPER CHIEF

This will be a restrained account of another small but exhilarating adventure that came to me, a long time ago, in the dining car of an extra-fare train running between Los Angeles and Chicago. Back yonder somewhere in this book is a chapter telling about some of the characters I used to encounter aboard the transcontinental luxury trains I enjoyed riding in the golden days of long-haul railway travel. I mean those trains where, say, in Colorado they took on rainbow trout fresh from the mountain streams, and melons from Rocky Ford, and a man rolled along in a state of contentment and in the presence of world-famous movie stars and robber barons and Croesus-type kooks.

In those days, let me repeat, it was as much fun to ride the Twentieth Century and the Super Chief as it was to go on an ocean voyage. Quite often my wife and I would have no particular reason to go to California, but we'd go anyway. There was no experience on earth, in those times at least, compared to getting a haircut *and a singe* on the Super Chief. Hell's farr, a man didn't even get a *singe* on solid ground!

When I spoke of a single adventure in the dining car, I was not being fair to the rest of the train, for I used to have epical encounters and dialogues and confrontations from end to end of the Santa Fe as well as the rolling palaces of the Union Pacific. In addition to the epicurean foodstuffs, the sumptuous fittings of the

Copyrighted 1971: The Chicago Tribune. Originally published as "Mr. Puncher, Where Are You?" in the Chicago *Tribune*.

cars, the proficiency of the hired help, and the exquisite pleasure of that *singe*, there was always the chance of meeting and talking with untutored glamor-pusses out of Hollywood, gentlemen-rankers out on a spree, the previously treated champion duck caller, and the incomparable Chicagoan I have always remembered as Mr. Puncher. Many, many more . . . but let me say without hesitation that Mr. Puncher was my favorite of them all.

He was having a go at a luncheon dish of *tournedos Bordelaise* when I sat down across the table from him. We nodded at each other and then went through the required ritual of not speaking until about five minutes had elapsed. He was a plump citizen close onto fifty, dramatically bald, and he had on a busy Hawaiian print shirt (almost daring in those times) with no jacket and no tie.

At length I broke the ice by asking him if he lived in Chicago. He said he did. When he spoke his voice had authority. His tone and his manner, including the use of many gestures, were all calculated to give the impression that he was a man of parts, well-informed, poised, and tax-ridden.

We talked about how sandy the desert looked this time of year and what a mess Los Angeles was getting to be, and he asked me if I lived in Chicago, and I said no, but that I came originally from a small town in Southern Illinois. I said that after an absence of many years I had gone back to see my hometown and the experience had been disillusioning.

"Thomas Wolfe," I rambled on, "said that you can't go back again, and I remember that Odd McIntyre always said you should avoid going back to your hometown because it would very likely prove a sad disappointment to you."

There was an interlude of silence, and then he said, "Mind if I ask you a personal question?"

"Not at all."

"You in the newspaper game?"

"No," I said, "but I spent about twenty years in it. How the hell did you know that?"

"I could tell," he said knowingly. "I could tell by the way you said 'Odd McIntyre.' Ordinary person would say 'O. O. McIntyre.' I been around newspapermen all my life. Spot you guys in a minute."

It quickly developed that we had something in common—personal acquaintance with an assortment of well-known newspapermen—and now in the dining car the conversation galloped.

At this point I find it necessary to digress, to mention a couple of facts about myself, facts that I hope will be accepted as expository rather than boastful. If there is such a thing as erratic, eccentric competence, that is what I had in my years as a newspaperman in New York; I acquired a certain notoriety for doing such things as needling great statesmen with embarrassing questions and goosing beautiful movie actresses. *Raffish* was the word *Time* magazine used to describe me, after which *Time* magazine assigned a fairy poet to review one of my books. I need to add that I have long had an enviable and unsullied reputation as a non-fisted drinker. This reputation is international in scope and has been gossiped about by the Tashi Lama and his monks at Shigatse in the tablelands of far Tibet. Whole populations have believed that I spend all my waking hours hurling it down the hatch with almost incredible perseverance. And many of these people, noting the uninterrupted flow of books and stories and articles bearing my name, speculate at length on just who *really* writes my stuff for me while I'm laying numb. You should know about all this if you are to understand what followed with Mr. Puncher aboard the eastbound Super Chief.

He was having his coffee, and now he said to me, "Did you ever know Heywood Broun?"

"Sure," I said. "Worked on the same paper."

"Quite a guy. Quite a writer. But what a sloppy dresser! He always looked like an unmade bed."

He spoke that final line as if it were original with him, and I knew that it wasn't. He asked me if I had known certain other prominent newspaper people, such as Ernie Pyle and Fred Othman and Quent Reynolds and Bob Ruark and Westbrook Pegler and, by chance, I had known most of them and worked alongside some of them. He had little intimate comments to make about each of these people, indicating that he knew them well. By this time I was trying to figure him out—maybe an ad agency man, perhaps a sports promoter, a Hollywood press agent, maybe even a politician.

He was dawdling over his coffee when it came.

"Happen to know H. Allen Smith?"

I looked up quickly, suspecting that he was having me on, but I could tell from his bland expression that it wasn't a gag.

"Yeh," I said. "I know him. Slightly."

He raised his plump right hand above his head and swung it downward in a gesture of disparagement, and he spoke loud and clear.

"*What a lush!*"

I didn't say a word, and I managed to suppress a grin. He raised his hand again and swung it downward and amplified his declaration:

"What . . . a . . . *boozehound!*"

Now I had to speak.

"I know," I said.

"The things that guy's been gettin' away with!" he went on. "Listen to this. I had dinner with him one night in New York. Wish you coulda seen him. He showed up with a lot of bandages wrapped around his head. He'd been out to some joint and got barreled and got in an argument with somebody and next thing you know his own wife picked up a beer bottle and belted him alongside the ear with it." He raised his eyes and studied me a few moments and then something told him he'd better tread carefully—he was thinking that maybe this simple-looking guy across the table would turn out to be a close friend of H. Allen Smith and might resent such talk.

"You know him pretty well?" he asked.

"Pretty well," I said. "Been drunk with him a few times, but not lately."

He couldn't restrain himself any longer. He had to find out who I was.

"By the way," he said, "mind telling me your name?"

I had a weird moment of near-panic. Some strange psychological quirk took hold of me and I couldn't bring myself to speak my own name. I was actually feeling sorry for the guy. I thought first of giving him a phony name and saving embarrassment all around, thereby permitting him to get away with it. But something made me change my mind. I just had to break it off in him.

"Oh," I said airily, "I don't think you'd know *me*." I reached into my pocket and fished out the Santa Fe envelope which had contained my ticket. My name was written across the front of it.

"I'd be surprised," I added, "if you ever heard of *me*." I handed him the envelope.

He took it in a confident grasp, handled it in an attentive, businesslike manner as if it were a contract for three and a half million toggle bolts. He held it just above his coffee cup and then he glanced at the name on it. I saw his eyes bug out, and he paled a little, and then the envelope dropped from his fingers. He ducked his head down almost to the coffee cup, covering his face with both hands, and all the sound I heard from him was "Jeeeeeeeez!" which was emitted in a sort of agonized and muffled moan.

I was almost as embarrassed as he was—I actually sat there and suffered for the bum and I couldn't think of a single thing to say. Finally he began raising his head, spreading his fingers slightly and peering at me through them. I forced a big grin.

"Honestly," he said in a small voice, "I . . . I'm . . . well, I'm sorry. I apologize."

I summoned up a short laugh, but I don't think it sounded too genuine.

"Forget it," I said.

"I did meet you one day," he finally offered in a defensive tone.

"Where?"

"At the United Press office in New York. Al Greene introduced me to you. Must have been twenty-five years ago. You don't remember?"

"Well," I lied, "just vaguely." Then I asked him how he happened to be in the United Press office and he said he had worked in the Chicago UP bureau for ten years up to that time and he had been vacationing in Manhattan.

"What throws me," he said, "is that you don't look any older. Not a day older." Suddenly I had an eagerness to forgive him, to pick up his *tournedos Bordelaise* luncheon check, to get off the train at Albuquerque and buy his wife or his girl friend a handsome Navajo blanket.

He sat and stared at me and he still had a sickish sort of look on his face.

"How," he asked, "do you manage to keep lookin' so young?"

"Drinkin' whiskey," I said.

He paid his check and got up and spoke his apologies again and then scurried off to his quarters. I saw him only once after that. I was in the club car, keeping young, and he appeared in the doorway. As soon as he saw me he turned tail and fled. The thing would be eating at him for quite a while.

In Chicago I stopped by the United Press office to visit with the bureau chief, who was an old friend. I asked him about my dining car buddy in the Hawaiian shirt. The guy was a puncher —a teletype operator. From that time on he was known to me as Mr. Puncher.

Said the bureau chief: "He's a nice guy. His father-in-law died in L.A., and he went out to escort the body back to Chicago. Just by chance, I guess, they put the coffin on the Super Chief, which is a train with many splendid facilities, including the time-honored baggage-car-ahead. I suppose being on the Super Chief threw him."

"No," I said. "What threw him is how I keep looking so young."

"Bull shit," said the bureau chief.

So there it was. I gave the over-all picture some thought and began feeling a trifle more tolerant toward the guy. Under similar circumstances, I might very well have gone into the same dissembling performance. Finding himself riding one of the finest of all the extra-fare trains, he had felt the need to pretend, to comport himself in the self-assured manner of a Hollywood big shot or a midwestern industrial giant. He just wanted to participate.

He never had dinner with me in New York. I never have had my head swathed in bandages. My wife has never clouted me alongside the ear with a beer bottle (she has customarily used a whiskey bottle, 86 proof). But let's give Mr. Puncher his due. He had a *little* something going for him. I'd like to meet him again some day, preferably aboard a long-haul Amtrak luxury train, where I would guide him to the club car and buy him a drink treetop tall. And have one myself.

CHAPTER 46

BACKING INTO THE ITALIAN LANGUAGE

I'm quite certain that Mrs. Mardsley was paved with good intentions when she gave me the little book. She had just come back from a long vacation in Italy and she was burbling with talk about Como, the wild *paparazzi* of the Via Veneto, donkey rides in Calabria, and *fettucine* Alfredo. More than that, when she spoke a word like *fettucine* she gave it the old pizzazz and said fett-tu-cheeeeeen-nih. Come up sharp on the *nih*. The moment she found out I was contemplating an Italian journey, she insisted on giving me the little book.

She hastened to explain that this was no ordinary language guidebook of the type customarily carried by tourists. It was a book with the subtitle, *Manuale di Conversazione Italiano-Inglese*. Italian talk translated into English, but not the reverse rendering also, as is the usual format. The book's main title, in my own smooth translation, was: *The English: How She Is Talked*.

"This little volume," Mrs. Mardsley told me, "will serve you far better than the standard kind of language guide. You will really learn Italian, and you will acquire a much better grade of language. What I mean is, you will learn to talk about things that Italians talk about among themselves."

I wasn't at all sure of what she was trying to say. I flipped open the book and my eye fell on this:

"What was that loud noise?"

"Oh, nothing. Just an explosion."

I didn't say anything. Obviously I was reading in the wrong column, my eye was somehow cocked linguistically off center. Meanwhile Mrs. Mardsley was chattering away about some kind of a long downhill walk she had taken in Florence. Pretending continental insouciance, I turned a few pages and came to:

"*Guarda com'e alta la giraffa! E che aria impassibile ha il cammello!*" I had the distinct feeling that somebody was trying to lure me into a false sense of security. Look how tall the giraffe is! And how impassive the camel looks!

What goes here?

Let me make it clear, I'm not afraid of any living creature. On the other hand I am a reasoning animal and I don't think a camel is being impassive just because he *looks* impassive. Come to think of it I am somewhat apprehensive whenever I'm around the cammello. Also around the leone, tigre, elefante, ippopotamo, mule, rinoceronte, coccodrillo, and even the struzzo, which latter is the point-after-touchdown ostrich. I made a mental note to stay the hell away from animals—tall, short, soft, hard, passive or impassive, during my happy jaunt through Italy.

Mrs. Mardsley was talking again about the little book, having arrived at the bottom of the hill in Florence. "The way you work it," she explained, "is you look first at the expression as given in English, and then you know that this is a thing that an Italian wants to know, so you are beginning right off to get into the Italian frame of mind . . . you are *thinking* the way an Italian thinks . . . and then you hop over to the expression as given in Italian so the Italian will be able to find it in the book, and now you penetrate deeper into his consciousness, and the English phrase becomes firmly embedded in your mind, and . . . but here, let me demonstrate. Open it up, just anywhere."

I opened it up and using that hatpin system of picking horses jabbed my finger at the right-hand page. It said: "*Non potete insegnare alla nonna a bere le uova.* You can't teach your grandmother to suck eggs."

Mrs. Mardsley bent over and inspected the lines and then scowled at me, as if I had put them in the book, as if I had written them.

"Now," I said quickly before she could come up with some

justification for the suck-egg line, "how about *that*? Am I going around the streets of Rome and Ravenna and Naples saying *that* to the Italian people?"

"Hmmmmmmm," she murmured. "That's one that I hadn't even noticed. I think perhaps that it means something in Italy that it doesn't mean over here."

"What does it mean over here?" I asked. "I don't even know what it means in the U.S.A. I have heard the expression that so-and-so's grandmother sucks eggs. It is spoken, I suspect, as a reflection on the grandmother. I would judge that in Italy they go out of their way to *teach* egg-sucking to their grandmothers, except when the grandmothers are too deep in senility to grasp the first principles of——"

"Please," Mrs. Mardsley protested gently. "Turn to some place in the middle—hotels and railroads and the post office." I did, and arrived at a section dealing with signs: BEWARE THE DOG! BEWARE OF SHEEP! BEWARE OF PICKPOCKETS! And my eye picked up a startling line: "My collarbones are broken." I was reflecting on this when I thought I heard a loud noise, just an explosion, and it was Mrs. Mardsley urging me to try another section of the little book. She, too, had perseverance and so I went to work and quickly discovered that if I am to enjoy myself to the fullest in Italy I should be prepared to plead heartwrenchingly as follows: "I am cold. I am hot. I am hungry. I am tired. I am ill. Can you help me? It was not my fault. I cannot find my hotel. I have lost my friends. I forgot my money. I have lost my keys. I have missed the train. They are bothering me. Go away. I have been robbed. Where is the Lost and Found desk? The razor scratches. No, I part my hair on the other side. Take me to a hospital." Jesus!

I was getting into a state of nerves, just reading. Mrs. Mardsley was talking about a most delightful experience that had been her lot in the marketplace at Verona where she had come upon a set of *persiane avvolgibili* and she had started to haggle with . . . I stopped her and asked her the nature of the item and she said Venetian blinds with diagonal stripes in purple and orange, just right for her music room back home, and I thought to myself, humpf, some place to go for Venetian blinds with

Venice just down the road a piece, so I left her gubbling along and returned to the book.

It had been my aim to *noleggio di automobili* in Italy so I flipped through and found: "Excuse me, I was confused by the traffic; I am a stranger here," quickly followed by the question, "How much is the fine?" Same as everywhere else—you can't win. And then: "My tire has collapsed. It is a slow leak. My engine skips. There is a grinding. There is a diminution of power. It stops. You must change the bush of the engine, register the tappets." A bit farther on and I found: "I came in from your left and so I had the precedence. It was your fault." Oh boy. Splat! Right in the kisser!

The notion now occurred to me, why go to all that bother of renting a car? How about, instead, a nice side trip by boat in the lovely shining Adriatic? My enthusiasm restored, I turned to matters *marittimo* and there it was, consistent constancy: "I am sick. Please show me the quickest way to my cabin. Are you sure we are on course? Where are the pills? Go away." Cruising the Adriatic—*out*.

Mrs. Mardsley had turned to talking about some cheese she had enjoyed in a Naples restaurant. "It may be," I interrupted her, "that I'll go to Hawaii instead of Italy, perhaps fly on to American Samoa, and then . . ."

"Don't you dream of it!" she responded. "Don't you give up Italy. It's gorgeous. Glorious. *Magnifico*. And that little book will make it all so pleasant."

And so I carried it home with me and remembering my customary concern for my health when traveling, I looked up the medical section and pretty soon I was suffering pains in tandem, maladies I had never known about before. The *conversazione* went: I have a pain in my back, in my stomach, in my head, in my kidneys, in some bones. Taxi, be quick! I feel these pains before eating. After eating. When riding. When I walk fast. Sitting down. I suffer from headaches, dizziness, nausea, colics of the liver, nettle-rash, *morbillo* (measles) and *orecchioni* (mumps). I fled right out of that chapter like a startled gazelle and found myself immediately in the dentist's chair. I am a man possessed of a great talent for linguistics so I noted that one essential expression was missing, and I telephoned the Italian who *mieteres* (mows) my *prateria* (meadows) and told him I was going to Italy, maybe, and wanted to know the Italian word meaning "Ouch!" He mumbled a bit through his mustaches and came up with something that sounded like *mee-fah-molly!* Which, he said, "mins, you hurts me too a-motch!" I explained that *mee-fah-molly* was a good deal to have to holler in the dentist's chair, too spread out, too extensive, so he recommended *Fermatti!* which he said mins "Stop! You hurta me too a-motch!"

I felt glum (*sconsolatamente*). It seemed unreasonable to me that a vacation in sunny Italy should be so fraught with disaster, unprogrammed interruptions such as colics of the liver, dissembling cammellos probably with rabies, collarbones cracking in pairs, man-eating sheep, and withered old grandmothers sitting around sucking eggs and complaining about the guv'ment.

Then suddenly the truth hit me. The little book was not about Italy at all, had nothing whatever to do with anything in Italy. The dangers and disasters I had been reading about were not endemic to Rome or Milan or Como or Calabria. They were put into print for the benefit of Italians getting ready to travel among *us* . . . in New York and Washington and Miami and Chicago and Denver and San Francisco. That perfidious cammello is in St. Louis and grandma is sucking her eggs in Beverly Hills. A great oppression lifted from my spirit and a heady eagerness seized hold of me. I wanted to head out for Italy right now . . . *immediatamenta*. It is good for the soul to get away from one's own kind for a while, from one's own barber who can't even locate the part in one's hair, and where *I* can't even locate the Lost and Found desk.

CHAPTER 47

ZOË AND MR. JACK AND
THE ORINOCO GUNBOATS

Nobody ever wants to leave well enough alone any more. From the time when I was fifteen and first made the acquaintance of a side-wheeling Oliver typewriter, I was always satisfied with the classical test line: "Now is the time for all good men to come to the aid of their party." It is my firm conviction that old Christopher Sholes pecked out that sentence immediately after he invented the typewriter in 1867.

I do know that I have used that old-reliable test line fifty years in the face of continuing innovation and reform. Occasionally in the old days some cane-carrying smart aleck would come along and flout tradition by typing a ridiculous line about a quick brown fox that jumped over a lazy dog, accomplishing nothing. Around the newspaper offices where I worked we usually ostracized such show-offs, consigning them to the same general category as Harvard men. (It is a fact that when I was a boy, in the middle part of our country, a graduate of Harvard was popularly thought to be the ultimate in human uselessness. It is not my desire that this information be used politically.)

In recent years I have heard of a typewriter test formula that has been brought to our shores by the immigrant secretaries and receptionists lately installed in the offices of many Manhattan oak-panelly executives. These imported girls, no matter how pallid, no matter if they employ the rhyming slang of the London cockney, are alleged to heighten the tone and the style and the dignity of an American business leader's private lair, and one of the ways they do it is by testing their typewriters with this limey line: "A quick movement of the enemy would jeopardize six gunboats." Those crisp English broads would very likely scoff at my old-fashioned test sentence, pointing out that it is technically inadequate because it contains no b, j, k, q, u, v, x, or z. I never take no lip off of no Englishers. My answer to them is: their jeopardized gunboat line is technically inadequate because it contains no 9, *, &, ?, 6, $, ½, %, ¢, or ⅛. More than that, we Americans, when we sit down to a typewriter, know what we are actually doing; we are not testing the typewriter—we are testing ourselves.

Just a month or so ago I got a further surprise when I chanced to meet a neighbor who has been with the same typewriter company for twenty-seven years. He told me that the technicians in the factories scorn the stereotyped sentences the rest of us use and, when they are making their final check, they write a line of their own devising: "Amaranth saseususos Orinoco initiation secedes Uruguay Philadelphia." You think I am trying to wax comical? I josh you not. Those typewriter mechanics contend that those words (I don't think *saseususos* can even qualify as a word), set down in that order, will always show up any faulty alignment in the type bars.

It required little effort for me to reject, out of hand, that *Amaranth saseususos Orinoco* sassafras. I don't think I'd care to have my typewriter tested by men who employ such degenerate language, on or off the job. They either don't understand the English language at all, or they know more about it than all the rest of us put together.

Finally, just last week, along came an entirely fresh test line. Another import. I was trying out a new portable typewriter, a machine manufactured in the French-speaking part of Switzerland. There was a sheet of light green paper in the carrying case and someone had typed lines of capital letters and then lowercase letters and then punctuation marks. Beneath all that were two sentences in French as follows:

ZOË MA GRANDE FILLE VEUT QUE JE BOIVE CE WHISKY DONT JE NE VEUX PAS.

monsieur jack veut que vous dactylographiez bien mieux que votre ami wholf.

I readily recognized that these were test sentences employed by the check-out technicians in the Swiss factory. I tried to translate them, but my French is a patois known only to the Chinese merchants of Tahiti and not understandable in any other French community on earth. So I took the green paper and called on the only French-born person I knew in my neighborhood, Mme. Christiane de Milly Halle. She looked at the sentences and quickly translated the first:

"Zoë, who is my oldest girl, wants me to drink the whiskey, which I do not wish."

Mrs. Hale elevated her eyebrows and said: "This Zoë. Who is this Zoë? Is she a friend with you?"

"No," I said. "She is no friend of mine. Any damn girl who would treat her mother like . . ." Then it came to me that my explanation of the test lines apparently hadn't been clear to Mrs. Halle, so I tried it again, and she went on to the second sentence.

"Mister Jack," she translated, "wants you to typewrite much better than your friend Wholf." She studied the last word a moment and then added: "Even I know this is one dumb way to spell the name of a man's name Wolf. The way this one spells, you would have to say eet Whooluff. No?"

Her husband Stanley, who had been sitting nearby engrossed in a bawdy book—my own very latest—now tore his eyes away from its magnetic pages and said:

"What the hell is going on here? What are you two talking about? I'm trying to concentrate on this marvelous book and all I hear filtering in to me is something about a girl trying to force whiskey on her old lady. And what's eating the old lady, she doesn't wish it?"

I advised him to go back to his book, back to savoring its double entendres and the choicest of modern dirt. He wouldn't understand about typewriter test lines. He is a Wall Street guru

with little or no personal experience in the science of dactylographiez.

As for me, now that both sentences had been made clear to me,
I promptly lost all interest in the depraved girl Zoë and the
busybody Mr. Jack. I stand steadfastly where I stood before. Now
is the time for all good men to come to the aid of their party.
God knows it needs it.

CHAPTER 48

MURDER

All over the face of this bright and shining land foul murder is being plotted, homicide that is actually fouler than foul.

Right at this moment, as you are reading these words, people are pacing floors and walking around innumerable blocks and sitting at desks and lying on studio couches . . . each one trying to devise a special method for slaughtering people, some diabolic way of rendering a person null.

These killers come from every walk of American life. The man who shares your seat in the train or bus may be plotting such a plot, and the house or apartment next door to you may harbor such fiendish, murderous schemings as would make your toes curl if you knew about them.

These malevolent contrivers are the murder mystery writers of our national scene, both pro and amateur, but chiefly the latter. The amateurs, to be sure, far outnumber the professionals and there is no way of estimating their total strength. They worry and torture themselves no end, but they worry other people, too. Among those they used to worry is Isabelle S. Taylor.

Mrs. Taylor once was boss-editor of the Crime Club, the Doubleday adjunct which publishes three mysteries a month. She stayed with the job for something over thirty years and read about fifty manuscripts a month to get the three she would publish. Thus, out of sixteen manuscripts, one is found to be publishable. This ratio holds good not only in the Crime Club but in the offices of the many other publishers who issue murder-detective novels. There is no way of telling how many are written, or started, or planned, and never submitted to a publisher. Some mystery novel authors, on the basis of personal conversations with people they know and people they meet at random, are convinced that half the adult population of the United States is quietly engaged in murder plotting. It has been said that there are as many people writing mystery stories, or trying to write them, as there are people who chew gum. I myself am certain that the remainder of the populace is hard at work on books of humor. I hear from most of these.

"People write mysteries," says Isabelle Taylor, "and never tell their closest friends about it. I have known wives who wrote them without telling their husbands and husbands who didn't tell their wives. It seems entirely possible that such stealth, such domestic huggermuggery, may have at one time or another resulted in actual murder." Mrs. Taylor says, incidentally, that a great many people who get the urge to become writers usually start off with a mystery. They have some weird idea that it would be easy.

"For some reason," says Mrs. Taylor, "all these amateurs believe they must have a fantastic method for doing their victims in. The Rube Goldberg devices they figure out used to drive me to the edge of madness. They come up with dry-ice bullets and dry-ice daggers. They have the empty hypodermic for injecting the bubble of air. I remember a young man who turned in a mystery in which the victim was deliberately scared to death."

As any pro knows, the method of killing is not important. A plain bullet, or a push off a building, or some ordinary dime-store rat poison is adequate and neat. Philip MacDonald, the mystery writer, has put the matter quite succinctly: "It is not quite correct to call them whodunits. Better to call them how-catch'ems." (Minor digression: If you are aching all over to become an author of detective novels, and successful at it, one of the easiest courses is to get yourself born with the name MacDonald or Macdonald.)

And so we have all these people wandering around, trying to think of bizarre methods of killing folks. Mrs. Taylor told me about one woman whose chief concern was the method for murder and who almost got her bustle in a sling because of it.

She wanted to kill her victim by having a charge of dynamite wired under the hood of his car, rigged to the starter—not a very extraordinary procedure. This woman, a stickler for accuracy, went to the du Pont plant—through some family connection she gained access to the offices of the top du Pont executives. She walked in and began asking just how much dynamite she should use in the murder car, the exact amount needed to blow the driver to shreds when he hit the starter. She had neglected, however, to explain why she wanted this information. There were eyebrow-raisings and little hand signals and secretaries began telephoning the cops and even the FBI; the du Pont executives figured they had a real homicidal maniac on their hands. It took a little doing for her to get things squared around.

I asked Isabelle Taylor to recall the most fantastic murder technique ever to come to her attention in a mystery novel. She had to think a while. She began rearranging things on her desk while she ruminated, leaving telltale fingerprints all over the joint.

At last her frowning concentration ended and the smile came back to her face. She remembered a certain British author's how-catch'em.

The dead man was found lying in the middle of a small pasture. Snow on the ground. No tracks of any kind in the pasture. Gentleman had been done to death by a terrific blow on the head. Couldn't possibly have been dropped from an aeroplane or balloon.

Well, you on the edge of your chair? Wanna know how it was done?

The murderer had a smart horse, and he trained this horse to perform the black deed. When Mr. Unfortunate wasn't looking, the horse turned around and let go with both hind feet and kicked him clean over a fence and into the middle of that field.

Cute? Well, if you don't think it's cute, just conjure up a picture of the possible payoff—a horse in the electric chair.

CHAPTER 49

CHRISTMAS LIST

I don't want any more gadgets. Got a god's-plenty of clothes.
I already have three bathrobes and I'm opposed to neckties on
general principles; I don't wear them except on State Occasions,
such as when I go to a Mexican restaurant in Marfa, Texas, or
when I head out for Sweden to accept the Nobel prize. My
wristwatch is adequate and I have a drawer full of belts. The
things I want Santa Claus to bring me are things that won't go
under the tree or into the stocking I hang by the chimney with
care.

It will be a truly beautiful gift if people will pronounce Caribbean properly when they are in my presence. I cringe every time
I hear it spoken with the accent on the *rib*. The name comes
from the Carib Indians, who inhabited the islands when Colum-
bus arrived. Carib is pronounced Care-rib, with the accent on
the *care*. Caribbean should be pronounced with the stress on
the *be*. I have a dozen or so dictionaries and they all agree. Even
the thirteen-volume Oxford English Dictionary has the emphasis
in the right place, which is surprising because, as everyone knows,
the English are lubberly and maladroit in the way they handle
the English language. They call a halfpenny a "hayp-nee" and
threepence, even in their dictionaries, is "thruppence." What
clods!

There are other stupidities in the area of pronunciation which bug me no end. Many people still say Rews-uh-velt instead of Roosevelt and if they'll kindly quit it I'll consider it to be one of the best Christmas presents I ever received.

There is, too, the word pantomime. Vast numbers of slovenly and ignorant talkers pronounce it panto*mine*. The best pan-tomimest in the land, Red Skelton, stubbornly refers to his art as panto*mine*. I have been ragging him about it for years, but he believes that the word *ought to be* pantomine and that, by god, is the way he's going to say it. I must mention also the vast num-ber of people who say *momento* instead of *me*mento, e.g., "I'd like to take this home with me as a momento of the occasion." That's dumber than pantomine.

In the same Christmas package I would enjoy getting an or-dinance passed against those who insist that Horace Greeley said, "Go west, young man." An editorial writer in Terre Haute, Indiana, said it, and three years later Horace Greeley (whose comical style in chin whiskers is being copied nowadays by so many of our male citizens, young and old) quoted it in his news-paper.

I would enjoy even more having Congress enact a law against people who commit the hideous crime of saying: "As Mark Twain once said, everybody talks about the weather but nobody does anything about it." Mark Twain didn't say it. Never. God damn it to hell, he didn't say it! I have been inveighing against this atrocity most of my adult life and such is my influence with my fellow man, I hear it or read it somewhere at least once every week. I have written endlessly trying to get it corrected, and I've bellered about it on radio and TV. In the spirit of Christmas then, let me say that something should be done to the perpetrators, although I don't think we should hang them. A brisk bastinado will do.

A similar gift I would cherish would be the jailing of all people who contend that W. C. Fields said of himself: "Any man who hates dogs and little children can't be all bad." I hear that one, and read it, almost as much as I hear and read what Mark Twain said about the weather which he didn't. The line was spoken by Leo Rosten, the distinguished editor and author, at a testimonial dinner given for Fields in Los Angeles. Anyone with just minimal perception should recognize the fact that a man would not say such a thing about himself, that the statement in itself testifies that it was spoken by another person. I have tried for two decades to correct it, and Mr. Rosten at my urging has written the true facts, but people go on attributing it to Fields. Godfrey Daniel!

There are so many other requests for intangible things I would like to put in the hands of Santa. For example, death by firing squad for anyone who uses the word *confrontation* which has been worn to a frazzle lately. No, wait. I take that one back. I used the word in the title of a recent book of mine, used it without compunction and without shame. For this transgression I am going to put on a hair shirt and go into the desert and build me a pillar sixty feet high and sit on it, the way Simeon Stylites did in the olden time. I sometimes wonder how, after building the pillar, he ever managed to get on top of it, but he did, and he stayed up there thirty years. If he could do it I could do it. We have better machinery and better heads than they had in the fifth century. Make that just better machinery.

I would appeal to the people who write the scripts for TV Westerns to do me a big favor for Christmas: for Xt's sweet sake quit using present-day slang in stories that are laid in the nineteenth century. I watch Westerns quite a bit and it startles me and offends my ear to hear a cowboy or a lawman or a hired gun employing words and phrases that had their origin in my own time. The writers who compose the Westerns are all too frequently guilty of committing these frightful brain-jarring anachronisms. Just last night I heard a *Gunsmoke* character say, "Well, ya can't win 'em all." I've winced when a lawman operating just after the Civil War has said, "Spell it out for me, will ya?" I recall a rancher arriving back from town, asking his ramrod how things have been going. Says the foreman: "Ever'thing's copacetic." I've heard a Black Bart character order an underling, "Go git me thet sawed-off shotgun"—the term and the weapon originated during the gangster wars of the 1920s. I've never kept a list of the anachronisms I've heard in TV Westerns, but they are quite common and suggest to me that the script writers are either indolent or stupid. Any day now I expect to hear some cowboy use one of my favorite words, *rhubarb*, as descriptive of a brawl in Miss Kitty's Dodge City saloon.

A person shouldn't be a pig, shouldn't expect too much in the way of Christmas gifts, so I think I'd better close out my list with one final request. I would be real happy if people who put things at angles would put them occasionally at something other than 45-degree angles. I have never heard of anything being at an angle unless it was a 45-degree one. Why not, just for novelty's sake, put something at a 25-degree angle? Or a 63-degree? I'm beginning to get bored with 45-degree angles.

That'll about do me for this Yuletide although, for sentiment's sake, I'd like to get two items I always found in my Christmas stocking when I was a child back in the Middle West—gifts that had a little substance to them—one orange and one banana.

The foregoing composition appeared originally in *West*, which is the Sunday magazine of the Los Angeles *Times*. Almost immediately there was an uproar among the lesser anthropoids of Southern California. They wrote bushels of letters to *West*, leading off with one by a Ruth Fried of Canoga Park, giving me holy hell for committing a redundancy, to wit: "the true facts." This Ruth Fried, when she wrote her letter, was probably her last name. Many others jumped me about "the true facts" and called me ignernt and I tell you I spent three nights sobbing into my pillow.

An act of necessity on all of them.

One letter, however, came direct to me from Cedric Worth, a former New York newspaperman who lives now in Claremont, California. Mr. Worth has given me an opportunity to correct the record in the matter of W. C. Fields and dogs and little children.

In the November 1937 issue of *Harper's Magazine* he had an article reporting on a cocktail party held in New York City seven years earlier, a gathering at which a man named Gastonbury monopolized the conversation with an eloquent attack on dogs. When the party was ending, Mr. Worth found himself in the elevator with several other guests, including Mr. Byron Darnton of the New York *Times*. In that elevator this Mr. Byron Darnton uttered a remark which Mr. Worth promptly wrote down. The remark was:

"No man who hates dogs and children can be all bad."

Mr. Worth of Claremont states firmly: "Darnton made his electrifying observation in the elevator at 30 Fifth Avenue (corner of Tenth), at approximately the sixth floor, in the summer of 1930."

Years later, working as a war correspondent for the *Times,* Byron Darnton was killed under air attack off the coast of New Guinea. And Mr. Worth is deeply pleased that his friend is to be given recognition for speaking the famous line eight or ten years before Leo Rosten used it at the W. C. Fields testimonial dinner. He sent me, incidentally, a copy of the *Harper's* issue for November 1937, in which Byron Darnton was quoted.

In my letter of thanks to Mr. Worth I tacked on a postscript saying:

> I correspond with a lady who lives on West Bonita in Claremont. She used to teach English at, I think, San Jose State and no doubt advised her students that an accurate gauge of a great writer lies in his frequent use of the phrase "the true facts."

CHAPTER 50

DELUXE HARDSHIP TOURS, INC.

Worldwide tourism, having burgeoned into a gigantic economic complex since the end of World War II, has also grown more than a trifle daft in some of its major phases. Offbeat characters are sitting around these days thinking up new ways of luring some of that lovely lucre away from their competitors. And some of them are reaching pretty far out.

There are African safaris for unattached ladies, and bachelor tours for soigné young men who have a strong weakness for vintage wines and belly dancers. Groups of travelers are hauled up to Baffin Island to smush noses with the Eskimos and eat blubber *béarnaise*. We are offered tours in which the traveler is required to have his appendix out and his wisdom teeth removed before shoving off for isolated archipelagoes. A Pacific shipping line has just announced special cruises for checker players.

Much of this travel planning is predicated on the notion that people want to travel with people who are like themselves. Hog breeders like to go vacationing with other hog breeders and inspect the procedures in hog breeding among foreign breeders of hogs, and so clannish hog tours are being set up for them. Bridge players like to travel with other bridge players so they'll have something to do at night. Bird watchers and spelunkers and jazz buffs and karate choppers and flower arrangers and golf fiends all enjoy global traipsin' in the company of their own kind.

I once heard of a girl in Hawaii named Shirley Belz who worked for hotel people and who was continually on the prowl for new ways of enticing people to go traveling. One day in a whimsical moment Miss Belz came up with an idea for a travel agency which she would call Mystery Tours. The traveler would pay in his money and receive a large sealed envelope. He would be told to board a certain plane or ship at a stipulated hour and once on board, to open his Cracker-Jack package. Only then would he know where he was going and what he was going to see.

The New York *Times* has described the travel industry in the United States as "a $30 billion sleeping giant." The phrase is poorly wrote but it suggests that important money is involved, and I would enjoy getting some of it; this is the principal motive for my organizing a specialized travel service to be called Deluxe Hardship Tours, Inc.

In recent years I have been roaming quite a bit and in the course of my journeyings I've become acquainted with a great many other travelers on terms of restrained intimacy. I've been surprised at the number of men and women I have encountered whose mission in life is to suffer-on-the-go. They are the ones who yearn to travel to out-of-the-way places which they describe as "unspoiled." Typical of their kind were the Arsenaults of Pennsylvania, a man and wife I met one day in a Tahiti hotel. I wrote a brief bit about them in a book about my own languorous pursuits in Paradise, and at this point I would like to describe the Arsenault Syndrome again, even more briefly.

When I met these two Pennsylvanians a hard rain had been drenching Tahiti for three days and they were bitter about it, because it had fouled up their plans for suffering. Over rum drinks they told me they wanted to organize an expedition to Lake Vaihiria and capture a Giant Eel. Getting to Lake Vaihiria is about as difficult a proposition as you could lay out for yourself in Tahiti. You start from the shore road and strike inland along the Vaihiria River. It is jungle all the way—fetid and sweaty and stinking and aswarm with clouds of voracious mosquitoes. Lake Vaihiria itself is about fifteen hundred feet above sea level, which means that you've got to walk steadily uphill to get to it. I had talked to several people who had been there. They said don't go. You've got to carry machetes and chop away the jungle growth that blocks your path and a good part of the time you are slithering around in mud, often up to your knees. After two long days of this fun, you arrive at the lake. It is a spot to which some people are attracted by the legend that its waters are inhabited by eels as big around as men. I wouldn't want to be in the same hemisphere with such eels and I am happy to advise you that they don't exist.

So, what else is there to see and do at Lake Vaihiria? Nothing. Nothing but sweat one minute and shiver the next and bat mosquitoes and claw through the mud and acquire multiple welts and abrasions and knots on your head. I tried to describe all this to the Arsenaults of Pennsylvania. The more dramatic I made the horrors of the trip sound, the more eager they were to get going. The beaten track is not for them and their peculiar ilk. They are happiest where the food is ghastly, the accommodations primitive, the snakes ultravenomous, the tigers saber-toothed, the natives unfriendly, and the malarial whim-whams available at every turn. It is foreordained that they shall suffer and bleed; that they shall take down with diarrhea resembling the hot blast that emerges from the bottom of an Apollo rocket during takeoff at Cape Kennedy. And then go home and talk about it. I might add that they are held in much higher esteem back home than those of us who have no desire to beard a Giant Eel in his native bog.

So it came about that, after listening to the Arsenaults and many others of their stripe, I quietly swam upriver and spawned my plan for Deluxe Hardship Tours, Inc. I say without hesitation that any traveler who signs on with our agency will be guaranteed the highest quality misery and discomfort available anywhere on earth. This is going to make me rich.

Our beginning project is a harrowing, heartbreaking tour of the Pacific. Our vessel, the S.S. *Happy Slough*, is a gaff-rigged schooner eighty feet long, flying a troublesome flag-of-convenience, sailing under questionable registry, with destination unstated and the whole venture seemingly underfinanced. My seafaring friends tell me that this concatenation of afflictions will invite heavy shellings from shore batteries all along the route.

We will try to synchronize our sailing dates with the typhoon season and, in the Caribbean, the girlish hurricanes. Our first voyage will be for men only, but if the ship survives the initial cruise, later voyages will be open to small but wiry American women.

I have already engaged Captain Wardell Stone as master. He is no Laughton-style Bligh. Alongside Wardell Stone, the captain of the *Bounty* was a spineless milksop. Thus every person who signs for our cruise may have ample confidence in our skipper; he will make them miserable during every hour they spend aboard the *Happy Slough*. Their agony will be constant. There will be no lolling in deck chairs with novels of espionage; no skeet shooting off the taffrail; no bingo in the lounge; no lounge. Everyone on board (I will not be going) will be assigned to rough and unpleasant duty of one kind or another. Holystoning the decks, for example, using the bare hands in place of holystones. There will be an ample store of seasick pills, by which is meant pills that *induce* seasickness. No person among our clientele would sign on if he wasn't sure of getting seasick—just enough so that when he returns home he can say, proudly: "I tell you, I wanted to die."

The ship will have a slow but continuing leak, so that there will be round-the-clock pump manning with rusty pumps. We plan for evening periods when one and all, in jolly spirits, engage in sewing patches on the ragged sails, using needles made of Javanese thorns. Our travelers will sweat out their nights in an unventilated forecastle with two men occupying each bunk. Mattresses will be stuffed with unginned cotton and a few lively baseballs. By means of a patented syphoning action, bilgewater will trickle steadily across the warped decking of the fetid fo'c'sle. There will be imported cockroaches of outlandish size and vigor, each with its own certificate of warranty. And magnificent Tasmanian devil rats whose nightly travels through the interstitial areas of the ship's structure will resemble, to the ears of our passengers, the charming patter of children's feet.

And the food. Ah, the mouth-watering food! A hideous Abyssinian warthog would turn his back on it. If there is one thing our type of traveler demands above all else, it is lousy food, lousily prepared. His culinary wants will be catered to religiously aboard the S.S. *Happy Slough*. Our chef, an alumnus of truck-stop cafes in south-central Mississippi, will prepare steaks of the general consistency of top-grain leather. Bacon strips that could be used to pry the lids off oil drums. Eggs that all hendom would renounce. Mildew gravy. And all fish will be served up raw. As I said, I am not going; I intend to stay home and run the office.

We'll rig it, of course, to have periodic water shortages, at which time there will be plenty of finnan haddie on the menu. Pemmican tidbits and Texas jerky and sassafras tea will be served on deck each afternoon at four. I have not yet drawn up a final program, covering every hour of every day, because I want Captain Stone, out of the hardness of his heart, to improvise little punishing activities along the way.

There will be at least one Night of Romance, at Papeete, when a bevy of slightly tainted Tahitian girls will swim out to the ship, climb aboard, and offer to trade for nails. Then too, we will visit Australia because our travelers are certain to be nature-lovers. They worship Mother Nature in her most evil aspects and creations. They want her to gnaw on them. They will be given opportunities to prove their stamina and courage and to find out if they are personally good to eat. They will be tested to see if they are capable of outrunning the vicious wild dogs of nearby New Guinea. They will be put into the arena with adult emus and spur-tailed wallabies. If they survive this last event, they will be matched against disgruntled and misanthropic kangaroos—the outback species capable of punting a grown man forty-five yards.

In the South Pacific Captain Stone will make it a general practice to dock in such ports as Pago Pago and Suva and Papeete at noon on Sundays. This is the sacred time, in that part of the world, when all the bureaucrats are catching up on their sleep. The arrival of a ship will require that these irascible gentlemen leave their couches and go to work. It is their custom to discourage Sunday dockings by subtle nastiness toward the ship and everyone on it. They will fumigate until passengers, crew, and Tasmanian devils are close to asphyxiation. They will arrest and imprison some of our travelers and call them dirty names.

There will be other planned tragedies, organized disasters, charted catastrophies, all made to look spontaneous and unrehearsed. A secret lottery (rigged) will be employed to select individual passengers for specific adventures. One will be chosen, for example, to be left behind in a foreign fort without money and without papers. It will be necessary for him to use his own ingenuity in squaring himself with the authorities (impossible) and in catching up with the S.S. *Happy Slough* (unlikely). If he fails . . . well, he has *lived*.

With no concern for the expense involved, I am scheming up many other distressing, frightful, harrowing, and sickening events and undertakings, all designed to quicken the hearts of our customers. We solemnly promise them one great service that is absolutely essential: no where, during the entire cruise, will they be compelled to face up to a bathroom equipped with adequate plumbing. We do not intend that they shall have a single moment of unhappiness through an encounter with fixtures that work. Did I mention, earlier, that I am not going?

The financial profit to me will be great. That is the way I want it. I like to eat the ten-dollar spread, stay at the top hotels, ride the luxury liners, and lie almost motionless in beach chairs for long periods of time. Man's unflagging spirit of adventure, his urge toward hazardous pioneering, his yearning for the rugged and bug-infested path . . . all these things are not for me. I don't want to ride the rockets to the distant planets. If invited to go to the moon, I shall make my excuses. If *required* to go, it will take eight professional football players, four male nurses, and a bulldozer to get me aboard the space ship.

Yet I recognize the fun that many others get out of misery-travel. I'm inclined to be tolerant toward them. Live and let . . . well . . . let suffer. Well-heeled people beyond numbering yearn for the kind of cruddy travel I am offering them. On the forthcoming cruise of the S.S. *Happy Slough* they will never want for the kind of adventure they love. If Captain Stone and I should fail them, they have their own resources to fall back on. Let us not forget that they are the most ingenious and inventive people on earth when it comes to planning out amoebic dysentery and broken legs and other disasters for themselves.

They know how to travel.

CHAPTER 51

MENCKEN: A MEMORANDUM

The first time I ever visited with H. L. Mencken on his home grounds came on a summer day in 1941. During the 1930s I had enjoyed meetings with him in New York but now he agreed to a session in Baltimore. As soon as I got back home I typed up my notes, wrote a brief newspaper column about the interview, and then stuck the papers away in my files, where they disappeared. I have always kept voluminous reference files and many interesting items disappear into them from time to time. Recently, in the summer of 1969, twenty-eight years after the fact, I found out why the Mencken notes had vanished. I was looking for something in my "Maryland" file and out popped the Memorandum. I had filed it under "Baltimore" rather than "Mencken."

Somewhat late, then, I offer it to you—precisely as I set it down in 1941:

Monday, July 28, 1941, when the official temperature stood at 104, I met H. L. Mencken in Paul Patterson's office at the Baltimore Sun. I had suggested that I see him at his home on Hollins St., but he said it was "too god damn hot out there." Later when I told him I had hoped to do a piece about the home life of HLM, he was apologetic and said we could grab a cab and go out, but it was too late, since I was catching a 4:40 plane back to NY.

I had not seen Mencken for several years and he looked now, for the first time, like an old man. Through our long talk, which lasted an hour and a half or two hours, he remarked on his age, 61, several times, and spoke of death more than seemed necessary, using such expressions as "I may not last long," and "If I last."

He wrote a weekly piece for the Sun up until January of this year but quit then. He described his house—the old Mencken place, a 3-story house fronting on a city square.

"The neighborhood has been going down steadily," he said. "In the last few years I've noticed that the Okies are moving in. They are the mountain morons from Appalachia and most of the old-timers are moving out as they come in. Not me. I intend to stay as long as I last. I'm 61 and I may not last long, but that's where I intend to finish out my days. I've lived in that house since 1883, save for the five years of my marriage." In those five years he and Sara Haardt lived in an apartment on Cathedral St. There are stories that the death of his wife was responsible for his so-called change in attitude—the change which wrought him into an intense reactionary. I judge this theory to be wrong basically and specifically. He spoke occasionally of his wife with no show of emotion and quite impersonally. "My wife," he said, "was a southern woman, the yielding type." This comment was made during a discussion of his old friend Jim Reed of Missouri, whose first wife was, in Mencken's description, "a domineering old bitch."

Mencken lives at the house with his bachelor brother, August, an engineer, who is about ten years younger. They have a couple of colored servants. HL says August looks like him. "We keep house together and enjoy life. We have plenty of room for our respective jobs. He needs lots of room for his drawing boards and other such stuff, and I have acres of space for the junk I have accumulated throughout my life." Mencken has a secretary, a lady who comes in mornings, takes dictation, and goes home to type it. At one point he described her as being "in her fifties with asbestos ears."

I have often read that Mencken has always been a hypochondriac and he still seems to worry about his health. He is robust and has a flushed face and a red nose. His hair is gray at the sides but he still has that funny wild part in the middle where the hair is black. He dresses like an Iowa farmer bound for a funeral, giving off an impression of black broadcloth. His eyes are still remarkably blue, and he wears glasses when he has to read anything. He's a cigar smoker.

"I worked like the very devil all last year and through the winter," he said, "so I was worn down when spring came. The quacks put me in the hospital for a week and then told me I ought to get away for a while, so I took a trip to Cuba, chiefly for the boat ride. I've been feeling good since then."

He discussed his most recent work—the second autobiographical book, Newspaper Days, which is coming out this Fall, and the 1,000,000 word dictionary of quotations which he has been accumulating for 25 years. It has been turned in, and is in type.

"It's a book of quotations for a civilized man, not a schoolteacher," he explained. "It won't be of much use to a schoolteacher or a suburban pastor, but it'll be a nice bathroom book. It'll be something nice to read on the can, just as The American Language was a first-rate stool-book."

He is now starting a supplemental work to American Language, based on the wealth of material that pours in on him year after year. And he is forever occupied with the job of trying to get his records in order. He was vague about plans for further autobiographical books, though he is trying to straighten out all the material dealing with his magazine days, which he said represent probably the most interesting period of his life.

"The chief pleasure I get out of life is my work," he said. "I get no pleasure in games. I hate sports. The one thing I love to do is travel, but a man can't travel any more. I don't want to see South America. I might get down there and get stuck in one of those rat traps. Europe of course is out. And I've seen all of the United States I want to see. I've been everywhere and know people in every town in America. It becomes a tough proposition for me to go to a town and try to see it and soak it up. People I know in each town want to entertain me and meet their friends, and what I really like to do is just wander around the streets and look at the morons."

His most intimate friend, Raymond Pearl, a biology professor at Johns Hopkins, died recently. "He left a great gap in my life," said Mencken. "We saw eye to eye on almost everything. He was my chief buddy for 23 years. He was a member of our little Saturday Night Club."

This is made up of a small group of amateur musicians. Mencken plays second piano. Pearl was the French horn player.

The group has been meeting every Saturday night since 1905. They gather in a room in a downtown office building and start making their music at 8:15. They play until 10, and then adjourn to some beer resort and sop it up for the remainder of the evening.

"I'm the only original member left. There are no written regulations and no officers. To become a member a man has to meet with unanimous approval. There are no guests permitted to wander into our concerts. A member may bring a guest but he's got to be sure of his man and he's responsible for the guest's behavior. A guest is not permitted to criticize the music. He can sit and listen to it, but he can't say he likes or dislikes it. If he says anything at all about it we throw him out. We have this room for the meetings exclusively and keep the piano and bull fiddle there."

Mencken comes to New York about once a month, but never unless he has specific business to attend to. He still has a few cronies in town. Usually he sees Edgar Lee Masters, who lives in NY now and is in his seventies. They go to Luchow's. On his most recent trip Mencken saw the Stork Club for the first time, with Paul Patterson, and when I talked to him he flung back his coat to display the bright red suspenders Sherman Billingsley had given him.

"When I have a woman on the string," he said, "I take her to 21. It's a good place. Has good food. It's expensive, but what the hell! Expense is no consideration when it comes to having good food now and then."

Mencken gets out of bed at 8 a. m. He is the board of directors at the Sun and goes there frequently though he has no office at the paper. He generally rides a street car or takes a taxi and has not owned an automobile since 1919. He speaks of the cheapness of taxis in Baltimore.

"People have always commented about my luck with taxis," he said. "I can be in any city in the world, at any hour of the day or night, and if I want a taxi, I no more than mention it, or think of it, when a taxi comes in view. It's just dumb luck."

Speaking off the record, Mencken said he represents the Sun management in talks with the Newspaper Guild. "If I were eligible," he said, "I'd belong to the Guild. I've always believed some such thing was needed." But I didn't quite believe him. He doesn't like the idea of the Guild at all, and let drop the observation that "it's run by the Jew boys in New York." He said: "Years ago when I used to hire a new reporter, I'd ask him out to the house and have some of the fellows in and we'd sit around and get acquainted and everyone would feel better for it. Nowadays I don't dare go in the city room. I don't dare sit down beside one of the reporters. We might get to talking, and he might say something about the Guild. You know I'm not a man to hold back. I'm not tactful under such circumstances. I might let loose with something about the Guild and get the paper in bad."

He is, of course, a thorough Roosevelt-hater. He speaks of the "ja ja" convention in Chicago, "the dirtiest piece of business in years." He says he really doesn't believe the United States will ever see another presidential election.

"This country doesn't fully realize what it's getting into. I know just how it's going to work out. Roosevelt is going to shove us into this war. It'll be a bloody thing and when it's over, after we get our brains kicked out, the people are going to open their eyes and start asking, 'Who done it?' We'll have the old who-done-it campaign. And out of the mess a demagogue will arise. He'll be a bold man, and he'll signal the end of so-called democracy. It's a sad prospect but I refuse to worry about it. If I had children I'd worry myself straight into the tomb, but when I go I'm gone, and I leave no descendants to suffer. Today I can say the hell with it, but there are a lot of people who can't."

Mencken still uses "boob" and "boobs" throughout his conversation. When we prepared to leave the Sun building, he said he'd go with me to the Lord Baltimore Hotel across the street where I was to catch an airline coach. Our watches didn't agree and he stepped into another room and asked a couple of office boys about the exact time. They looked out the window and said, "It's a quarter to four by that clock."

"What clock?" Mencken demanded, looking around the room and seeing no clock.

"Out the window," said one of the boys. "The clock on that building over there."

Mencken stooped over and peered out the window.

"Good God!" he said, turning to the boys. "Don't ever believe that clock. That clock's on the Hearst Tower."

In the elevator he spoke almost affectionately with the Negro operator, asking about his health and family, and said, "I missed you around here the other day. I thought maybe you were in Europe fighting the Huns."

He crossed the street with me and we stood at the entrance to the hotel for about ten minutes.

"I'd go in with you till you make the arrangements about the coach," he said, "but if you noticed, the chiropractors of America are in convention assembled at this hotel. You know how I have loved chiropractors down through the years. If I so much as stepped into that lobby they'd ambush me and take my spine apart bone by bone. And anyway I would not be caught dead beneath the same roof with one or more chiropractors."

We talked a bit about the book business and the heat and train travel versus plane travel and then he left, swinging briskly up the street beneath his stiff straw hat, nobody paying him a bit of mind in spite of his being, in my estimate, far and away the greatest man in Baltimore. Inside at the transportation desk I talked to a Baltimore taxi driver. I was thinking of HLM's magic with taxicabs and I asked this one if he knew H. L. Mencken. Sure.

"Newspaper guy," he said. "His column ain't as popular as it used to be though. He's agin Rews-uh-velt."

CHAPTER 52

THE WHERE-I-WANT-TO-GO GAME

I have never considered myself to be a widely traveled person. By this I mean I have never said to myself, "My, I am really a widely traveled person!" Recently, however, I made a most pleasurable discovery during a conversation with some people who got to talking about the wonders of Hawaii. I reminded myself that I already know Hawaii pretty well, and can even talk a little Hawaiian, and that if I'm going to do some traveling soon, I ought to pick a place I haven't been yet.

So I began running over in my mind a variety of places I have not seen and where I would love to go. I let my mind rove over the nation, over the entire globe, and it soon dawned on me that I've been a travelin' man from who-tied-the-pup. I am, in cold fact, a widely traveled person.

I've been to Palm Springs and Las Vegas; Tahiti and the Kona Coast; the Michigan bean country and deep-frozen Port Arthur on Lake Superior; the Cotswolds and Dover and Oxford; Bowling Green, Ohio, and Bowling Green, Kentucky, and Bowling Green, Florida; the top of the Eiffel Tower and the palace at Versailles and a balcony at the Negresco in Nice; beautiful Lugano in Switzerland and the château of Ferney where Voltaire once lived; the Panama Canal Zone and Chiapas in southernmost Mexico; Monaco before Grace Kelly married into it and the fabulous island of Bora Bora; Concord Bridge and Walden Pond; Sinclair Lewis's Sauk Centre and Theodore Dreiser's Terre Haute; Australia and

New Zealand and Fiji and Samoa; Old San Juan and Sausalito . . . on and on. That's real place-droppin'.

I've never traveled in Russia or the Orient simply because I've never had any great itch to do so. I indulge in all this traipsin' because I love it and because I am usually able to pay the freight by writing books and magazine articles about my wanderings. I'm now past sixty and a person in my age bracket is not going to live another sixty—his number might very well be posted conspicuously just around the next corner. He's not going to make it to all the places he'd like to go . . . but he can dream.

Out of my own dreaming came a little game. I played it myself and then I had several of my friends play it and we called it Where-I-Want-to-Go. The player takes a sheet of paper and sets down the names of a dozen places he would enjoy visiting. He can make it twenty if he feels up to that much dreaming. He must not choose any locality he already knows—each place must represent a new travel experience.

The people to whom I introduced the game all made a satisfying discovery: as their minds ranged over the globe they came to a realization that they had traveled far more than they thought. This is a discovery that brings on an inner glow. It is pleasant to find out suddenly that you are not an old poop, and old stick-in-the-mud, but rather that you are a cosmopolite of sorts, a sophisticate, a man of parts, dern neart a candidate for membership in the Jet Set.

To demonstrate for you how Where-I-Want-to-Go is played, I shall now set down some trips I chose for myself, and why each place was selected. So, away we go to . . .

1. HANNIBAL. In Missouri. All my adult life Mark Twain has been my Number One Boy. I have been to many places with which his name is associated, but never to his boyhood home, the home of Tom Sawyer and the immortal Huck Finn. I simply can't understand how I ever missed Hannibal.

2. The *Land* of BADEN. For the reason that my grandfather came from there; also because of the beauty of the Black Forest, the legends of Heidelberg, where they have a wine barrel that holds 50,000 gallons, and because they named one of their rivers the Oos. I have been told that there are characters galore in the *Land*, such as Ignatz Mueller, who was called Nussbaumnatz after a big

walnut tree that stood before his house. He hated his nickname and wanted to be called Muellernatz so he cut down the walnut tree, and thereafter he was known as *Der Abgesägte*-Nussbaumnatz, meaning "the sawed-off Nussbaumnatz." Black Foresters are not without humor.

3. BERMUDA. For its beauty and also because Mark Twain spent much time there, as did James Thurber, another great man. Please keep in mind that I am in the same trade pursued by both Twain and Thurber, though functioning forty light years down the scale from them.

4. KEY WEST. Twice I have started for this southernmost city in the United States, but each time I've been sidetracked, so I have never made that spectacular drive across the Forida keys. I'm attracted by Key West's strong West Indian flavor, which must give it a romantic aspect, along with such exotic flora as the ilang-ilang tree, sapodilla, night-blooming cereus, banyan, frangipani, tamarind, East Indian palm, monkey-fiddle cactus and the dead-lady lily which is also known as Moses-in-the-bathtub. I think I could make it through life without inspecting the town's cele-brated turtle crawls.

5. GOTHAM. Not New York City, but the village in Notting-hamshire, proverbial for the foolishness of its people. A long time ago the citizens of Gotham wanted to discourage the King from buying a castle in the neighborhood because they thought it would turn into a great expense to them. When the royal messen-gers appeared as advance agents for the King, they saw the people of Gotham engaged in various stupid and idiotic pursuits. And so the village acquired its reputation for being a community dedi-cated to daffiness. I have wanted to visit it from the time I first heard the legend. Why? Because I would find myself amidst fa-miliar surroundings. Some of my wisenheimer friends say other-wise: that I would be absorbed into the community quickly and become mayor within a year.

6. TEL AVIV. Because Paul Forchheimer, whose judgment I respect, went there not long ago and blew his chimney over it. Mr. Forchheimer has been in many of the world's leading cities and he rates Tel Aviv to be the most colorful and the most cos-mopolitan town he's ever seen. More important, he's offered to

present me with a new passport holder made of genuine iguana hide if I'll go. Why fight it?

7. IRELAND. I've always maintained a disdainful attitude toward people who waste their time with genealogy and now: get *me!* First, the *Land* of Baden, and now this—the country of my mother's ancestry. Yet, that's not the whole story. I admire the Irisher's reputation for wit and good humor as exemplified in such men as Oscar Wilde and Bernard Shaw. It doesn't bother me what kind of charades Oscar Wilde chose to play on Saturday nights. He knew how to write good.

8. LIMA, PERU. A foreign correspondent, long my friend, spent several years in Lima and considered it to be the most fascinating city on earth. He was forever urging me to go there and observe the eccentric behavior of the populace. As an example, he told of the time he witnessed the burning of a large hotel in the heart of Lima. The firemen were making some progress when a water main broke and their hoses went limp. Quickly they hooked those hoses up to the city's sewer system and proceeded to stucco the burning building. Later on I read a book called *Grandfather vs. Peru* by Walter Beebe Wilder. It was a book that both entertained and informed, which is what a good travel book ought to be. I'll make it some day to Peru and if I can get up enough courage, I may even set fire to my hotel.

9. MONTANA. It seems unreasonable that I've been in Wyoming six or eight times but never once in this state which has more character and depth (and height) than most. Books written in recent years by John K. Hutchens and Chet Huntley, hymning the glories of the years they spent in Montana, have buttressed my determination to have a look at the state. There is an authentic individuality about its people, a true western ruggedness. They still drink ironmongers' cocktails—whiskey with a beer chaser—and eat something described fancifully on the bill of fare as Sowbelly Supreme. Their untrammeled spirit is reflected in an old Montana proverb: "Live every day so you can look any man in the eye and tell him to go straight to hell." There is another saying that touches on their hardiness: "The only way you can kill a Montana man is to cut off his head and hide it from him."

10. VIENNA. Once upon a time, I waltzed.

11. NORFOLK ISLAND. Ten years ago, discussing certain

islands of the Pacific, I wrote: "Many people have their own private dream island, a place they plan to visit before they die, and Norfolk is mine . . . I have read everything I can get my hands on respecting its physical aspect and its famous pine trees and its somersetmaughamish administrators and its people who are descended from the Bounty mutineers." I got as close to it as Sydney, but I still haven't made it to Norfolk. I intend to keep trying.

12. WINK. This is a town in West Texas. Pop. somewhat under 2,000. In the last year I have met two different people who came from Wink. They are not loyalists—they both told me the town ain't much. Many people and some publications say that Wink was ruined by urban renewal and this is its sole claim to fame. The town got its name not from the flapping of an eyelid, but from one Winkler, a Confederate officer and a member of the Texas legislature. Any town bearing the name of Wink can soon rope me in as a tourist.

That's enough to demonstrate how our game is played. It is not a competitive sport, though several players can set down their lists and afterwards all hands can indulge in heated argument.

I could stretch out my own list indefinitely, citing Amsterdam and Warner Hot Springs, Iceland and that towering German castle that sometimes appears in the magazine ads, serene Aruba and wild Patagonia, Luxembourg and Pitcairn and Nome. But something urgent is in the wind right now—I've suddenly decided to climb into my car and head out for Wink. It is only 136 miles from where I'm sitting. And after my visit there I think I'll just hop on up to the town of Fink, Texas, which lies close to the Oklahoma border. Fink has a population of three, the last I heard. It's quiet there.

Flash: I've just made it to Warner Hot Springs. Nice country up around in through there.

CHAPTER 53

YOU, TOO, CAN SET A WORLD'S RECORD

There isn't really a lot to it—this business of establishing a world's record. Hens have done it, and so have hogs. It's not necessary to be a Lindbergh wheeling down at Le Bourget, or a Marie Curie picking up her second Nobel prize, or a Valeriy Brumel sailing over the crossbar in a Moscow stadium. There are easier ways of setting world's records and some even come to a person when he's got his eyes shut.

Customarily there are two ways of establishing world's records. One is by outdoing someone else; example: Eddie Arcaro riding his fifth winner in the Kentucky Derby. The other is by doing a difficult or unusual or idiosyncratic thing for the first time in history; example: Johann Huslinger walking on his hands all the way from Vienna to Paris, a distance of 871 miles. The latter type of world's record is usually the most interesting. Be the very *first* person to do a thing. There is great satisfaction in it, as I myself know and as many other holders of world's records have testified.

This urge to be first is one of the principal reasons why mountain climbers climb mountains that have stood, through the centuries, cleanly unclumb. Babe Ruth beat out a lot of other ballplayers when he hit No. 60 in 1927, and that was a thrilling thing, but somehow it doesn't stand up against the performance of Lincoln Beachey, who looped the loop in an airplane for the first time in history in the air above San Diego back in 1913. There

© 1966 Curtis Publishing Company. Originally appeared in *Holiday*.

is some question whether he *meant* to do it, but the fact stands that he did.

Some years ago in New York City there was a young man named Omero C. Catan who became widely known as "Mister First." It was his practice to show up several days in advance of the opening of a new tunnel or birdge or highway, settle down in his car in the Number One getaway position, and become the first person to traverse the tunnel or cross the bridge or race onto the highway. The trouble with Mr. Catan's type of heroic operation is that it tends to beget imitators. He kept at it for years and reaped many columns of newspaper publicity as "Mister First" and was justifiably proud of himself. Then dozens of other young men began turning up, and beating Mr. Catan to the starting line. He retired, an unbeaten champion, but the others are still at it. We see them in large numbers at bridge dedications and tunnel openings and highway ribbon snippings. Sometimes they jostle one another. But their spirit is usually chivalric, the same as the spirit that imbues those noble souls who arrive at the ballpark gate a week or two before it opens for the first game of the World Series.

There are a few important things to keep in mind if you want to become holder of a genuine world's record. For one, a certain amount of perseverance is generally needed. Think of Captain Ahab in *Moby Dick*. He clung to his ambition with passionate determination and in the end achieved his immortality: the first peg-legged New Englander to be et by a white whale—a world's record which, we firmly believe, stands to this very day.

Unless you are a professional athlete, you should choose a performing area that is somewhat on the bizarre side. Philip Yazdzik of Chicago, for example, ate seventy-seven hamburgers at a single sitting and his name appears as world's champion hamburger-eater in the Guinness *Book of World Records*. We have drawn upon this splendid volume as well as upon Kane's *Famous First Facts* for some of our information regarding championship performances. Such as the achievement of Mrs. Alton Clapp of Greenville, North Carolina, who won the women's non-stop talking championship in 1958 by talking for 96 hours, 54 minutes, and 11 seconds. It is not specified what she had to say. As well as Philip Springer and Nita Jones who, in 1961, captured the cham-

pionship for writing a song with the longest title in the history
of Tin Pan Alley, namely, *Green with Envy, Purple with Passion,
White with Anger, Scarlet with Fever, What Were You Doing in
Her Arms Last Night Blues.* An enviable accomplishment, indeed,
and it somehow reminds us of the world's record established in
1846 by John Banvard, who created the largest painting in the
whole history of art—*Panorama of the Mississippi,* four and a
half acres of canvas measuring 15,000 feet in length. It burned up.

Authors, as a general thing, are not noted for constructive
achievement outside the realm of beautiful letters, although
Anthony Trollope devised the first street-corner mail box. There
have been other exceptions and out of fealty to my profession,
I would like to mention two or three. Edgar Allan Poe first suggested four-tracked railway lines with local and express service.
Lord Byron invented male cleavage, being the first man of
fashion to wear his shirt wide open clean down to his belly
button. Gilbert Murray, the great English scholar, loved to baffle
his friends with a trick he alone knew—taking off his sock without
removing his shoe. I, myself, hold several substantial world's records but I choose, at this time, to mention only the most recent
one.

This great honor came to me on the day I paid my first visit to
the new Pan American Building in the Grand Central area of
Manhattan. This tremendous structure is widely regarded as the
architectural wonder of the middle months of 1963. It is fifty-nine
stories high and is said to be the largest commercial office building
in the world.

The skyscraper was already occupied by a great many tenants
on the day I was first there, although construction work had not
been completed and droves of workmen were hustling back and
forth in the ground-floor lobby. I was walking toward a newsstand
and my course took me alongside a huge square pillar. As I strode
from behind this pillar, into the open, a workman pushing a
steel wheelbarrow, loaded to the very lip with about three
hundred pounds of soupy concrete, arrived at the same spot. The
wheelbarrow hit me and ran over me.

The fact that its inflated tire pinned down my right foot kept
me from plunging headlong into two and a half feet of concrete,
and for this I was grateful. If I have to drown, I prefer plain

water. As it was, the embarrassed workman pulled the wheel off my foot and I noted that only a small quantity of the gray soup, about a half pint, had sloshed onto my trousers. I wasn't at all indignant or feeling litigious, as is traditional in such contingencies. It was as much my fault as it was the workman's. I had, in a sense, been guilty of reckless walking. I didn't howl for a lawyer, which is the patriotic American thing to do. I didn't do much of anything—I couldn't very well ask a building *that big* to dry clean a pair of pants for me.

That episode, which was unplanned and hit me like a bolt from the blue, constitutes my most recent world's record. As I stand today, I am the first person in history ever to be run over by a wheelbarrow full of wet concrete in the largest commercial office building on earth. It is my hope that the management of the skyscraper will furnish me with a proper certificate and that my accomplishment will be emblazoned in the pages of the Guinness and Kane record books. I want my descendants to know about this thing.

In the event you go questing for world's records, let me recommend extreme caution in certain areas of operation. Don't, for example, attempt to set a new record for swallowing metal objects. There are two reasons for shying away from this field. The present world's champion went to a doctor and complained of swollen ankles. It was discovered that he had in his stomach a three-pound chunk of iron, twenty-six keys, three sets of rosary beads, sixteen religous medals, a bracelet, a necklace, three pairs of tweezers, four nail clippers, thirty-nine nail files, three metal chains, and eighty-eight assorted coins.

Now, the temptation might come upon you to go for this fellow's championship by consuming all that he consumed and then topping it off by gulping down a brass doorknob. Don't do it. Don't do it even if you have no objection to swollen ankles. Your victory would be a hollow one. The man's record is written in the books, but not his name; in cases of this kind the medical people don't use names—they just say "male patient, age 54." No glory in it.

There are other unpleasant and even painful ways of achieving world's records. For instance, two Russians named Bezbordny and Goniusch became world's champions at Kiev in 1931 by slapping each other in the face for thirty consecutive hours. Their match was declared a draw.

In this last connection I must mention another record-holder, Mrs. Beverly Nina Avery. She was forty-eight in October of 1957 when she obtained her sixteenth divorce. That in itself was a world's record. But Mrs. Avery, a California barmaid, was not satisfied with her achievement. She testified that five of her husbands had broken her nose. This made her holder of a *double* world's record. Not many people can lay claim to that.

CHAPTER 54

A FRIEND TO IDAHO

When I was a small boy in Illinois I had a friend named Whiney
Mueller. I remember Whiney quite clearly for one thing, a declaration he was inclined to make when he was in a pensive mood,
as follows:

"Time I grow up to be a man I'm a-goin' acrost the ocean to
Idaho."

In those years I did not know the nature and the quality of
an Idaho, but Whiney Mueller spoke his ambition with such
quiet fervor that I, too, felt a great yearning to go acrost the
ocean to Idaho. In time I found out what an Idaho was and
that there wasn't any ocean to go acrost to get to it, yet I still
had strong feelings about it. I have retained those feelings all
through my subsequent life.

It has been, for the most part, an untrammeled and whole-hog
admiration, though I have found myself on occasion entertaining
compassionate feelings toward Idaho. In those faltering moments
she has seemed to be a desolate and forlorn commonwealth.
Through the years I never heard much, if anything, about her.
People didn't talk about her, the way they didn't talk about
Kazakhskaya of Manitoba. Until I deliberately began investigating
the matter I had never heard of anyone who ever came from
Idaho, unless maybe Borah and he was born in my own native
Southern Illinois. And I never heard of anyone who ever went

there, except maybe Hemingway, also a native of Illinois. Oh, indeed, I had heard of Sun Valley, but back in New York we were under the impression that it was in Utah or Jackson Hole or Banff.

Hemingway killed himself in Ketchum, giving the state some publicity, and a California friend of mine named Fred Beck, whose name has been mentioned elsewhere in this book, actually moved to the same town in Idaho and lived there. Mr. Beck is a writer like Hemingway, only better. I now had knowledge of two people who had gone to Idaho, so it wasn't an impossibility. It wasn't against the law.

My friend Beck was bewitched by the state and planned on writing a book about his peculiar adventures within its borders. I proposed that the book be patterned after Carl Carmer's classic *Stars Fell on Alabama,* and I suggested a title for it: *Igneous Rocks Fell on Idaho.* Mr. Beck said thanks just the same but he already had a title. He thought of his title before he ever thought of writing the book. He told me that one of the principal agricultural products of Idaho is a forage crop called rape, a brassicaceous plant whose leaves are favored by sheep and whose seeds yield up a commodity called rape oil. Mr. Beck said he planned on calling his book *Idaho: Land of Rape.* I told him I thought it would have a good chance.

Since then I have had occasion to chide him about his title. The phrase "Land of Rape" could be confusing to some people. A word-man named Otto Whittaker told me he knew about the rape that tosses and shimmers in the slanting fields of Idaho, but he said there was another definition of the word. "Rape," explained Mr. Whittaker, "is the guck that's left in the bottom of the vat after the juice is pressed or tromped out of the grapes." This definition had not been mentioned to me by Fred Beck, who is big in wine, tastes it professionally, and has even written books about it. His own California, said Mr. Whittaker, could be called "Land of Rape" by reason of its grape guck.

When I wrote Mr. Beck about his oversight, he quickly replied:

"Forget about rape. I have a new title and a new plan for the book. Let us convene at Picacho Pass on the eleventh and talk."

He and I enjoy occasional meetings midway between Lindero

Canyon in California and Persimmon Gap in West Texas and in
recent years, at this two-man think tank, we have talked about
"The Idaho Book." Both Mr. Beck and I, as suggested, have long
contended that Idaho is a commonwealth that has been un-
reasonably neglected. Poets, we feel, have been remiss.

And so once again we foregathered at Picacho Pass in Arizona.
After toasting a few Idaho mountain peaks, plus some attractive
valleys, we got down to business. Mr. Beck now proposed that we
collaborate on the book about how big boulders fell on Idaho. A
man named Irving Stone was largely responsible for this change
of course; he had unwittingly given us a brand-new title and a
whole new approach.

Fred Beck had recently been reading Mr. Stone's latest book,
Passions of the Mind. In its pages he came upon an unusual word,
a word he had never encountered before. It was highly descriptive of himself, meaning Mr. Beck, and it applied with equal
cogency to me. More than that, it was a word that could be
used to designate a good many stalwart citizens of the Idaho
that Mr. Beck used to know and love.

The word is *potator*. The dictionaries say it means drinker,
or heavy drinker, or toper. And our book would be shamelessly
titled: *The Idaho Potators*.

There is, of course, a possibility that Mr. Beck will never
be allowed back in the state. Matt Weinstock once asserted, in the
Los Angeles *Times*, that citizens of Idaho "generally are suspicious of invaders with California license plates." Mr. Weinstock
blamed this condition on the bizarre conduct of Fred Beck and
Californians of his ilk. "They've heard awful tales about us," Mr.
Weinstock wrote, "and some visitors from Los Angeles manage
to tarnish our already smudged reputation as a boorish lot, spoiled
by success and luxury." The thing that was fretting Mr. Weinstock was the story of Fred Beck and the fishin' worms.

Mr. Beck got off to a shaky start in Ketchum by getting caught
in the act of using worms to catch fish. This set him apart from
the town's leading fisherfolk (including the aforementioned
Hemingway) who were sages and philosophers and fished with
flies. Artificial flies, bearing such names as peacock's doodad, spent
gnat, cock's hackle, and green drake. Grown men of Ketchum
spoke of such things with awe and reverence.

It is a cool fact of life that fly fishermen look upon worm people with pervasive disgust, that worm people consider fly folks to be snobs and opera-goers, that a man who favors the dry fly would not give the time of day to a man who baits his line with a wet fly, and that Idaho people think that Southern California people have mislaid their marbles. This interstate warfare is known to science as the precarious balance of nature. Fred Beck was not totally condemned for worm fishing but the practice put him under suspicion and the Idaho banks wanted a lot of collateral out of him.

There came a time when he decided to build a cabin separate from his house and a man with a bulldozer arrived to clear and smooth down the site. On this particular day Mr. Beck decided he would have a try at some Idaho trout, so he took a spade and a coffee can and went out to gather bait. On impulse he asked the bulldozer man to run his blade over a certain spot where he usually found a lot of worms lurking, and the bulldozer man did it, and Mr. Beck looked upon more night crawlers than he had ever seen before in his life. As he began gathering worms in his coffee can, moving along behind the bulldozer, he noticed that a car had stopped across the way and two citizens of Ketchum were watching him curiously. He thought nothing of it. But the next day, down at the post office, Mr. Beck found himself being pointed out and contemplated with new interest by the locals.

"That's him," they'd say. "That's the fella from California not only fishes with worms, but hires a bulldozer to dig up his bait." And as an afterthought, "On toppa that, he's got two different toilets in that house of his'n."

Mr. Beck was never able to live it down and so in time, rather than skulk through the back alleys of Ketchum, he moved away to the Palm Springs area. There he soon became a man of distinction; he was looked upon as being strange in his ways and in Palm Springs such regard is considered to be a sort of accolade. Then he began noticing that other people, including his neighbors, were getting strange in *their* ways, and so he sold his house and packed his books on demonology and moved to Westlake Village, where he found a whole new set of people to confuse.

Thus the two people I knew who had gone to Idaho, Beck and Hemingway, had taken their departure. Still my interest in the state continued, amounting almost to a fascination. I became a sort of walking encyclopedia on Idaho. Consider the Snake River. Did you know that it rushes through a much deeper canyon than that piddling Grand Canyon they have in Arizona? Hell's Canyon in Idaho is almost 8,000 feet deep whereas Arizona's gully is a mere 5,650 feet. Bang the fieldpiece, twang the lyre, for Idaho my Idaho!

People will tell you that the Snake got its name from the circumstance of its winding along like a serpent or because a lot of snakes are to be found along its banks. Nonsense. It got its name through error, the way the kangaroo got its name. When the early navigators reached Australia and saw their first kangaroo they said to the natives, "What in the name of time is *that* thing?" The natives replied, "Kangaroo." And kangaroos they became. What those natives were actually saying when they said "Kangaroo" was, "Whad you say?" It was much like that with the Snake River. The white people, probably the Lewis and Clark party, asked an Indian on the river the name of his tribe. He made serpentine motions with his hands and so the palefaced ones figured he meant he belonged to the Snake tribe, and so they called the river the Snake. The Indian actually belonged to a tribe known as the Basket Weavers. Not a very good name for a river.

The acquisition of place names can sometimes get pretty weird. The Nez Percé Indians belong to Idaho, and they acquired their tribal name through white man's error. "Nez percé" means "pierced nose" and these Indians are called Nez Percé, the books say, because they never have their noses pierced.

There was another interesting tribe of Indians who wandered in and out of Idaho in the olden time. They were the Diggers, of whom Mark Twain wrote: "They would eat anything they could bite." And, in reference to myself, let me quote another Mark Twain remark: "Information appears to stew out of me naturally, like the precious otter of roses out of the otter."

I need not dwell on the fact that scenically Idaho has no superior among the forty-nine other states. The words "magnificent" and "grandeur" and "breathtaking" are peppered through all travel writing about the state. There are vast areas where no roads have been cut and the only access is by trail. Any substantial guidebook to Idaho is an unending hymn to her natural beauty and needs to be composed by a person with a command of purplish prose; such a guide is almost altogether concerned with wild grandeur, and descriptions of gorges and lakes and incredible peaks and scores of ghost towns and tremendous forests and breathtaking waterfalls. And seldom even a mention of the fine fishin' worms of Old Ketchum.

The people of Idaho don't do much bragging about their superb homeland but they do have a saying that goes: "This would be the biggest by-god state in the union if it was ever ironed out flat."

It's really something. And there is one more pertinent fact you might want to know. All these years I've been entranced by the beautiful Land of Rape, the Country of the Idaho Potators. I've traveled pretty widely, and I've been almost everywhere in the United States. But . . .

Never once have I set foot in Idaho.

CHAPTER 55

"THIS IS BETTER THAN
GETTIN' DROWNDED"

A few years before he died of a heart attack, the incomparable Gene Fowler and I were discussing famous last words. We talked about deathbed utterances as collected by Clifton Fadiman and Barnaby Conrad and other connoisseurs, and then Fowler said: "I've always felt that someone ought to put together a collection of the last words spoken by people on the gallows, or sitting in the electric chair, or awaiting the headman's ax."

Fowler then mentioned several classic examples of gallows humor, his favorite being a line spoken by a man about to be hanged in Chicago. Fowler's old friend Ben Hecht was present at the execution as a reporter and enjoyed recalling the victim's parting words. The sheriff asked him if he had a farewell statement and the man replied: "I have nothing to say at this time."

Fowler sometimes gave speculative thought to what he himself might say at the end. His first heart attack felled him at sixty-five and when his wife reached his side he blurted out: "Agnes, don't let the undertaker rook you." He recovered from that attack and expressed keen disappointment over his "final words." He said he felt that he had done well enough for a dress rehearsal, but he hoped to do better the next time. Ten years later, when he had his fatal seizure, his last words were quite prosaic. Just before he collapsed he said: "It's probably indigestion."

At the urging of Fowler, I began to look into the subject of true gallows humor and I found that the farewell utterances of condemned men were not hard to come by; there were always witnesses, and usually the witnesses were newspaper people intent on every detail of the drama. A surprising proportion of victims have been defiantly arrogant *in extremis,* although those who have sermonized and pontificated at the end seem to have been in the majority. Strangely, the meaner and ornerier the victim, the more likely he would be to grovel and whine and express repentance. Big Steve Long, proprietor of a saloon actually called "The Bucket of Blood" and one of the meanest men who ever watered whiskey, was hanged many years ago in Laramie City, Wyoming. As the noose was being fastened around his neck, Big Steve spoke to the crowd as follows: "Go to church Sundays and mind your mama."

Ned Kelly, a man whose name figures prominently in Australian folklore, went to the gallows in 1880. As he stepped onto the trap he remarked philosophically: "Such is life." Around 1915 a Tennessee fellow was being hanged and Irvin S. Cobb was present as a reporter. Cobb said the victim's last words were: "This is sure gonna be a lesson to me." Nobody has ever figured out what was in the mind of Adolf Fischer just before he took the drop in Chicago in 1886 for his part in the Haymarket riots. His final words were: "This is the happiest moment of my life." And Charles Pence composed a feeble apothegm out of his final words in England in 1879, saying: "What is this scaffold? Nothing but a short cut to heaven." A triumph of realistic thinking was the final statement of Charles Norton, lynched in 1880 for killing a policeman in a Colorado saloon Mr. Norton observed, just before they strung him up: "I oughta been hung long ago."

Voltaire once observed that "nothing is more annoying than to be obscurely hanged." It is pure conceit, then, that leads men to display bravado on the gallows or to preach sermons. Many of them show a strong inclination to ham it up at the end. And some strive for a witticism and a laugh.

One of the most nonchalant characters ever to enter the death chamber at Sing Sing was Frederick Charles Wood, a suave and gentlemanly individual, confessed killer of five. He marched in, took out a handkerchief and dusted the seat of the chair, turned to face the fifteen witnesses, and spoke a pun that the governor of the state would never have commuted. He said: "Gents, I got a little speech to make. This is an educational project. You are about to witness the damaging effect electricity has on wood."

In that same grisly chamber a man named Hendricks, a vicious murderer, sat quietly for a moment while the harness was being strapped on. Suddenly he glanced at the black helmet in the hands of the executioner, then turned and glanced at the witnesses, jerked his head toward the helmet and grinned, and then said: "This'll sure cure my dandruff."

That medical observation by Hendricks was reflected long before in the words of Three-fingered Jack McDowell when he was lynched in Nevada Territory by vigilantes in 1864. His final statement was: "I got bad rheumatism anyway." And this in turn calls to mind Wick Fowler's story of a man who was hanged in East Texas. Before dropping the hood over his head the sheriff offered him a cigarette. "No thanks," he said, "cigarettes er bad fer muh cough."

I like, too, the last letter written by a condemned man, which went: "Dear Governor: They are fixin' to hang me on Friday and here it is Tuesday. Yours truly."

Early in this century one of the famous hangings in the West was that of Tom Horn in Wyoming. Sheriff Eddie Smalley was strapping Horn into a special hanging harness when Horn felt the lawman's hand tremble.

"What's the matter, Eddie?" he asked. "You ain't nervous, are you?"

"It's my first hangin'," said Sheriff Smalley.

"Mine, too," said Tom Horn, and those were his last words.

A man whose name I have unfortunately lost (he was of truly heroic stature) was awakened early in the morning in his Nevada cell. He dressed himself slowly. They brought him some coffee and asked if he wanted eggs. He did, and he ate them. Then they brought him a copious snort of whiskey. He drank it. He had to walk half a mile to the gallows, and he took his sweet time. When at last he was standing on the trap he remarked: "Well, so far so good."

The concluding remarks of the ancients were usually quite dull. The old-timers said things like, "Prithee, let me feel the blade." The only chopping-block case I can locate that contains anything approaching wit was that of Sir Thomas More who, when he placed his head on the wood, drew his long beard to one side and remarked, "This hath not offended the king."

In former times it was not unusual for politicians to take advantage of the crowds assembled for hangings and to use the occasion for campaign speeches. One condemned man, when told there would be a delay because a politician was coming, begged that he be hanged forthwith and instanter so he would not have to listen to the speech. This is one story I refuse to believe; it implies that a politician could influence a law enforcement official. A thing that could never happen in this great land of ours.

General Eisenhower often told a story about a man sentenced to hang in Louisiana where the law prescribed that he would be given five minutes to say what he wanted to say. When the time came, the doomed man spoke: "I haven't got anything to say, so get on with it." Whereupon a gentleman in the crowd spoke up: "If he doesn't want his five minutes, Sheriff, let me have them because I'm running for Congress."

There have been many instances in which condemned men, in their final declarations, have tried to gloss over their black deeds. A generation or so back there was a notorious killer-bandit named Gordon F. Hamby who was paraded to the death chamber in Sing Sing prison. Along death row the condemned men had often talked about "going through the Little Green Door." When Hamby arrived in front of the electric chair he faced the witnesses and said: "Tell the boys back there that the Little Green Door is brown." Then he sat down and his final words were: "Everybody got an even break in front of Hamby's gun."

Fuller Carson, a horse thief, was strung up to a telegraph pole in western Kansas in the 1870s. Before he stood on nothing and kicked at the United States of America, he spoke an irrefutable truth: "There's a lot worse men here than me." And not long afterward a scholarly desperado named Rogers spoke feelingly to a vigilante group as they adjusted the rope around his neck. "I don't mind," he said, "bein' hung by you ignernt people—they's not a single person in this crowd knows that five plus five eekels ten."

The general run of badmen of the Old West spoke with more originality than their brothers in the East. Jim Gates, for example.

Gates was four and a half feet tall and weighed 180 pounds. He had wild black whiskers, wore a ragged coat and a slouch hat, and carried an unloaded horse pistol and a butcher knife. He stole a mule in Colorado in 1880 and for this he was lynched. His parting remarks, an attempt at justifying his crime, went this way: "I was clean up there in the Oh-Be-Joyful Basin, three miles from Irwin, and I'd already walked my feet sore, so don't blame me for doin' what I did when I found they was a ride available."

Details of the crime for which Slim Coulter was lynched in New Mexico are not available, though I'd like to know them. Coulter's last recorded words were: "All I done was kilt a newspaper fella."

Samuel Johnson, in a discussion of the executions at Tyburn, said that "the principal was greatly admired if he carried it off with a swagger." The literature of executions in America is not lacking in characters possessed of swagger and thespian skills.

Clubfoot George Lane met an interesting end at the hands of vigilantes in Virginia City, Montana. Chairman of the vigilante committee was a man named Paris S. Pfouts. A fact. Clubfoot George was compelled to stand on a large wooden box in a barn and the rope was attached to a rafter. Before Paris S. Pfouts could kick the box from under Clubfoot George's feet, Clubfoot hollered: "I'll beat you bastards at yer own game!" and kicked it out himself. A while later a citizen approached John X. Beidler, the man who had adjusted the noose.

"When you fastened the rope around that poor fellow's neck," said the citizen, "didn't you feel for him?"

"Yes," said John X. Beidler, "I felt for his left ear."

Black Jack Ketchum, one of the most famous of western highwaymen, was hanged at Clayton, New Mexico, in the spring of 1901. He spoke sharply to the men who were supervising his execution. "Hurry up with it," he ordered. "I'm already late for my supper in hell."

Cherokee Bill Goldsby, one of the uncouthest creatures ever to come out of Oklahoma Territory, was paraded to the gallows in Fort Smith, Arkansas, in 1896. He was asked if he had any final words. "Hell no!" he barked. "Cherokee Bill came here to get hung, not to make no speeches."

Jack Gallagher, who was a member of the Plummer Gang in Montana, expressed displeasure toward the citizens who assembled to see him hanged. He said: "I hope forked lightning strikes every last one of you." On the other hand, the most diffident and meek-hearted man to be hanged in Arizona's Gila County was one Arlo Gillky, who killed a saloon filly with a beer bottle. Just before they dropped the hood over Arlo's head, he remarked rather disconsolately, "Well, here goes nuthin'."

Bob Augustine, a Texas cowboy and expert pistol shot, was possibly the most optimistic victim ever lynched in his state. He tried to shoot up the whole town of San Antonio one day in 1863, a proceeding which displeased the citizens, and they hauled him out to a chinaberry tree and prepared to string him up. Perched at the brink of eternity with the rope already around his neck, Bob Augustine advised the crowd: "I'm warnin' you. If I get out of this alive I'm gonna make every one of you bite the dust." He was quickly dead. Carl Pangram, who was hanged in 1930 for killing twenty-three persons, was far from contrite about it when he stood on the trap. He said: "I wish the whole human race had one neck and I had my hands around it."

A man named Cicero Simms spoke with some eloquence in Fairplay, Colorado, as they dropped the noose over his head. He said: "This is better than gettin' drownded." His emotional reaction was not too distant from that of a character in a recent Western movie, a young desperado who was shown a crucifix by a priest. The boy looked at it for a long moment and then said: "That looks worse'n hangin'." It was a man named Kenneth Neu, hanged in Louisiana in 1935, who gave thought to the technical aspects of the operation and remarked to the executioner: "It's not the drop that bothers me, it's the sudden stop."

Emerson wrote of the humorous English thief who drank a pot of beer at the gallows and blew off the foam, remarking that it was hell on the liver. Another London thief, Jonathan Wild, amused himself in his last moments at Tyburn by picking the pocket of the clergyman who was trying to give him final consolation. James Rodgers, a brash-mannered murderer, stood before a Nevada firing squad in 1960. He was asked if he had any final request to make. "Yes," he said. "Bring me a bulletproof vest." And when William Palmer arrived on the gallows in a western state he studied the improved trap door that was being used for the first time and then spoke apprehensively to the sheriff: "You sure this thing's safe?"

Finally, the case of Jesse Smith of Houston, who killed a man in a holdup. Ed Bartholomew tells the story of Jesse's execution at Huntsville prison in his book *Hard Cases*. Said Jesse at the end: "They's lots of Smiths in this world. Ain't nobody really cares if another Smith lives or dies." At which point they lowered the boom.

That story somehow depresses me.

CHAPTER 56

THE UGLIEST WORD

Lullaby. Golden. Damask. Moonlight. Do these words seem aesthetically attractive to you? They have appeared with some regularity on lists of "the ten most beautiful words in our language." Along with *luminous, hush, anemone, mother,* and various others. These lists appear from time to time in the public prints, and there is almost always disagreement among the scholarly people who mine the dictionaries looking for lovely words. Sometimes these disagreements reach a point where ugly words are used. I can't recall ever having seen a list of the ten ugliest words in the language but I do remember that the late Ring Lardner, coming upon one of the beautiful-word lists in a newspaper, remarked with chagrin and bitterness: "Why did they leave out *gangrene?*"

The people who assemble these lists actually can't make up their minds what they are after. Is a beautiful word beautiful because of its musical sound or because of the thing it describes? If *moonlight* was the name of the diamond-back rattlesnake, would *moonlight* be considered a romantic-sounding and pretty word? If there were no such word as *mother,* and your mother was your *sludge,* would *sludge* be poetically beautiful? You ask my opinion and I'll tell you that *gangrene* is a downright lovely word, provided you keep your mind off gangrene. You want to hear a *real* ugly word? *Ugly.*

My own choice for the most beautiful word of them all would not appeal to the generality of people; it is a word of glowing, glimmering loveliness and arouses intense feelings of well-being and even sensuality within me. The word is *End*. With a capital "E." As a professional writer of books and magazine articles, I almost swoon with gladness when, on the last page of the third draft of a long manuscript, I write: *The End*. I sit and stare at it, and the longer I do so, the more excruciatingly beautiful it becomes. *Lullaby* my ass! I have left instructions that *The End* be chiseled on my gravestone.

As for ugly words, almost every literate person has in his head an agglomeration of them—words that can cause him to wince, and even shudder, such as *agglomeration*. I lay claim to several hundred of the uglies. *Mulcted* almost nauseates me (as I've indicated in an earlier essay in this book). I cringe in the face of *albeit, and/or, yclept, obsequies, whilom,* and *tinsmith*.

My own nomination for the meanest and low-downdest and ugliest word of them all is *Oh*. Said twice, with maybe a hyphen, this way: *Oh-oh*. In its maximal ugliness, it is customarily spoken softly with inflections that would curl the toes of a South Georgia mule.

Something is wrong, let us say, with the engine of your car. You take it to the garage. The mechanic lifts the hood and pokes around a bit and then you hear him murmur: "Oh-oh." The wretched creature says it in such a restrained dramatic manner that you know instantly that your whole motor has to be derricked out and thrown away and a new one put in.

Oh-oh almost always suggests tragedy, or impending tragedy. I remember standing with another man at a cocktail party when he, glancing across the crowded room, said, "Oh-oh." I followed his gaze. A prominent actor and an equally prominent newspaperman were squaring off, and blows began raining, and a nose was bloodied, and it took some doing to pry the two gentlemen apart.

Consider again our friends the dentists. Most of them have enough gumption to conceal their opinions and judgments, but sometimes you'll run across one who forgets his chairside manner. He'll be inspecting a big molar in the back and suddenly he'll say, "Oh-oh." Or he'll come out of his darkroom carrying an

X-ray taken a few minutes earlier, and he'll put it up against the light, and he'll look at it briefly, and then his head will give a jerk and he'll say, "Oh-oh." You know at once, without ESP, precisely what is meant. Out. All of them. From now on, plates. And you know what Aunt Gert says about plates. No apples. No corn on the cob. No a lot of things. You are a captive in the dentist's chair but you feel like busting out of the place and hiding in the woods.

Physicians as a general thing have schooled themselves carefully to conceal any sinister condition they may find during an examination. Yet I have run across one offender in my checkered medical career. He was giving me the annual checkup. He took my blood pressure and tapped me for knee jerks and scratched me on the bottoms of my feet for God knows what and stethoscoped me front and back and had me blow into a machine to test my "vital capacity" and then he turned the electrocardiograph loose on me. As he studied the saw-toothed dossier on my heart, his brow crinkled and I heard him say quite softly but with an undercurrent of alarm, "Oh-oh." Everything inside me suddenly bunched together in one large knot.

"What is it?" I gulped. "Whad you find there?"

"Nothing really," he said. "Nothing important."

Nothing! Cancer of the heart is *nothing?* It had to be that at the very least.

"I heard you say 'Oh-oh,'" I told him. "Come on. Give it to me. I'm a man. I can take it. Let me have it straight."

"Okay," he said, and I steeled myself manfully for seven seconds and then began to turn chicken. He resumed: "I said 'Oh-oh' because I just happened to think that I haven't made out my tax return yet, and the deadline is tomorrow."

I quit him the next day. Took my aches and agues elsewhere. I can't use a doctor who is mooning over his income tax problems while he is looking at the record of my frightful heart disorders. I don't want a doctor *ever* to say "Oh-oh" in my presence, unless perhaps he has dropped his sphygmomanometer on the floor and busted it all to hell. Even in that contingency I think he should employ a more masculine and earthy expression. I surely would.

The saying of "Oh-oh" should be forbidden by federal statute. It is the most frightening, nerve-shattering locution to come into general usage since Noah Webster quit slopping pigs on his father's farm in Connecticut. It is, in fact, so low-down mean in its usual implications that even the dictionaries won't let it in. I scorn it, and deride it, and let my mind dwell on its opposite— that most beautiful of words . . .

END